Stanley Woodward

Paper Tiger

An Old Sportswriter's Reminiscences of
People, Newspapers, War, and Work

INTRODUCTION TO THE BISON BOOKS EDITION BY
John Schulian

UNIVERSITY OF NEBRASKA PRESS
LINCOLN AND LONDON

First Nebraska paperback printing: 2007

Library of Congress Cataloging-in-Publication Data
Woodward, Stanley.
Paper tiger: an old sportswriter's reminiscences of people,
newspapers, war, and work / Stanley Woodward; introduction
to the Bison Books Edition by John Schulian.
  p. cm.
Originally published: New York, Atheneum, 1964 [c1963].
Includes index.
ISBN-13: 978-0-8032-5961-4 (pbk.: alk. paper)
ISBN-10: 0-8032-5961-1 (pbk.: alk. paper)
1. Woodward, Stanley.   2. Sportswriters—United States—
Biography.   I. Title.
GV742.42.W653 A3   2007
070.4′49796′092—dc22
[B]   2006030514

Introduction

JOHN SCHULIAN

In case you are wondering, *Paper Tiger* is not kin to George Plimpton's *Paper Lion*, though I suspect Plimpton and that old tiger Stanley Woodward would have had a fine time swapping yarns. Both possessed a gift for anecdote and a love of characters, and besides, Woodward was mad for football. He played in college with eyesight so bad it made every game an adventure in Braille, and he wrote about the sport with great and sometimes booze-fueled bombast. It was as a sports editor, however, that he left his mark on American newspapers. There are those who say, in fact, that he was the greatest sports editor who ever trod the planet, but the whimsy in his memoir's title tells you it was for others to take him seriously. I count myself among those who do, so let me state for the record that at the very least he was the first Woodward to stand tall among ink-stained wretches. Sorry, Bob.

By the time the second Woodward, the one at the *Washington Post*, teamed up with Carl Bernstein to take down a president who was as out of control as an outhouse rat, Stanley had been in his grave for nearly a decade. But his legend survived in a way his beloved *New York Herald Tribune* hadn't been able to. In bars where newspapermen gathered, there was always someone who could recite what Stanley wrote after Michigan's powerhouse football team was upset and fingers were pointed at a lineman's inconsequential gaffe: "Attributing that catastrophe to such a cause is like blaming the Johnstown flood on a leaky toilet in Altoona, Pennsylvania."

Civilians and newspaper folks alike still trot that one out, though by now they seldom recall the author's name. Likewise, the passing of time has robbed Woodward of the credit for what he wrote when he returned to the *Herald Tribune* eleven years after being fired for the first time, but his words, and sentiment, are unforgettable: "As I was saying before I was so rudely interrupted . . ."

The funny thing is, Woodward never made much of his considerable virtues as a writer and wit. First and foremost he was an editor. The fact that he worked in sports, which newspapers have forever regarded as their toy department, may have galled him at times, but he never let it stifle his genius. He became the *Trib*'s sports editor in 1938, after eight years as a writer, and waded into a battle for scoops and survival among the city's nine dailies that was like something out of a hobo jungle. Four sports—baseball, boxing, horse racing, and football, particularly the college variety— dominated the landscape, and Woodward aimed to have a section that set the standard for covering them all, and more.

It took him seven years to find the writer who would define his section. He rescued Red Smith from slave labor in Philadelphia, where he was making ninety dollars for writing seven columns a week, and watched him become a press box colossus. Red, in turn, steered Woodward to an English professor named Joe Palmer, and Woodward had the good sense to not let his distrust of teachers prevent him from hiring a stylist who could turn horse racing stories into art. Woodward demanded from Red, Palmer, and the other prose masters at the *Trib* the same trenchant reporting that he himself had practiced in his days on the city desk and as a World War II correspondent in both Europe and the Pacific. Beyond that, he advocated irreverence, the kind that eradicated cheering in the press box. "Stop godding up those ballplayers," he told his troops. What he wanted, in addition to scores, race results, and elegant writing, was a good laugh. What he got may have been the best sports section ever. Certainly it was the most literate.

Red Smith called Woodward "the finest of craftsmen, a leader who commanded loyalties as fierce as the loyalty he gave, a giant of integrity, dedication, and honor, a brooder, a worrier, a fighter, and the dearest of friends." But when Woodward himself summed up his career, it was with characteristic understatement: "Over the years I tried to write English and see that others did, too."

Even when laid up in the hospital he could be a scourge, as Richard Kluger tells it in his splendid book *The Paper: The Life and Death of the* New York Herald Tribune. When a *Trib* sports writer called to ask how the boss was feeling, Woodward said, "Terrible. I've just been reading your story of yesterday's game." He had started grinding his teeth, it turned out, when he read a sentence that began, "The second half saw the tide of the game turn." Woodward proceeded to make sure the writer understood that a period of time can't *see* anything. "Do it again," he said, "and I'll jump out the window."

Woodward was at his most imposing, of course, when he was prowling the office. He stood 6'3", weighed 225 pounds, and was strong enough to throw open the huge, filthy windows that nobody else at the *Trib* could budge. He had a mastodon's jaw, delivered his pronouncements in a clipped New England accent, and wore glasses so thick they distorted his eyes. The scariest thing about him, however, was his rebel's heart. As Joe Palmer was fond of saying, "Stanley is frequently disdainful of his superior officers."

Once—and most likely more than once—Woodward bristled at a summons from the *Trib*'s publisher that came while he had a reporter in his office. "Can't you see I'm talking to this young man?" he said. And that was when he was minding his manners. Other times he was, quite simply, an ornery son of a bitch who, among other things, couldn't wait to butt heads with a particularly spineless managing editor he nicknamed "Double Rubber George." Such collisions were frequent, and Woodward knew that sooner or later one would prove professionally fatal. His day of reckoning came when the editor's wife, noticing that the *New York Times* had covered a society golf outing, asked Woodward to do likewise. He declined, pointedly. I like to think he even told the editor's wife what he always told his staff: "The *Times* can out-crap us, but they can't out-write us." Whatever he said, though, it was enough to get him fired from the *Trib* for the second and last time.

Woodward left in 1962 just as he had in 1948, "in rage and disappointment." And yet what lingers of his legend all these years later, in addition to high standards, fierce integrity, and devastating observations, is laughter. The man had a good time at what he did. There were days when he would use his column to pick a fight with a writer on another paper just to see what would happen. "He's smarter than I am," Woodward said of his target on one such occasion, "but I fight dirtier." It was the kind of confidence he usually shared over a bottle of Wild Turkey at Bleeck's, the bar that served as the *Trib*'s clubhouse. But he would follow a good time and a stiff drink just about anywhere. So it was that he wound up in Pittsburgh for a long, boozy dinner that ended with Dr. Jock Sutherland, the Steelers' coach, issuing a challenge that could not be ignored: "Stanley, would you care to wrestle?"

Red Smith was on hand as "chauffeur and male nurse" for the editor he called "the Coach," and here is what he wrote about the ensuing festivities: "They stripped to the waist. The Doctor was about fifty-eight then, the Coach six years younger. Stanley removed his thick glasses, lunged blindly for a head-lock, and missed. A quarter-ton of beef smashed to the floor. The house trembled. Stanley was pinned. He lay gasping.

"'Smith,' he said weakly, 'help me up.' I handed him a Scotch and soda where he lay. He knew I went on newspapers because I disliked lifting things."

Such stories captured the romance of the newspaper business as it still existed when I got out of the army in 1970 and took up reporting as a profession. It was a business full of writers who could transform facts into poetry and hard drinkers who somehow always managed to deliver an honest day's work—and everybody took out in laughter what they didn't make in dollars. I yearned to be part of their world, to know its characters and lore, to feel the rhythm of its best prose. Some of what I learned came from listening to old-

timers as they yakked between deadlines or at the bars
where they postponed their trips home. For writing
to inspire and teach me, I tracked down collections by
the men who remain my heroes: Red Smith, Jimmy
Cannon, W. C. Heinz, Jimmy Breslin, Gay Talese,
John Lardner, A. J. Liebling, and Joseph Mitchell. In
those days, most of their hardcover output had been
consigned to used book stores, but that turned out to
be a blessing because a used book store was where I
chanced upon *Paper Tiger* and stepped into the world
that beckons you now.

There are any number of reasons why this book's
return to print is so important, not the least of which
is this inescapable fact: in a business that may not realize how badly it needs another Stanley Woodward,
only two writers who worked for him—Roger Kahn
and Jerry Izenberg—are still plying their trade, and
only Izenberg still toils for a newspaper. In his fifty-
sixth year in the business, he pounds out four sports
columns a week for the *Newark Star Ledger*, the paper where he met Woodward in 1956. Woodward
was between stands at the *Herald Tribune* then, and
Izenberg was a headstrong youngster not long out of
the army and hungry to work for a legend. Inevitably
Woodward wound up asking him what he would like
to make of himself. Izenberg puffed up his chest and
said, "I really want to be a journalist."

There was an uncomfortable silence as Woodward
stared at him through those damn glasses. "Son,"
he said at last, "you may be at the wrong paper. You
should get yourself a three-piece suit and a Phi Beta
Kappa key and go to Geneva and cover financial con-
ferences for the *New York Times*. We don't have any

journalists here, we have newspapermen."

Izenberg ended up working for him anyway, and when Woodward returned to the *Herald Tribune*, Izenberg went, too. They hit some bumps along the way, as when Woodward yanked Izenberg out of spring training for spending too much time describing Arizona sunsets and not enough time finding out who was going to play second base for the then New York Giants. But Woodward also laid hands, literally, on the bookkeeper who tried to deny Izenberg a five-dollar-a-week raise. And when the *Star Ledger* sought to woo Izenberg back to Newark in 1962 by offering him his own column, Woodward sat him down for the most important talk of his life—at Bleeck's, naturally, over a bottle of Wild Turkey.

"What's this crap about you turning down the *Star Ledger*?" Woodward asked.

"I like working for you," Izenberg replied.

"Well, you're not going to for much longer," Woodward said. "They're going to fire me in a month. So if you don't take the job with the *Star Ledger*, I'll fire you now, and you'll *have* to take it."

Izenberg did, and soon afterward, as predicted, Woodward was out of the last newspaper job he ever had. He went home to write *Paper Tiger* and saw it published shortly before he died in 1964, while revolution consumed sports pages all over the country. Woodward never took credit for what was happening, but his spirit could be felt in the anarchy that two swashbuckling young editors, Larry Merchant of the *Philadelphia Daily News* and Jack Mann of Long Island's *Newsday*, began preaching in the mid-fifties. Merchant advocated "humor as the corrective for hype," and Mann urged his writers not to hesitate in demythologizing ballplayers if they were louts who dragged their private parts over the postgame cold cuts. Woodward, no doubt, approved. And how he must have laughed when he read the question that encapsulated the revolution's irreverence. The inspiration for the question struck when Ralph Terry of the New York Yankees mentioned that his wife had been feeding their baby while he was pitching a World Series game. Up popped one of Woodward's spiritual descendants, Stan Isaacs, who asked, "Breast or bottle?"

But the revolution that burned on into the eighties and even the nineties seems to have lost its heat as times have changed. Everything is different now. Athletes make the kind of salaries that once would have enabled them to buy entire teams, society shifts between adoring and loathing sports-page heroes as quickly as it downloads music on its iPods, and newspapers stagger toward an uncertain future, fixated on the bottom line, beset by staff cutbacks, humiliated by reportorial scandal. The Internet, meanwhile, looms larger every day, giving us information at warp speed, too often at the sacrifice of the literacy, wit, and regard for facts that were Woodward's religion. Sometimes my only consolation is to imagine Woodward rising from the dead to terrorize this onslaught of egomaniacs, moneygrubbers, cowards, and slaves to fashion.

Maybe that's the main reason I take such pleasure in *Paper Tiger*'s return, for here is a lesson in the kind of vision and courage it once took to count for something in the newspaper business. And if Woodward were indeed on hand for the occasion, I bet he would celebrate by grabbing the first likely candidate he saw and dragging him to whatever the twenty-first century version of Bleeck's is. There they could play an old Welsh miners' game, one of Woodward's favorites. One man would hold a mug of beer while the other kicked him in the shins. If the beer holder spilled so much as a drop, he had to buy a round for the house. Then they would trade places and do it again, and it would go like that all night, back and forth, again and again, until one of them surrendered. Crazy, I know, but that is the best way to remember Stanley Woodward: always kicking.

TO RICIE, MY WIFE

PAPER TIGER

1

THE BROAD-BEAMED AMPHION ROLLED GEN-
tly as she steamed steadily toward the
French coast. It was the thirteenth day
out and the convoy, led by an ancient
cruiser, was spread over the whole visible
ocean. A quarter-mile off the *Amphion's* port quarter
there was a ship that carried a load of TNT. A red flag
flew from her truck, and her crew was reported to be
drawing double pay instead of time and a half, which was
the reward of men on ships carrying less deadly cargoes.

The TNT ship seemed to have been loaded queerly.
She was down by the head and she frequently yawed and
bucked as if the quartermaster was fighting the wheel.
During the night she had once borne down on a virtual
collision course with the *Amphion.*

Our captain probably knew she was being ably handled but he didn't tell the crew, and the men of the *Amphion* were more ugly and nervous than ever as they goddamned their sister ship and scanned the horizon for
smoke from the destroyers which were supposed to protect the convoy over the final stage of the trip.

Kelly, the officers' pantryman, was on springs. He had
been torpedoed five times. Forgaad, the Danish baker, another multiple victim, had been drunk since we left Newport News. He had had the forethought to steal the stewards' supply of vanilla extract. A big surly coal passer
reacted with unbearable truculence. We kept away from
him—most of us—as we carried on the grueling routine
of four-and-four watches.

The coal passer looked so formidable that many a
tough guy took bumps and insults without calling him.
However, he was finally called, and the fight that
resulted was the most remarkable in the unofficial his-

tory of the ring.

The watch which had just come off duty sat down to breakfast in the fireman's forecastle just after eight o'clock. It was a gruesome hole. Coal dust covered everything, including the men. The only light came from an overhead bulb hanging by its wire and the only air came from the door after bypassing the permanent blackout curtain at the end of the long, narrow compartment. The iron porthole covers had been dogged down with a heavy wrench to make sure that no ray of light could be seen on the ocean.

There were those of us who wondered why the dogs couldn't be loose and the ports cast open in the daytime, but that wasn't the way the mate wanted it.

Pat Shannon, the fifty-five-year-old alcoholic who had slid down the ladder to fireman's mess-boy, was shuffling around, pouring out second cups of coffee after the first rush of eating, when the coal passer raised his voice.

"Hey, old man," he growled at Pat, "get me some butter. . . ." By this he meant the glistening light-yellow precursor of oleo with which the Shipping Board regaled its mariners.

"Sorry, son," said Pat. "The ration is gone and the second steward won't give me any more."

"Listen, you old son of a bitch, you go and get some more butter or I'll break your neck."

"You'll what?" said Shannon in honest surprise.

"I'll break your lousy neck."

"Do you want to fight, boy?" Pat asked calmly.

"I'd kill you, old man."

"Come on and do it then."

In justice to the coal passer, who was thirty-odd years the younger, it must be said that he undertook the fight reluctantly; but Shannon, as the wronged and challenged party, insisted that he go through with it.

A small space was found amid the *Amphion*'s deck load of Packard trucks, and the contestants stripped for the fight to shoes and dungaree trousers. The spectators amassed on the trucks and climbed the ratlines to see over the closepacked crowd at ringside.

The coal passer was an impressive physical specimen. His arms were hideously muscular. He had a coal heaver's corrugated stomach, and ropy sinews ran from his lumpy shoulders to the waistband of his greasy blue pants.

Shannon didn't look like much when he took his shirt off. He had an old man's body. His chest was meager and his arms were stringy. The enemy obviously outweighed him by about thirty pounds. But when Pat shuffled into the fight, it was clear he had been there before. His left hand, loosely extended, jigged in front of the opponent's chin. His right, a battered shapeless member, was open and motionless in front of his face.

The coal passer rushed, swinging a mighty left. The old man drew back just enough to let the punch miss him, then moved in quickly and shot both hands to the face over the extended left. The young man rushed again, his right hand drawn back. The old one stepped inside it and delivered half a dozen piston blows to the stomach. He moved back and in again, shooting left and right to the face.

The coal passer was a beached whale. He moved with ridiculous slowness as he tried to hit the formidable thing in front of him. Shannon moved in and out, shooting straight punches at the openings. Finally the coal passer said he had had enough. Shannon put his arm around the enemy's shoulder and seized his right hand.

"All right, kid," he said. "No hard feelings."

They walked together into the forecastle where Shannon sopped the coal passer's face with the water he had hauled from the galley to wash the dishes.

Pat used the whole bucket, an act of extreme generosity, in view of the difficulty of getting fresh water on a freighter of that vintage. It was necessary for him to carry his bucket back to the galley amidships, climbing over the crates and trucks which comprised the deck load and the steel cables lashing down the trucks. The galley pump was the only source of fresh water. It was padlocked, and the only key was in possession of the cook, a saurian Cockney, who resisted all efforts to get fresh water. Pat had to find him, persuade him, and then carry his bucket, now full of water, back over the obstacles on the well deck.

After the fight the kid was civilized. He regained a little of his self-confidence when he learned that Shannon once was supposed to have gone twenty rounds with Jimmy Britt. His devotion to Shannon was complete. Ashore at Saint-Nazaire, when Shannon got drunk, as he did with clocklike regularity on each new day in port, it was the kid who extricated the old man from the trouble that inevitably accrued—whether with *les gueuses* or the shore patrol.

The day of that fight, incidentally, turned out to be the best day of the trip. The TNT ship mastered her steering problem and kept her distance. Just before six bells there were puffs of smoke on the horizon, and in no time our escort of destroyers was ripping through the convoy to protective posts on the flanks.

From that day on, despite smothering conditions below, dreadful food, cockroaches by day, bedbugs by night, and occasional touches of submarine warfare, the old *Amphion,* once the North German Lloyd freighter *Köln,* was a happy ship. And Pat Shannon, a sober man and true as long as he was surrounded by ocean, and obviously a hell of a fighter, was our hero. He disappeared when we were paid off in Norfolk and I've never seen him or heard of him since.

I was twenty-three years old when I saw Shannon fight, much too old, no doubt, to be impressed by an old drunk's mastery of the four punches. But as I look back on my prenewspaper days, practically all the people who impressed me were professional athletes, mostly fighters and ballplayers. The only exception which comes effortlessly to mind was Professor Bennett of Amherst College, who interrupted the drone of recitative Latin translation to read us the verse of the young F.P.A.—"Odes After Horace" and, most important, "Tinker to Evers to Chance."

Worcester, Massachusetts, was full of great athletes when I was a kid, and my father, a barehand catcher of the eighties, whose athletic addiction was as abysmal as my own, presented me to many persons whose names took my breath away. Kitty Bransfield, Jesse Burkett, Jack Barry, Rabbit Maranville, then playing for the Worcester minor league club which Burkett managed, and Major Taylor, the great Negro bike rider. As soon as I could write, my father taught me to score a ball game. I had gone to athletic events with him from the time I was housebroken. Until I started playing various sports on Saturdays we never missed a game at Holy Cross. We saw the first football game in Harvard Stadium (1903), which Dartmouth won, and subsequently we went there to see such colossi as Jim Thorpe, the great Indian, Tad and

Howard Jones and Ted Coey of Yale, Earl Sprackling of Brown, and Charlie Brickley of Harvard.

My birthday, from eight to eighteen, was special. I wasn't required to go to school. My father and I would be up early to catch the train to Boston forty-four miles away. He would go to his Boston office for half an hour to quiet his conscience, then we would take the boat to Nantasket Beach for a swim. We'd be back in Boston in time for lunch at the Winter Place Hotel or the Somerset.

The ball game was the big event of the day. When we started the birthday expeditions, the Doves, now the Milwaukee Braves, played in a tight little park called the Columbus Avenue Grounds, and the Red Sox were on Huntington Avenue across from the opera house. The opera played matinees on Saturday and the cast, when not on stage, would view the ball game in costume from the fire escape.

In spite of his addiction to sports, my father was remarkably erudite. In addition to an ability to read Latin at sight, an accomplishment I found very useful in high school, he could identify operatic roles by costume on the fire escape and sing their arias. Of course he only did this when the teams were changing sides between innings.

In 1914 the Boston Braves, ex-Doves, pulled up from last place in the National League to beat the Giants for the National League championship. Subsequently they whopped the Philadelphia Athletics four straight in the World Series. I couldn't see the Series because I was back at Amherst College playing football. My father saw all the games, both in Philadelphia and Boston.

That season we went together to see the Braves and Giants in the crucial Labor Day double-header at Fenway Park, new home of the Red Sox, which the Braves

were leasing halftime. Getting off the train at the Huntington Avenue station well before the morning game, we
had no trouble getting tickets and watched from the third-
base side as the Braves beat the great Christy Matthewson.
It was the first time I had seen Matthewson's fade-away,
a hump-backed pitch which traveled with the speed of a
fast ball and later became identified as a screw ball.

We delayed a little too long over our lunch at the Somerset, and when we got back to the park, long lines
stretched away from the ticket booths. It looked bad for
us, but my father, who was endowed with great resource-
fulness as well as the nerve of a burglar, saw no difficulty.

"You wait here," he said, then advanced on the ticket
window, politely but insistently shoving his way through
the mob in the entrance. He walked up to the third man
in line, slapped him on the back, and beamed at him.

"How are you, old man . . . Rufus Woodward from
Worcester . . . Remember me? . . . While you're up at
the window, would you mind getting me two? Here's a
ten."

My father returned with two tickets.

"Is that man a friend of yours?" I asked.

"He is now. . . . Come on, the Giants are having infield practice."

My mother was responsible for such religious education as I received. From childhood I was required to attend Sunday School at nine A.M. in All Saints' Episcopal
Church. After that I joined my family for the church
service. It was agreed, however, that my father and I
could slip out before the sermon to pursue our sporting
life.

This was a concession by my mother, influenced perhaps by the preposterous snores habitually given off by

my father during the rector's harangue from the pulpit.

We sneaked out the side door during the second-last hymn and took the trolley car to the boat club, where we played a couple of sets of tennis or took out the big double sharpie for a sail and went for a swim. My father could dive off the board with a short cigar in his mouth, turn it around with his tongue, and come up smoking.

On occasion we got out of church entirely, thanks perhaps to my father's new habit of taking short, loud naps during the first and second lessons and raising the roof in singing the hymns, all of which he knew by heart.

The occasion for total amnesty generally was an episode in the sailing series between the Quinsigamond Boat Club, to which my father belonged, and the Tatassit Canoe Club, another alcoholic and sporting organization at the south end of the lake.

We raced in small, wide, cranky centerboard sloops which capsized at the slat of a jib sheet.

The two Quinsigamond club boats were marked by a heart and a diamond stitched on the mainsails. The Tatassit boats flew the club and spade. My father and I generally comprised the crew of either the Heart or the Diamond. When I was little we were almost unbeatable in medium air. As I grew our impost rose alarmingly, for my father weighed 250, and finally we needed a whole gale to have any chance of winning, and the club commodore ruled us out of most of the races.

My father took no interest in horse-racing or boxing and gave me no education in either field. Such knowledge of horses as I acquired came through my Uncle Lem, a doctor who kept a couple of trotters, Mike and Nita, for his house calls. I drove him around on occasion and sometimes on winter Sunday afternoons we would go over to

the Boulevard, now Park Avenue, and race sleighs. I
learned to ride a horse under a stern German in the Oread
Riding Academy. My mother arranged this for ethnic reasons. German was her original language and she got a
chance to speak it when she took me to the school.

Boxing I learned in the street and later through association with Louis Scelercio (Kid Scaler), Seattle lightweight
who made Worcester his fighting headquarters for a year
or so.

He had a gym in back of a boot-black stand on Main
Street and gave boxing lessons to supplement his income.
I paid for one lesson and after that he wouldn't take my
money. It wasn't that I didn't need the lessons. It was that
I was about his size—he being a lightweight—as well as
tough and much honored to be knocked around by a battler I admired. I therefore was a willing, not to say an
avid, sparring partner, reliable too, for nothing would
keep me away from the gym when Scaler was getting
ready for a fight.

Most afternoons we would go three or four rounds.
Scaler was not regarded in the trade as much of a puncher,
but I got hurt sometimes, even with fourteen-ounce
gloves. Occasionally he would attack viciously, using his
whole repertory. More often he would content himself
with defense and belt me only when I committed an er-
rant departure from professional procedure.

My chief fault was advancing my right hand too far
from my chin, thus enabling Scaler to hook around it or
slam me with an overhand right.

"I told you fifty times, kid, to keep your right hand up
and in close. . . . Now no more telling . . . I'm going
to show you."

Whack! . . . "Keep your elbow close and take them

hooks on the back of your glove." Smack! . . . "Catch
them rights in your open glove and stick out your left."

Scaler's fighting was based on continuing left-hand
feints. The left, palm up, was always jigging with a bead
on the opponent's nose. . . . Extend, jerk back . . .
Extend, jerk back. There was an off-beat rhythm in the
feint which seemed to fascinate the enemy and render him
vulnerable to the jabs and hooks which Scaler launched
from the retracted position, turning his palm down as he
fired.

Scaler did not teach me anything about using the right
hand until I could make the feint as well as he and fire the
jab and hook with fair accuracy and power. Like Joe
Louis, terror of a later era, Scaler regarded the jab as a
real punch rather than a mere annoyer, and when I landed
a stiff one on his bent and limber nose he would praise me.

"Good punch, kid. Good feint, too."

I had been firing occasional rights for two months without eliciting comment from the master—that is, verbal
comment. Often when I threw a right I would catch a
savage counter or a fusillade to the body as Scaler slipped
it. One day when I came for the workout, he gave me a
handball and told me to throw it against the wall for a
while.

In the long, narrow gym there was a space back of the
boxing ring where limited three-wall handball games
could be played. It was about twenty feet in length.

"You ever seen a good pitcher work?" Scaler asked.

He was talking my language. I named off practically all
the great ones.

"Okay, you throw the ball at the wall the way a pitcher
throws it when he warms up. . . . Not hard . . . Just
go through the motion."

I won't use names here because I do not want to be guilty of anachronisms or bury myself in the baseball records. I was then sixteen years old and I'm not sure whether I had seen Matthewson, Walter Johnson, etc., before or after this incident. Anyway I was enthusiastic about throwing the ball against the wall because I was imitating the big pitchers and I admired them as much as the fighters.

After half an hour Scaler came out of his dressing cubicle and motioned me into the ring.

"While you were throwin'," he said, "you were learnin' how to throw a right hand. Now let's see you go through the motion.

"Okay. When you pitch the ball you come off your right foot. Your weight shifts and you come down on your left foot. The good pitchers put their weight behind their pitch and the good fighters do the same thing, only the fighters don't lift either foot off the ground, and they don't use the same arm motion. Pitchers whip their deliveries. Fighters drive them."

To me this was a lucid explanation, and in the course of time it made me a good right-hand puncher. First, however, there were other things to learn. The right must be delivered without warning from its normal defensive position in front of the chin, with the open glove facing the opponent. As the punch flies the fist must be clenched and the palm turned down. The left hand, always delivered in preparation for the right, must be retracted to a place in front of the face, ready to block a counterpunch or shoot through an opening.

All this sounds pretty theoretical, but it wasn't at all theoretical to me, for Scaler illustrated it in full accordance with his explanation. He biffed me a couple of beauts to show how it was done, and numerous others when I committed errors of execution.

In the course of a couple of months Scaler turned me into a fair right-hand puncher, then taught me the fourth punch and the only other one recognized by boxing purists, the right uppercut. This is the only one of the four punches which is delivered with the palm up. It is the shortest of all and is most effective in combination with a left hook against a rushing opponent. Scaler illustrated it by commanding me to rush at him and then practically lifting my head off.

Late in the winter of my work with Scaler, I was winning amateur bouts with fair consistency and actually had turned pro, fighting preliminaries in small New England towns where I didn't think I would be caught. My amateur standing was valuable to me on strictly unprincipled grounds. I was afraid I wouldn't be permitted to play baseball and football in college if I were declared to be a pro.

Traveling the local circuit with Scaler, I sometimes boxed a preliminary, sometimes not, but in any case I was errand boy, bag-carrier, and towel-swinger. In those days it was considered essential to fan the battler throughout the minute rest between rounds. The swinger grasped the towel by two corners and snapped it over his head at the fighter, stirring up a rush of bad air and tobacco smoke.

Scaler fought in tough, well-matched company, sometimes winning, sometimes losing, always by decision. He won and lost against Young McDonough of Manchester, New Hampshire, and Terry Brooks of New York, and took a bad beating from Young Dyson, a featherweight, when he ruined himself making 128 pounds.

Win or lose I never saw Scaler depart from the classic

boxing principles he taught me. I accepted them on faith and ever since have admired battlers who were confined in orthodoxy, never quite approving the windmills like Greb and Ambers, or those who thought an uppercut could be improved by telegraphing it and calling it a bolo punch.

From the days of Jim Corbett the classicists have been the best fighters. In the heavyweight division, since Corbett, there have been no outstanding successes who left the main track. As a sports writer I saw most of them and also those of the lighter classes. The greatest potential fighter I saw was the short-time featherweight champion, Chalky Wright. He was a wonder with all the moves and all four of the punches. He might have been the greatest of all if he had ever decided it was worthwhile to train.

I gave up fighting as a participant, except on special occasions, after one winter with Scaler. I had taken it up as a substitute for football and baseball because my eyes had started to go bad. In the seven years between my fistic winter and my tour in the merchant marine, I had undergone nine operations to restore my vision and had graduated from college. I had played football ineffectually and baseball badly on an intercollegiate (amateur) basis. I hated football and wouldn't have played except I was too cowardly to drop out and feel the scorn of undergraduate opinion.

When I saw old Pat Shannon outpoint the bruising coal passer who was half his age and at least doubly endowed with health and strength, a train of thought was set off in my head. From this I evolved a principle to which I have since adhered. A professional (skilled performer), whether paid or unpaid, is the man that counts. An amateur is a clumsy bastard.

2 I WAS WELL ON THE WAY TO BLINDNESS
when I finished high school. I did my
studying with a powerful reading glass
after dosing my eyes with belladonna. I
got my diploma mostly through the kind-
ness of my teachers who understood the difficulties I was
having.

I had to quit all the sports I liked and in desperation re-
sorted to rowing in the high school crew, which had a
dismal record—two races rowed and two lost. All nine of
us in the shell were (referring to prior definition) ama-
teurs.

This was the last step in my athletic retreat. The boxing
interlude had been another, because I could still see a personal opponent after I lost the ability to see small balls
flying around in the air.

My bad eyesight was discovered by my father when I
was fourteen years old. We were standing on the corner
of Main and Foster streets waiting for the Lake View car
for one of our Sunday expeditions.

"Come on," said my father, "here's the car."

"Is that it? I can't read the sign."

"Tell me when you can read it."

The car came nearly up to us before I could read the
words "Lake View." My father was silent all the way to
the boat club. He didn't suggest a game of tennis or a
sail. We had a swim, then sat in the bar where my father
consumed two quick gins and bought me a horse's neck,
which is a ginger ale with the peel of a whole lemon
wound around inside the glass—very expensive.

Until the episode of the streetcar, I hadn't realized
there was anything wrong with my eyes, but my father
had. Sitting in the club, I discovered that he was terribly

upset. I don't think it entered his head that I might go blind but the thought of my having to wear glasses seriously damaged his plans.

The old boy had played briefly for the Providence National League club before taking a job as a porter in his Uncle Sam's hardware store. A delegation of the family had forced him to quit organized ball. Uncle Sam even hated to let him off Saturday afternoons for semipro engagements. The substitute porter couldn't lift a three-hundred-pound keg of nails up on the dray. This was easy for my father. The advantage to Uncle Sam was obvious, for he could get along with one porter instead of two, which was the complement of other hardware stores in town.

Old Joe Waite, driver of the big bays which hauled the store's wagon, said my father was the strongest man he had ever seen. This may have been an honest statement, but such physical power was a handicap in the Worcester, Massachusetts, hardware business because Uncle Sam steadfastly refused to promote my father to a job requiring more than muscle. To get ahead, Father had to leave the store and enter another business.

But whatever he did, baseball was an important avocation. He coached Amherst and then Harvard, the latter as assistant to Colonel Samuel E. Winslow, who served as congressman from our district for many years. The colonel had been a Harvard pitcher and he and my father were battery-mates in Worcester County semipro ball.

When I came along, his greatest mission was to make a catcher out of me, and I had professional-looking equipment for the job when I was nine. There was no Little League fifty years ago but the kids of that era were capable of organizing their own activities, as they would be now if the papas weren't so anxious to butt in.

By the time I was fourteen, I was catching for half a dozen teams, including the West Side Willie Boys, the Providence Hill Jews, the Vernon Hill Irish, and the Greendale Swedes. Worcester then had a bigger percentage of Swedish residents than Minneapolis. The Swedes came to Worcester to work in the steel industry through arrangements made by two tycoons, Washburn and Moen.

My father and I never were on the Little League basis with each other. When he came to watch me play baseball or football, he stood on the sidelines and said nothing. He departed from this rule only once. I had seen players get hurt in the college football games and one day after being jarred by a tackle, I imitated their technique and lay on the ground groaning. Everyone was solicitous except my father, who walked unobtrusively in from the sidelines, gave me a gentle kick in the ribs, and said: "You're not hurt. Get up."

Mawkish behavior was anathema to him and there was no sentimentality in our relationship. My three sisters were permitted to employ the "dear old daddy" technique but as far as I was concerned it was out. From the time I was nine we were men.

Now I was fourteen and we were sitting in the bar of the Quinsigamond Boat Club finding nothing much to say to each other. Having finished the horse's neck, I chewed up chunks of the lemon peel. The old boy smoked cigarettes (Egyptian Prettiest) and looked out the window.

At last he said, "I knew there was something wrong with your eyes. You haven't been hitting the ball on the nose and you've been going for bad ones . . . we'll go and see Davie Harrower in the morning. Maybe he can fix you up."

Both of us undoubtedly had the same thought:
"You can't wear glasses under a catcher's mask."

Dr. David Harrower was a Scotsman and a most distinguished "eye man." He had studied in Edinburgh and
Harvard and heaven knows what he was doing in Worcester, Massachusetts. His office on Elm Street, one hundred
feet up from Main, was always stuffed with myopias,
astigmatisms, and glaucomas. If you didn't want to wait
all day you passed up the waiting-room door, walked
down a dark hall, and entered the inner office. Anyway,
that's the way my father did it, and I was soon sitting in
the examining room peering into a brilliant light.

The examination was comparatively brief. "The boy
has cataracts in both eyes, Rufus," he said.

"What does that mean, Davie?"

"It means we'll have to operate a couple of years from
now. We'll have to see how they develop."

I was sent to see Doctors Wadsworth, Jack, and Myles
Standish, top eye men of the era in Boston, and a few
weeks later the three came to Worcester for a joint look
at me and a subsequent consultation. Apparently I was a
celebrated case for cataracts generally are an affliction of
the aged. The eye men seemed to be principally interested
in what caused the cataracts. Dr. Wadsworth said they
were hereditary and later changed his mind. The others
reserved opinion while I was probed, bled, and urinated
for every disease to which cataracts had been attributed.

My own guess was that I was hurt by a blow. When I
was eleven, the West Side mob was having a pickup football game one day and I got my face in the way of the
hard head of a boy named Pie Wyman, later killed in

World War I. My nose was smashed flat and my eyes were turned outward so that I could see both side walls at once.

After Dr. Charley Wheeler had pried up my nose and the eyes had resumed normal focus, which they did almost immediately, the only immediate damage was a pair of shiners. Dr. Harrower said three years later that this probably did not cause the cataracts inasmuch as I hadn't been struck directly in the eyes.

The subsequent punches I took around the eyes during my tour of Scaler's gym had nothing to do with it because I was already a proven cataract case.

I continued to play baseball and football for a short time thereafter. Then my father banned baseball on the ground that my school work wasn't satisfactory. This was undoubtedly true and the old boy, in spite of his sporting interests, was strong for academics and intolerant of bad marks. However, I think the real reason he stopped me was because he couldn't stand watching me strike out.

Early in life I had started to learn the violin and was just beginning to make progress, under the impact of a severe drive by my mother, when I had to give that up because I no longer could read music. There was no more compulsion, no more painful practice sessions. Under these circumstances I turned to the fiddle as a means of pleasure and played more and more each day as my eyesight grew worse. I found I could play by ear practically any tune I heard, and I had the remains of a repertory which Professor William Howard, a Boston Symphony second violinist, had foisted on me during my years of required music.

The last time I tried to play ball was at Millbury, Massachusetts, during my third year in high school. I had been consigned to right field and right away someone hit a fly out there. I didn't see the ball and two or three runs charged around the bases. The coach pulled me out of the game, pointing out my shame to everyone. He damned me when I came back to the bench. I sat down for an inning, then sneaked away and took the car back to Worcester.

Cataract patients in the preoperation stage can see nothing but shades and shadows in bright sunlight. Dark days are much better. This is due perhaps to the contraction of the pupil in bright light. Doping myself with belladonna, I was able to keep my pupils in a state of dilation and thus to see well enough to play football. I continued to play through the fall of my senior high school year. In the spring I rowed in the crew, a most unpleasant experience, but apparently some form of athletics was necessary to me.

Dr. Harrower and his group of consultants decided I could have my first operation that summer (1912) at Worcester's Memorial Hospital. The board of strategy had decided against outright extraction of the lens in my case. They decided instead on a "needling" operation. This involved slashing the lens and causing it to absorb. The theory was that at seventeen the lenses would be soft and pliable and would disappear at the first slash.

That's what I hoped when I stretched out on the operating table and saw the knife coming into my right eye. There was nothing very painful about this operation, for my eye had been desensitized with cocaine. It's just hectic. The eyelids are retracted by a metal frame and everything in the room is focused on one eye of one man.

Dr. Harrower gave me instructions as he jabbed: "Look left . . . Look right . . . Up . . . Down . . ." It was over quickly but the aftermath seemed endless. Both eyes were bandaged tight and I was put to bed flat on my back with sandbags on either side of my head. I was required to stay in this unhappy position a week without even getting up to go to the bathroom. The pain was bad for a day, then there was nothing except darkness and boredom.

Lots of people have had cataract operations and most of them will tell you it doesn't amount to anything. But they don't keep you in dry dock more than a day now and the needling operation which was performed on me no longer is done. Now they extract in one motion.

I went through the needling operation eight more times and the operations were spread over three years. After that I could see as well as anyone, with glasses. The removal of cataracts means also that the natural lenses are removed and the glasses take their place.

After the first four operations I was fitted with a lens glass for one eye and wore an opaque shield over the other. The next spring I went to a boarding school in Connecticut so that I could get into college the following fall. I made it by the grace of God and what is more I pitched on the school ball team. My father had been advised by Jesse Burkett—who batted .400 three times in the big time—that pitching was my only hope in baseball.

I was seriously handicapped, and I was surly and hard to get along with because fate had turned me from a budding pro into a clumsy amateur. Playing against Newtown High School in Newtown, Connecticut, I committed a degrading piece of bad sportsmanship.

A big Newtown boy picked on one of my misplaced pitches and whacked it into the next cow pasture. Two runs came in and the big boy charged around the bases behind them. There wasn't any hope of getting him short of the plate but I moved to the third-base line on the pretense of backing up the bag. As he turned for the plate, I tripped him and he plunged on his face. Naturally he was outraged. He got up and delivered a vicious kick at me. Before I could respond, the umpire and others intervened. I should have been lynched for pulling such a trick, but I carried it off with an air of truculence and my fellow juvenile delinquents on the ball team considered me quite a hero.

At this stage of my life I had come to believe that anything I could get away with was justified and I engineered a coup with the aid of one of my instructors which might have won permanent disgrace for both of us.

Sanford School, Redding Ridge, Connecticut, whose main building now has been cut up into three houses, was a worthy institution which adapted its instruction to what was needed by the individual inmate. I needed to be crammed in a modern language, i.e., French, and also I needed to be brushed up generally so I wouldn't fall on my scholastic face at Amherst College.

My father had talked the principal of Worcester Classical High School out of certificates in most subjects. I had had no mathematics since my second year and it would have been impossible for me to have passed college board examinations in elementary algebra and plane geometry. Amherst would accept no certificates in modern language and it would have been impossible for me to have passed any examination in French.

My father went to Amherst to see the registrar. The old boy was one of the college's great athletic heroes. He was also an ingenious and persuasive man and he put over a coup on the registrar which was homeric. It was agreed that I would be admitted on probation in mathematics. I would take no entrance examination in the subject. If I did satisfactory work in the first semester of freshman mathematics (it was a required subject for one year and finished with analytical geometry) my probation would be removed.

My only surviving problem was to pass the college board examinations in French, which would be given at our school. Therefore I attended three French classes each day. I found it fun to study and I applied myself to learning the irregular verbs and improving my reading and writing knowledge of the language.

The instructor was a Swiss whose native language was German. He and I became close friends, probably because I was the only boy in any of his classes who showed any avidity for knowledge. I have neglected to state that our student body comprised behavior problems and other weirdies, many of whom had been heaved out of other schools.

I learned the irregular verbs so no one could stick me. Herr Muller found my translations apt and my composition excellent. He told me as the examinations approached that I would pass. Still I worried that I would in some way flop and nullify my father's heroic efforts to get me into college. If I failed in either of two French examinations I was out.

I told Herr Muller how important it was for me to get by and I guess he began to see that I was in danger of worrying myself into a state of blankness. It seemed to be catching me that way. Some day in class I would temporarily forget things I had had down cold.

I was obsessed with the need of passing the examinations, and could talk of nothing but the fatal day now only six weeks away. He tried to talk me out of the mood, even took me to the Hotel Green in Danbury and lectured me over forbidden drinks. He called me to his quarters one night after dinner and put up a strange proposition.

"If I can get you the examinations beforehand would you tell anybody?"

"I wouldn't tell God."

Three weeks later he summoned me, held out an envelope and said, "Here are the fatal papers."

He had got the examinations from Switzerland where they were given in early May.

When I saw the questions I was sorry we had cheated. They were so easy I could have scored in the 90's without illegal help. But I was involved and so was Herr Muller and I must act with caution.

When the day came I was handed the familiar examination sheets and I worked in a suitable number of mistakes. Subsequently I was notified that I had passed and that accreditation had been sent to Amherst.

I have never told anyone about this before and I may be kicked off the Amherst list of graduates. But perhaps Amherst has a statute of limitations. It happened fifty years ago.

When I entered college in the fall of 1913 it was nothing like its present thousand-student self. It had barely four hundred students and it was somewhat scrubby especially in the dead of winter when many of the boys wore mackinaws. Almost any high school boy who had not dropped his languages, living and dead, could get in and there was no particular rush at its classic gates. It was and still is a beautiful place, in spite of some of the architecture committed against it in the early years.

The chapel and the two old dormitories which flanked it were plain New England barn architecture and quite acceptable, but most of the other buildings were of the early Fisher Body school. They were, however, well spaced under the big trees of the knoll on which they stood, and the whole effect was neat if not pure.

At this time Dr. Alexander Meiklejohn, who was regarded as a demi-Bolshevik in liberal education, was in his early years as president and was supposed to be inaugurating the elective system. This, as far as I could see, permitted the freshman to choose between French and German, chemistry and biology. All were required to pursue for two years the ancient language he had presented and to take the set freshman courses in English and mathematics.

By postponing the modern language to a subsequent academic year, a freshman could take Dr. Meiklejohn's course in logic or one in European history. I chose biology and French. I wanted English and I was stuck with Latin and mathematics. The last turned out to be a combination of solid geometry, trigonometry, and advanced algebra with analytical geometry the second semester. At least at the outset it was easy.

I was pleased with all my courses and my teachers. It was a new thing to be able to read freely again. Two more operations in the summer had given me one good eye. I still had one blind one. I wore an opaque lens over the left eye. The first of three operations on the left had rendered it temporarily blind.

3 FOR TWO WEEKS MY LIFE AT AMHERST WAS pleasant, then the freshman football coach came to see me. He heard that I was a good player and wanted me to come out for the team. I explained that I had played football but that my eyes had failed and that I had had to quit. I said I didn't want to play because I could not see without glasses and would not be able to play well.

He said that everyone should participate in college activities and that if I had any specialized abilities like playing the flute or football, it would be disloyal to the college to keep them under a barrel. It was impossible to make him understand that cataract victims who have been operated upon are amputees. They have had part of their body removed, the natural lenses, and can't focus without glasses or, in current times, contact lenses.

To get rid of the coach I agreed to come out and try it. I had been a running passing quarterback when I could see, but the coach planned to play me in the line where my lack of eyesight wouldn't be as severe a handicap as in the backfield.

The next day freshman practice began, and I reported with the rest. The dressing quarters were in the old grandstand on Pratt Field. When we arrived, there was a pile of torn and sweat-stained jerseys, pants, shoes, helmets, and pads in the middle of the floor. We were instructed to pick out our equipment. I burrowed for things as unnasty as possible and put them on over a clean undershirt and jockstrap, the last items grudgingly handed out by an assistant manager.

The varsity worked on Pratt Field near the dressing quarters. We walked to a cow pasture half a mile away for our workout. The picture was discouraging beyond conceptions of Beelzebub and it was the start for me of a four-year career which was as unpleasant and as frustrating as anything I can imagine.

For three years I played blind, never seeing the ball. The fourth they wanted to move me from guard to tackle and a clumsy mask was devised so that I could see well enough to maneuver outside the central crush. The mask—made in a local bicycle shop—was devised so I could wear my glasses under it. I could see well enough straight ahead but all side vision was shut off and the contraption pinched my nose so that I had to breathe exclusively through my mouth. By this time, however, vacation-time operations had fixed my blind eye and my sight with glasses was normal.

But the memory of football as a freshman, sophomore, and junior is fresh and horrible. The first few days, while our freshman team was doing calisthenics, running around the field and falling on the ball, a maneuver much in vogue at that time, I wore my glasses.

Then scrimmage began and I was plunged into a world of vague shapes and thunderous cracks that I never saw coming. I devised a method of playing that presupposed that my opponents did not realize I couldn't see. If a shape came right at me, I sidestepped. If it tried to get away from me, I went after it. This system worked well enough so that I made quite a few tackles under punts and kickoffs. The coach soon got over playing me at center, because I couldn't feed the ball on direct passes, but he moved me to guard, where I played out the season at 156 pounds.

After a few days of practice and while I was still playing center, we were summoned to Pratt Field to scrimmage against the varsity. As I walked over I started to hate the varsity. Here was a bunch of third-rate football players who thought they were going to show me up because I was handicapped. I resented my rancid uniform and the impossible position into which I had been maneuvered.

I was in a rage when the scrimmage began with the varsity on the offense. At the first sign of movement across the line, I went in with a fury no one expected. I slashed into the backfield and stopped the ball-carrier in his tracks. Spurred by this success, I got wilder and wilder. My system was drenched with adrenalin and my mind— if such you could call it—was bent on murder. I smashed into play after play with fists, elbows, everything going. After twenty minutes it was over. The coach took me out and Dr. Nelligan, an understanding gentleman who trained Amherst's athletic teams, walked me to the dressing room with his arm around my shoulder.

"It's only a game, boy," he said.

To me it was much more than that. My ideal athlete was a smooth, skillful man with fast reactions and exact training, i.e., a pro. I had been on the way to becoming that kind of an athlete when I was brought up short. Under enforced college patriotism and—it must be admitted—a yearning to be recognized as the athlete I couldn't be, I was trapped in a smalltime football world which I could not dominate and therefore didn't like.

Psychiatry was in its infancy but I was a worthy subject. I was denied preeminence in sport, but through participation in it, I sacrificed making a mark in scholarship which I might have accepted as a substitute. Few were good enough to go through the galley-slavery of 1913 football and have anything left for scholarship.

I found I had responsibilities to the DKE fraternity to

which I had been pledged, principally, I am sure, because I was a "legacy," son of a member or "brother." After the six-weeks marks came out I was urged by the head of the house to make a try for Phi Beta Kappa. I had modest marks, three B's and two C's as I recall, but that was good for DKE, which enjoyed the lowest scholastic standing on the campus.

I explained to Big Brother that I was not Phi Beta material in the first place, that I couldn't do anything in scholarship if I was going to play football, and that my marks would be worse at the twelve-week period after daily scrimmages had further dulled my brain.

I never did strike a balance between football and scholarship, never failed to sink out of sight scholastically during the fall and barely made the alkaline side with furious study between the Williams game, our finale, and the mid-year examinations.

Late winter and spring were my normal college periods. It was then I enjoyed Amherst and learned to love the place. Baseball, which I tried to play again, was recreation, and the coach, George Davis, former Chicago White Sox shortstop, was a pleasant, intelligent man who showed me pitching moves I would never have known about. He taught me to turn my hand entirely over and let the curve go off the end of my fingers, and he gave me a good pick-off motion for first base. But he couldn't cure my wildness and didn't fully trust me in a game. Consequently I was not a factor in Amherst baseball.

An all-American tackle from Yale named Heinie Hobbs coached Amherst football during my freshman year. For the next three years, the coach was Tom Reilly, who had been a great player at Michigan and left his law practice at Escanaba each fall to coach football. I toiled at guard for him two years without making any kind of a mark. Having acquired a mask in my senior year, I played right tackle and so had one season of sighted football. It was the only year I was a regular and it was the worst team Amherst had ever had. We defeated Trinity, period. Trinity was helpless thanks to a housecleaning which had eliminated the pros and semipros who had played on the strong team of 1915.

In those days everyone played as long as he lasted. I played sixty minutes in all games, except the one with Brown, when I was on crutches with a knee injury and didn't play at all. This was one of the good breaks I had, because Brown, anguished by the fact that Amherst had defeated its Rose Bowl team, 7-0, the year before, ran up a telephone-number score. I sat on the bench and watched the great Negro, Fritz Pollard, and a big power-runner named Purdy murder the Amherst line.

The Amherst-Brown game of the previous year (1915) was one of the marvels of the age. Brown, later picked for the Rose Bowl, was beaten in a flukeless game in which Amherst not only performed the feat of stopping Pollard, who was the best back of his time, but marched eighty yards for the only touchdown.

In case you think I am trying to seize upon a little geriatric credit, I hasten to announce that I did not play in this game. In the year 1915 I was THE substitute on the Amherst team and I never played unless someone got hurt. In those days the coach picked his eleven best players and played them until they were dead or until the score got lopsided enough to be safe or hopeless. As I recall, I played in all the games that year except Brown when our eleven starters went sixty minutes.

As twelfth man on the Amherst eleven, I was a complication. I couldn't play any position except guard because all I could see were vague shadows. So if the left halfback was hurt, I would go in at guard and the following additional moves would be made: Butch Hobart would move from guard to tackle; Tom Ashley would move from tackle to fullback; and Stu Rider would move from fullback to left-half. Similar chain reactions would be set in motion if one of our ends or the center was hurt. The only simple substitution occurred when one of our guards was the corpse. This seldom happened because they were awfully tough.

This team that beat Brown—and I feel I can brag about it now that I have disassociated myself from participation—averaged less than 170 pounds. The only men who weighed more than 180 were the tackles, Ashley—killed in the war three years later—and Clark Knowlton. One of our ends, Billy Washburn, weighed less than 140. Billy Tow, the quarterback, a Brooklyn smartie, weighed 123 and was the toughest human being I have ever known. He was our best blocker. He died of a malignant bone disease a few years after graduation as a member of Phi Beta Kappa.

Billy talked Coach Reilly into putting him into the Wesleyan game at Middletown in the fall of 1914. Things were not going well on the field and he virtually demanded the chance to try his hand. Up to this point the coach had ignored him because of his ridiculous size.

But this time he put him in the game and things began to pick up immediately. Billy ran the team, carried the ball, blocked and tackled like a fury, and finally drop-kicked a field goal, employing a talent nobody knew he had.

From that point until Williams was defeated, 31-0, at the end of the 1915 season, Billy was the Amherst inspiration as well as one of its most valuable executors.

He and Shell Goodrich, another wonderful little man, were the boys who put the hooks into the Brown Bowlers, who outweighed Amherst at least thirty-five pounds to a man. Coach Tom Reilly, however, had equipped them with a weapon which proved lethal.

Goodrich was about five feet five and 138 pounds. He was tremendously muscled and covered with wiry black hair, except on the soles of his feet. He was our best sprinter on the track team, which meant that he could run the one hundred in about 10.2.

He started like a rocket in football and hit with a fierce impact. If he broke through the line he was inordinately hard to catch. The only back I have seen who was like him was Glenn Hardiman who played for Georgia Tech in the fifties. This fellow, somewhat bigger, also hit the line like a .22 bullet and was gone when he broke through.

In my college days the art of defensive football had not been developed to any extent. It was considered suicidal to play your tackles tighter than the offensive end's outside shoulder and there were only two alignments that were normally seen, the seven-diamond and the six-two-two-one. Notre Dame's great teams played the seven-two-two and the man-for-man pass defense almost throughout Knute Rockne's career.

Set defenses permitted a coach to plan an attack with scant worry as to where he would find the offensive men. So our Tom Reilly schemed darkly and came up with the attack which pried apart the Brown Bowlers.

His scheme was to double team every man in the defensive line by employing one back as an eighth lineman and spreading the enemy further by posting a wingback outside the strong end of an unbalanced line which had five men on this side of center.

Billy Tow took the normal blocking position. Goodrich, occasionally relieved by one of our other backs, Stu Ryder or Bill Taber, would line up three and a half yards deep behind the strong side, in position to take the direct pass from center.

The Amherst line was drilled in the wedge charge so that it could deliver a shattering wallop, low and fast, when the ball was snapped. Coach Reilly's theory was that the defensive line would break somewhere and that Goodrich, or his stand-in, would see the place and shoot through it.

Amherst started its scoring march on its own 20-yard line, catching Brown unprepared for such an unorthodox method of attacking football. Goodrich took the direct pass from center, standing stock still, paced a step or two to the right, then shot for the hole. Tow called a direction on each play and he, or whoever was at blocking back on that play—for we had to distribute the labor—would lead through the called hole looking for the line-backer. Goodrich's first step would be in that direction, but he picked his own hole, and frequently he broke clear, the line-backer having been lured away by his original step and the course of the blocking back.

There weren't any movies then, so Amherst's victorious 80-yard march is lost to posterity. I saw it, for I could wear my glasses sitting on the bench, but I saw it from a bad angle. It was a weird situation with Amherst shooting four, five, six, seven, occasionally ten yards at a clip through the huge Brown line. Wallace Wade, later coach at Duke and Southern athletic administrator, was the Brown captain and right tackle.

After the touchdown had been scored and the goal

kicked, the admirable Amherst heroes nearly blew the advantage they had gained. The ensuing kickoff was caught by Pollard and he almost got away from the whole Amherst team. There was no one left in front of him, but Bill Taber took a dive from the side and got him by one foot.

Pollard hopped on his free leg and tried to shake loose. He was in a highly vulnerable position when six or eight pursuing Amherst players landed on his back. Not only was he deprived of the tying touchdown but was knocked out for the rest of the afternoon.

If he had been able to finish the game I doubt that Amherst could have held its advantage, for he was a supreme halfback, perhaps the best of the great Negro football players.

In those days a team which employed the shift was supposed to come to an "appreciable" halt before starting a play, but most of them didn't do much more than brush the ground with one hand and keep going. Rockne's Notre Damers were supposed to be nonstoppers, and I can say from personal experience that Dartmouth, another shifting team coached by the formidable Frank W. Cavanaugh, later called "The Iron Major," was seldom caught in the act of stopping after executing its flying shift.

Dartmouth and Amherst concluded a long home-and-home series in 1915 when one of the really good Green teams came to play at Amherst before a packed house of four or five thousand.

Doc Spears, 250-pound all-American guard, was the great player on this team. Jack McAuliffe, who had been captain and fullback at Worcester High School, was captain and left tackle of the Dartmouth team. Other names I recall were: Worthington, a great track athlete, at quarter; Gerrish, Duhamel, and Thielscher in the back line; Dussosoit, the champion tumbler at one end, and Slats Baxter, a fiery 155-pounder at center.

Some years later when I was working for the Boston *Herald* I asked Major Cavanaugh who was the best football player he had ever coached and he unhesitatingly named Baxter, though he had coached many who had won more notice. Cavanaugh added, "There was no one on earth who could make him quit."

Fortunately for us this fellow didn't play in the last game at Amherst. Nevertheless, Dartmouth came down with enough power to knock us into the Connecticut River (four miles).

The team was followed by the whole Dartmouth student body, dressed in overalls, sweaters, lumberjackets, lambskin coats, mackinaws and navy watch caps, and covered with straw and wood shavings. The Hanover mob got to the field just before the game and went to sleep in the sunny north bleachers.

It developed that a couple of smarties had arranged the expedition by cattle car at a low per capita price. Each doubledecked car would hold approximately one hundred "animals" and two "herdsmen." The Dartmouth rooters were "loaded" at five o'clock Friday afternoon and spent the next eighteen hours or so making slow progress to the Boston & Maine siding in Amherst. A Dartmouth fraternity brother told us that it was like a mobile combination of the Black Hole of Calcutta and Dr. Cooke's arctic expedition with heady overtones of the pig-sty. The slatted openwork cars freely let in the November weather of northern New England.

Some of the Dartmouth brethren gave up while the cars were being shifted in the Northampton yards and made the rest of the trip by trolley car. Here they encountered bundles of Smith girls and their escorts who were enroute to the game and the subsequent dances at Amherst. Our Big Green informant said he had never been so thoroughly giggled or sniffed at. It was before the day when smelly and uncouth males became attractive to the dames. Even now it may be that eau de barnyard would not make a hit in female collegiate circles.

We were flattered that the Dartmouth contingent regarded the game as important enough to warrant a migration comparable to those of the lemmings. The Amherst students didn't see much hope for our little, if able, team. The Big Green was regarded as an unstoppable force and so it turned out to be. But a unique scouting job and a defense, plotted by our coach in the middle of a brainstorm or after six dry Martinis, made it a contest until the last period. By then many of the Amherst regulars were expended and half a dozen virginal substitutes were facing up to the Big Green and a fifty-mile gale which sprang up inopportunely out of the northwest.

The early victory over Brown was a strategical handicap in that it warned the Dartmouth general staff that Amherst was not going to be as easy as usual. Moreover, Major Cavanaugh, even then a veteran in the coaching profession, had had three weeks to analyze our eight-man line attack and, no doubt, had seen its weaknesses, i.e., that it posed little strength against the flanks and that it took one receiver out of the pass attack. He may have noticed that we didn't have one (pass attack), anyway.

Cavanaugh was no stuffy traditionalist, and as our coach expected, he played an inordinately tight seven-man defensive line with three backs close up behind it. Our coach threw away the eight-man line attack and we did little except run the ends from kick formation. We gained a lot of ground, too, before Cavanaugh regrouped his defensive forces.

Our main problem, however, was defense, specifically devising a way with insufficient manpower to stop the Big Green bread-and-butter play which was an off-tackle drive from the nonstop shift. This one had butchered every defense it had met.

The Dartmouth formation was the *T*, with the quarterback under center and the three other backs in line. After giving the signals—the huddle had not been invented—the quarterback shouted, "Hike," and the three backs would shift rapidly right or left. The lead halfback would take a big jump nearly up on the line and outside the end. The fullback would shift forward and to the side, and the tail halfback, Gerrish or Duhamel, would jump behind center. On attaining their new positions the three backs would brush the ground with one hand, then go. There was no time to shift any forces to meet the play. You had to be ready on the right and on the left.

The halfback hit the hole with amazing speed. He didn't hang around waiting for the quarterback to hand him the ball. This was accomplished by something known as "the Dartmouth floating pass." The quarterback tossed the ball out, right or left, so that it hung in the air for the carrier as he made his cut.

It was rudimentary but effective, very much like the Notre Dame attack of Rockne's early days. Incidentally the Great Norseman never fiddled around with shortside plays and such falderal until the rules committee enforced the one-second pause.

Dartmouth had only five or six plays. The fullback would hit the middle of the line once in a while if it started spreading out, and if it tightened up too much the quarterback would fake the tackle play and run around the threatened end.

This was the engine our coach set out to stop with his 166-pound football team, and he almost did it with the six-Martini defense, an alignment which never was seen before and never since.

The basis of it was the use of double tackles and double guards. Our tackles played just inside the Dartmouth ends, our ends just outside. The guards were the key. They lined up in the slot between the Dartmouth guard and tackle. The fullback and center lined up behind the Dartmouth guard and tackle. The fullback and center lined up behind the guards in tandem with them. Their principal job when the ball was passed was to shove the guards through the slot and into the Dartmouth backfield.

If I were asked to describe the feeling a guard has when he slices with the power of two men, I would paraphrase a latter-day radio blurb—"Am I a bird? . . . Am I a snake? . . . No, I'm Superman!"

This was one game I got into quickly. Clark Knowlton, our right tackle, was knocked cold, which meant that our guard moved out to tackle and I took the vacant post.

The shover on this side was Stu Ryder, our fullback, and he was most vigorous, so vigorous that I almost beat the ball into the Dartmouth backfield on my first play. The quarterback's "floating pass" hit me on the shoulder. I saw a brown blur bouncing around and I grabbed it. It turned out to be the ball.

The first half was scoreless. We had the better of it, thanks to the end runs of Ryder and the six-Martini defense. Dartmouth couldn't keep our guards out of the backfield, couldn't even get its quarterbacks around the ends. One guard or the other would force him deep and our halfback and safetyman would drive him over the sideline. He tried to pass, but when he did get the ball away it was wild and wobbly and two were intercepted. Fumbling was chronic and we recovered at least half of them.

It would be nice to give this episode a happy ending, but I feel limited to some extent by the truth and therefore I shall have to say that things got worse and worse as the afternoon advanced.

The first blow was the loss of Knowlton. The second was inflicted by the dean between the halves. Charley Matthews, an outstanding player, had been declared eligible the week of the Dartmouth game and had played a great first half.

The score was 0-0 and the coach was exhorting us between halves to fear God and keep the tandems fast and vicious, when a messenger of doom knocked on the dressing-room door. He carried a note for the coach from the dear old dean in which the latter said that he had been in error and that Mr. Matthews was still on the floor after encounters with Quintus Horatius Flaccus and Marcus Tullius Cicero. At this, our educated tough guy, Billy Tow, exclaimed, *"Time deanos dona ferentes."*

We should have strangled the messenger, thrown his body in the bushes, and denied the note was delivered, but no one thought of it, and the coach supinely told Matthews he was through for the day. As a matter of fact that was the only thirty minutes that football Charley ever played for Amherst for he couldn't outbox Gaius Valerius Catullus either.

Charley would have been a help in the gruesome second half, but nothing could have saved us in the face of continuing Dartmouth pressure, increasing casualties due largely to exhaustion and the rising fifty-mile gale which stopped our punts at the line of scrimmage in the fourth period.

We went along all right for a while, but Dartmouth scored near the end of the third period. At this point about half the Amherst first team had gone by the board. Now a big, awkward character dashed on the field. It was Lee B. Wood, later executive editor of the New York *World Telegram*. He was an enthusiastic striver and a pretty good hurdler on the track team. But he was no asset on the gridiron. Tow saw him coming and exclaimed, "Boys, the coach has given up. Here comes Wood!"

Following the Dartmouth debacle which ultimately turned into a four-touchdown horror, Coach Reilly gave our regulars a couple of days off. Furthermore, he decided he would take the whole first team to see Williams play Wesleyan on Saturday and would send the also-rans down to keep a commitment with Springfield College at Springfield.

This appealed to some of us as a rather dirty trick because Springfield had a good team and was entitled to a crack at the Amherst first-string line-up. However, Mr. Reilly was concentrating on the climactic game with Williams, which was less than two weeks away. Needless to say, guard Woodward was one of those designated to play Springfield and took another unholy and somewhat vindictive licking.

We set out for Williams the day before the great game and stayed in a fleabag in North Adams, a trolley ride from the scene of conflict. I recall the feeling of grandeur when I discovered that we had a special trolley car. This was really big-time.

Williams had one of its worst teams that year, and before long we were twenty-five points ahead. The Amherst team started to loaf and the coach, catching the spirit of the occasion, sent in some of the subs who had lost their virginity in the Dartmouth game. I was in action a good part of the game. Like my more important teammates, I gradually stopped whamming the poor old Williams players and merely went through the motions.

When the fourth quarter was about to start, one of our linesmen called the team together and proposed the first case of cabalistic point adjustment known to intercollegiate sport. You may think point-shaving started recently, and in basketball. Well, it didn't.

"Look, you guys," said the linesman. "I bet fifty dollars on this game and I gave thirty points. . . . Now for Christ's sake let's get another touchdown."

I can report that the Amherst team immediately responded, abandoned the live-and-let-live policy, and started once again to knock the whey out of the Williamses. The touchdown that made it 31-0 was forthcoming and when Coach Reilly, bursting with good will, started sending in substitutes, the players on the field refused to leave and the tyros returned crestfallen to the bench. The score had been nicely adjusted and the friends of the betting linesman wanted to keep it in status quo and wouldn't trust the custody to a bunch of rinkydinks.

We rode back to the Williams gym smoking cigars in a four-horse station carriage, and subsequently many of us got stiff as planks and tried to take a delegation of ladies from the local thread mill into the train back to Amherst. The girls liked the idea but the coach vetoed it. A number of North Adams grandmothers of the present day probably now are glad of the unfriendly offices of Mr. Reilly.

Even in the pleasures of the victory over Williams, the coach probably was organizing his forces for the ensuing campaign and eliminating what he thought might be deleterious influences. Cruelly it put an end to the only real fun I had as a college football player. The next season was sheer horror. Most of the assault troops had graduated or left college, leaving the sad remnant plus a pitiful bunch of sophomores.

Mr. Reilly, gray, bald, portly, and fifty, came back with a bride. The lady was pretty gorgeous, being tall, statuesque, and greatly less burdened with years. The coach installed her in his suite in the Amherst House, where she entered upon a three-months' period of boredom. The coach proved to be a jealous bridegroom. He was busy all the time and he was having a miserable time with his football team, which didn't show any signs of winning, not even from Bowdoin and Union.

Occasionally when he returned to the hotel he would catch Mrs. R. talking to the owner, a Lothario of seventy-two or -three. This he disapproved of and he made it pretty obvious. The football players got the play virtually first hand, for the training table was in an anteroom off the hotel dining room.

Our sympathies, right or wrong, were with the coacher but when we sat down to eat we forgot everything but the chow which surpassed anything I have yet experienced. Before service began, the table would be loaded with platters of fruit, pitchers of milk and cream, two-pound lumps of butter, jars of jam and marmalade, dishes of celery, olives, and scallions.

Then they would start bringing the *pièces de resistance*, slabs of roast beef half an inch thick that would cover a twelve-inch plate, with all kinds of vegetables and stacks of fresh toast. There was ice cream every night. None at noon, though, but the lunchtime provender was otherwise just as Lucullan.

And for breakfast . . . fruit and fruit juices, hot and cold cereal with cream, milk, coffee, toast, jam, eggs, bacon, and, if you wanted it, a medium-sized rare steak.

Let's skip back to dinner for I neglected one feature. About mid-season we got licked by Union, which, incidentally, had its only undefeated team that year (1916). It was decided by the coach and trainer that our team was overtrained. No thought was given to letting up on the scrimmage which went on every evening until it was too dark to see and which kept our casualty list full and made even the unwounded dull and unhappy. Scrimmage was the sole training method in those days. It was supposed to make you rugged and mean.

It may have accomplished these ends for we all felt mean enough and we had to be rugged to survive the ordeal. The most I can say for myself is that I survived, for in the years following college, I had to have five major operations to correct the after-effects of football. A case of osteomyelitis persisted even after the advent of penicillin.

I got the worst injury of all when I wasn't playing. I had just been taken out of the scrimmage and was standing back of the substitutes who were on the defense against the freshmen. I had my face-mask off and was wearing a blanket, but I can forgive the freshmen blocker who leveled me because it was almost totally dark.

He knocked me down with a beautiful Indian block at the knee line and put me on crutches for ten days. Whatever this may have had to do with subsequent bone and

cartilage difficulties, it had one supremely good effect
. . . it put me out of the Brown game, which proved to be
the worst drubbing given Amherst in the twentieth century.

The coach and trainer, not considering that rest might
do a good deal for this ball club, decided to increase the
team's caloric intake by adding two bottles of Bass ale per
man per day to the menu at the Amherst House.

Most of the boys dipped right into the ale as soon as
they got to the dinner table and practically all of them
were plastered by the time the coach started his post-
dinner lecture.

Billy Washburn and I took our second bottles back to
our quarters in the fraternity house and had the ale with
our only cigarette of the day, smoked behind a locked
study door. When we finished the second bottle we
couldn't stay awake another second.

Studying was out of the question so we devised a new
schedule. We got up at five o'clock and worked until seven
thirty, when we turned up at the Amherst House for our
steak and eggs.

Occasionally we would vary the routine. We would
stop on our way home at the College Drug Store where
Bill McGrath, the proprietor, would allow us smoking
privileges in his backroom, reserving the right to tell us
how lousy our team was.

He had a son at the other college in Amherst. It is now
known as the University of Massachusetts. Then it was
"Mass Aggies" or "Amherst Aggies." Our critic made
invidious comparisons between our team and the Aggies.
We did not have football relations with them, because of
the fact that the last game had resulted in a riot so ferocious
that the rival faculties joined in, breaking umbrellas over

each others' heads.

Usually Bill McGrath's criticism involved generalities, but one night he went into details.

"Your coach doesn't know what he's doing," he said. "How can a little end like Washburn here block a big tackle? Doc Brides up at the Aggie says no end can block a tackle by himself. He thinks Reilly is crazy."

Back at the fraternity house, Washburn and I allowed ourselves another cigarette, drank our ale, and discussed between yawns the matter that Bill McGrath had brought up.

"You know, he's right," said Washburn. "I can't block a tackle if he's any good. The only thing I can do is hold him and it's fifteen yards when I get caught."

My own assignment was to block the guard in. I was the tackle on Washburn's side of the line. If we could get Heinie Knauth, the guard on our side, to take the enemy guard instead of the center or backer-up I could pull around Washburn and help with the tackle.

We enlisted Heinie and that afternoon we tried the combination while the coach was talking to a reporter on the sideline. It seemed to work pretty well but we didn't dare risk detection so we never did it again until we played Wesleyan, which was supposed to beat us by twenty points.

Wesleyan got a field goal early and then Amherst came romping up the field ten and twelve yards at a clip and scored a touchdown. The revised tackle play was the big gainer. Washburn attacked the tackle head-on, attracting his full attention so that I could duck around to the outside and crack him with a high shoulder block. The coach, on the bench, having the worst possible view of the plays, didn't notice.

We used homemade shoulder pads to save money. The assistant trainer shaped them out of papier-mâché and glued felt on them inside and out. They were tied on with little strings under the arms and were held in place principally by the jersey.

It always hurt to make a head-on tackle or block, but that was regarded as normal in Amherst circa '16. I got really hurt in this game. The back long muscle tore and hemorrhaged. Driving blocks on the enemy tackle were painful and my left arm became almost useless. I kept on trying to help Washburn with the tackle, using my head and the wrong shoulder but the play didn't work as well.

Between the halves the coach and trainer looked at my injury and decided I could continue playing if they put an extra pair of shoulder pads on me. So I went out for the second half looking like Quasimodo and in no mood to give my all for the old school. Defense was the worst. There was nothing to do but stick it out, for though I was playing a lousy game, no substitute came in from the bench.

In the end I personally blew the game. The second half was pretty even but we were always in danger from a stocky fast little fellow named Hap Harmon who was one of the best halfbacks of his day. He caught a punt and Washburn tackled him at once but insecurely. Billy had him by one leg and Harmon was churning to get loose. I was coming down the field not far away and by putting forth all the speed and competitive fire I did not have, I certainly could have drilled Harmon and ended the play then and there.

But I let up and Harmon shook loose and ran for the touchdown that won the game. Afterward, I was neither praised nor censured for my part in it. The coach saw neither the series of blocks I made on the tackle play nor the dismal failure to nail Harmon on the punt. I was content to have the whole business forgotten. The next week Washburn, Knauth, and I went back to running the tackle play the way the coach wanted it run, and I don't recall that it gained an inch in the concluding games with Springfield and Williams.

THE AMBITION OF MOST STUDENTS OF AM-
herst College in the pre-World War I era
was to drop Latin and mathematics as soon
as it was possible under the rules and to arrange the academic schedule in such a way
that it wouldn't interfere too seriously with college life.
That is the reason this former Amherst student doesn't
know a thing about chemistry and physics. This is a grave
admission in these days, but these two subjects looked
"mathematical" at the time and therefore were avoided.
Two years of biology, plus one course each in geology
and astronomy fulfilled the scientific requirement for an
A.B.

Astronomy I was a celebrated course in Amherst for
many reasons, the most important of which was that it
was the least exacting phase of the curriculum. Professor
Davy Todd, who taught it, realized that his enormous
classes were not attributable to avidity for astral calcula-
tions, so he spread an atmosphere of restfulness, lecturing
steadily, requiring practically nothing in the way of
papers or laboratory (observatory) work. Each class included four or five who were interested and to these he
opened the gates of heaven. The rest were there to get
scientific credit and he gave it freely, flunking nobody,
handing out no mark lower than B.

Davy didn't even care whether or not his students came
to class. He called the roll perfunctorily and when two
voices answered simultaneously for an absent brother, he
said, "One at a time, gentlemen," and marked the brother
present.

He was a distinguished astronomer who looked the
part. He wore a short beard which was mowed to a point
and the clothes of a country squire. After he finished the

roll he stood up and jerked his right thumb upward. The class would intone, "Zenith." Then he would point down with the same thumb and the answer would be "Nadir." He would stick his finger straight out and bend it upward. . . . "Right Ascension."

"Very good, gentlemen," he would say. "You are becoming astronomers."

Many of us used Davy's lecture time to prepare classroom material for less comfortable instructors but it was hard not to listen to him. While he gave us nothing in the way of celestial mathematics, he explored the romantic phase of astronomy such as the rings of Saturn and the Martian canals.

The second semester was navigation, and while Davy could not rule out computations in teaching such a subject, he kept them merciful. He was greatly loved by the members of his classes, as witness the eclipse of the moon which occurred early one winter morning.

"There will be a total eclipse of the moon, starting at three forty-two tomorrow morning," Davy told his class. "I shall be at the observatory from three o'clock on and shall be happy to see any of you gentlemen who are interested."

It was snowing at two forty-five and the thermometer at the fraternity house registered ten below when my roommate, Raymond Ross, of Crawfordsville, Indiana, routed me out to attend the eclipse. Ross was a determined man, an idealist, as witness the fact that he fought and survived three years of World War I in the French Foreign Legion.

"We've got to go," said Ross. "If we don't poor old Davy will be all alone up there."

The fraternity was at the extreme northern end of the

town, the observatory beyond the southern edge. We slogged through the snow for two miles and arrived half frozen. Inside it was like Times Square. All hands had turned out to keep Davy from lonely melancholia. We should have been good enough astronomers to know that we couldn't see the eclipse in a snowstorm. However, Professor Todd was there and Ross and I both thought he recognized us as students when he greeted us.

One of the features of the second semester course in navigation was a cruise during Easter vacation on the yacht of Mortimer Schiff, a rich and distinguished graduate. Each year the cruising party assembled in New York and put in at Jack's and other ports of call before undertaking the main voyage. However, the cruise was called off in our year. The boys had made such a shambles of the yacht the previous year, it was reported, that Mr. Schiff and President Meiklejohn had decided against continuance. I cannot therefore confirm personally the thesis, advanced by earlier classes, that Davy Todd was the world's outstanding shipmate.

He was one of a group of redoubtable old boys who attempted to knock the corners off the Amherst youth of the era. Others of his ilk were: Professor Emerson in geology; Tip Tyler and Mud Puppy Loomis in biology; Charley Bennett and Billy Cowles in Latin; "Nungy" (Professor Genung) in Biblical literature; Grovy (Professor Grosvenor) in government; Crock Thompson in history; Billy Baxter in Spanish; Manthey-Zorn in German; and Stowell in French.

A faculty member to whom I was devoted was Professor Utter of the English department, a stooping red-bearded Harvard man who guided me into a great deal of good reading I wouldn't have discovered by myself.

Anatole France, to this day my chief literary hero, I encountered in a French course under Professor Stowell. The required reading, supposedly in French, *The Red Lily* and *Revolte des Anges* started me on a spree which carried me through France from *Penguin Island* to *The Queen Pedoque.* I sloughed off Henri Bordeaux and other psychological novelists to stay with Anatole. His double entendres and sentence inversions had me mesmerized.

For a football player pleasurable study was limited to the second semester. The two months between the end of the football season and midyears were a wild scramble to make up for the neglects of autumn. I found myself running far behind the pack in philosophy and Spanish. I tried to study philosophy solo but bogged down in the prose of Immanuel Kant. I needed help, so I engaged Bill Avirett, a senior with whom I later worked on the New York *Herald Tribune.*

"Kant believes this," said Billy, waving "The Critique of Pure Reason" at me.

"In that case, why doesn't he say so?" I responded sullenly.

I don't think Coach Avirett was particularly pleased with his pupil but he got me through the course.

I took another tack in Spanish grammar. Here was a subject which required mere spade work and memory. There was one other complete delinquent in the class, a pleasant man named Lozier who was having a tough time with all his courses.

I decided I would learn Spanish the hard way by tutoring him. I didn't say I wanted to tutor him. I said I wanted to study with him. We put in many hours learning grammar and irregular verbs. Lozier's opacity and good nature were unfailing.

We recited to each other. We went over and over the stuff day by day and when the midyear exam finally came we entered the room with confidence and finished our books before anyone else. Both of us passed the course.

I met Professor Billy Baxter on the street and he rejoiced over me.

"You made the highest mark on the examination," he said . . . "I regret I can only give you a B. Your early work was poor."

Social life in Amherst, which did not begin for me until late February, was governed largely by the rules of Smith College, located in Northampton seven miles west and, to a lesser degree, by those of Mount Holyoke, at South Hadley Falls seven miles south.

I'll have to approach this problem from a Smith point of view inasmuch as I had only one date at Mount Holyoke, batting for a brother who was in the hospital. I found the lady, who was supposed to be a blue stocking, to be strictly atypical.

I would say, however, that the Smith girls of the era —kind old grannies of today—were on the average greatly snappier. To have and control one of this breed to such an extent that she would pass up the weekend goings-on at Yale or Dartmouth for a simple fraternity dance at Amherst was to rate as a Man Who.

To protect these lovelies from the wolves of Amherst and other groups, the Smith College authorities enforced a code of rules modeled on those of a women's reformatory. If you had an ordinary date you could call for the lady at seven thirty and were required to bring her back undamaged at ten o'clock. On reentry she reported in some detail to a person who looked like Ilsa Koch.

Activities on dates were strictly limited. You could

take the lady to dinner in one of three or four approved teahouses. You could walk around Paradise Pond or up Dippy Hill. If the local movie was not on the Index you and the lady could see it. In any case, cloture was at ten.

This may have been just as well because the last trolley car back to Amherst left at ten twenty-seven. By running like a deer you could squeak in two beers at Rahar's and catch the car on the fly at Rahar's corner.

When there was a dance at Amherst the Smith girls who had gone through all the steps of temporal conditioning could get an extended night out terminating at eleven o'clock. When there was a game, the fraternity dance started as soon as it was over. The girls and their escorts would walk the mile or two from Pratt Field to the scene of the dance. If no game the dance started at three thirty.

This gay affair would end at ten o'clock, when a formidable group of chaperons would latch onto the girls and march them down to catch the last car for Hamp.

Before coming to Amherst each girl had to make a formal call on the chaperon. Her Amherst date would tell her the name of the one to which she was assigned. Before anything was done the fraternity made sure of its chaperons and when the old girls came to the dance they were treated with great deference on the theory it made them less tough.

A stooge would be assigned to pick each one up in Hamp and bring her to the House. Reluctant stags were told off to play auction bridge with them and each brother who had brought a girl was required to list one chaperon dance. This was known as smashing baggage.

It was all carefully organized and there was no booze, except for the orchestra. It was assumed that no orchestra could play without a few slugs. This was the era of the double-downbeat, just before the sax and horn supplanted the banjos, tenor banjos, and fiddles in what we shall anachronistically call the dance combo.

The orchestra that everyone wanted was Whitstein's of New Haven. This outranked costlier New York combinations in the Amherst rating. The featured player was a violinist who wandered around among the dancers playing the air an octave high. Among the thump songs, "Maori" was the favorite Amherst number. This was a syncopated tom-tom job which started nowhere and went nowhere.

The dances, which occurred rarely, the weekly home basketball games, weekends at home, and some studious endeavor occupied us during the cold months.

The winter in western Massachusetts is characteristically brutal and we hadn't learned to enjoy activities like skiing which the rugged modern college boys seem to like. In my day you were considered a "wheat" (same as a "lep") if you had any truck with jolly outdoor sports. The fashionable attitude was to curse winter and get indoors as fast as you could.

A catastrophe hit in my junior year. Hamp went dry and jolly groups no longer could sit around Rahar's or the Draper bar. The exercise of local option was a blow not only from the alcoholic point of view but because Dick Rahar would sell you, in nondry days, a wonderful planked steak with fixings for one dollar a man and would add a large decanter of port with two drinks of brandy in it for an additional seventy-five cents.

There were lectures in College Hall which some of us attended on the theory that we were improving ourselves and various student activities like the dramatic society and the mandolin club. I was interested in getting in the latter for the trips it took but was turned down, though I could play well enough, because I couldn't strum the thing with my wrist humped up, and this was the accepted fashion.

Spring is particularly beautiful after a New England winter and when it finally came, joy increased in Amherst and marks went down. The "wheats" went on long healthy walks through the Pelham Hills accompanied by the "leps." The rest of us played baseball, tennis, even golf, or participated in bull sessions on the porch.

The vernal routine was interrupted in my senior year by a declaration of war. Immediately the college became savagely patriotic. A known pacifist was dunked in the town horse trough and the students virtually stopped academic work and talked into the night about the merits of various branches of service.

By this time my roommate, Ray Ross, who had left college the previous fall, purportedly to be an ambulance driver, had switched to the Foreign Legion and had received the first of several wounds. He wrote me from the south of France to say that his wound was minor and that he would soon be back in action. I received a letter from my father in which he advised me to apply for officers' training and one from my mother in which she said the German people were *gemütlich,* but that Kaiser Wilhelm, who was leading them astray, was full of *Schrecklichkeit.*

The only practical things done at Amherst were the organization of a military company and a faculty ruling that each student who signed up for military training would be allowed to drop one course. I hastened to drop a course in ancient Frankish drama, which was written in a language I frequently couldn't find in my French dictionary.

The agricultural college on the northern edge of town was a state school and so had regular military training. The major in charge was ordered to take on Amherst as well and called a meeting at his house of all Amherst students who had any military training. I had been to two student camps at Plattsburg Barracks and came out of the meeting with a simulated commission as second lieutenant.

The major had applications for the war training camp for officers, also at Plattsburg, and I filled one in and sent it off. At that stage I might have been accepted in spite of my eyes, for confusion reigned and I could see well enough with glasses, but calamity swarmed over me.

In those days there was a game the girls and boys used to play. The boy would light a match and if he could burn it up entirely it was proof that the girl loved him. The boy had to change his grip to the burned end of the match to complete the incineration, and custom demanded that the girl make every effort to blow out the flame.

I had shifted ends and was back-pedaling after the manner prescribed by Kid Scaler for guys who have been tagged. The girl was chasing me with great show of spirit. At this point I tripped over a rug and broke my right leg.

So I had to write the army and say I couldn't be with it at Plattsburg.

By the time graduation came there were only half a dozen seniors left. The rest had gone to Plattsburg or joined the navy. I was on crutches and that's why I sat through the first half of the address delivered by Governor Calvin Coolidge, class of '96. By that time I had renounced the Republican party and could take no more. I hopped out of the row, resumed my crutches, and escaped. I found my father sitting on a bench under a maple tree smoking a cigarette.

"What an old seed!" said my father.

That's what Cal seemed to be, but, to look ahead a little, he did Amherst more good than all the Pratts, Plymptons, etc., who bequeathed all that lovely money. When he got on the ticket with Warren G. Harding on the strength of the myth that he did something good and noble in connection with the Boston police strike, people began to notice him.

When he succeeded Harding the right-thinkers all knew that he had gone to Amherst and hastened to send their sons. The college grew to twelve hundred in less than one undergraduate cycle. It numbered about two hundred regular students when Cal Coolidge delivered the graduation address to the class of 1917, most of whose members, having returned on furlough, were wearing khaki or blue under their academic robes.

I was called in the draft and turned down. I made the rounds of the recruiting offices and failed all eye examinations, even those of the French and Canadian armies. I felt that the biggest show I would ever have a chance to see was going on and that I was being left out of it.

But what could I do? . . . I accepted a job as an "executive trainee" in a textile mill. There I joined a squad of miserable draft-dodgers who were happy to be in essential industry. They paid for their safety. The mill schedule, like others at the time, was ten hours a day, fifty-five hours a week. They, and of course I, frequently were called on to work three hours more at night without compensation. We were business trainees and as such were paid nominal salaries—fifteen dollars a week.

I was very unhappy, more anxious than ever to get into some kind of active war service. I finally heard that the

United States Shipping Board was enlisting neophytes for the duration to make up the shortage of professional hands in the merchant marine.

The Shipping Board doctor passed me—but only for work in the steward's department. I found, however, that the Shipping Board exerted practically no control over its new men once they had been inducted. Therefore I made one trip as gunners' mess boy, then shipped over as a seaman without any objection from anybody.

That's how I happened to be aboard S.S. *Amphion*— the interned German ship *Köln*—when this book began.

5 IN THE COURSE OF MY SERVICE IN THE merchant marine I visited all the ports of France between Le Havre and Bordeaux. I steered ships into New York harbor, learned to splice and to tie a rolling hitch and a bowline-in-a-bight and shivered in my boots when our six-incher opened up on a periscope half a mile astern. The *Amphion* kept her posterior to the enemy as her Navy E (excellent) gun crew streamed shells at him. I was told off in a bucket brigade which passed ammunition up from below and didn't see much of the action. They say fire was coming out of the ship's stack as she reached three knots above her supposed flank speed of 11.5 knots.

That was my only real action of the war, though occasionally convoying destroyers dropped depth charges on supposed U boats which might well have been whales.

I was halfway home from Europe when the war ended. The *Amphion* had been put in dry dock and I had shipped over in an ocean-greyhound called the *Pawnee* (ex-German *Harbourg*), which needed twenty-one days to make the mouth of the Garonne River and nearly as long to get home under light ballast.

We weathered a gale on the return trip though heaven knows why. The captain, a de-retired old man whose name might have been Queeg, kept her on her course at all risks and there were times when the man at the wheel could look straight down into the ocean. The captain insisted on steering from the bridge.

When the war ended we were having better weather. The captain rang the submarine alarm and shouted through a megaphone, "The war is over!"

The watches below, pouring out of the forecastle and struggling into warm coats and lifejackets on the well deck, looked sullenly up at the bridge.

"Why did that old son-of-a-bitch have to wake me up?" a pitch-black fireman growled.

I paid off the *Pawnee* in New York and went back to Worcester, Massachusetts, where my mother, father, and sisters welcomed me as if I had personally routed the Kaiser. They all expected, apparently, that I would relax for a while and then settle into a nice peaceful job in Worcester or its environs.

My mother said she thought I should "write," a prospect that filled me with alarm. Personally there would have been no question about my future if I hadn't been an optical cripple. I would have stayed at sea the rest of my life.

But I couldn't get an able seaman's ticket, let alone a deck officer's license. I was qualified in most ways, but I couldn't pass the eye test. I might have transferred to the engine room but I hated machinery as I had always hated mathematics.

I decided to take one more trip and joined John Wofford, a pal from the *Pawnee*, in Boston to look for a ship. We registered in the union hall and put up at Phineas Snow's Boarding House, which provided bed and board for sailors for a dollar a day.

Eventually we were sent to Portland, Maine, to join the crew of the *Lake Govan*, built for the New York to Cuba Mail Co., a Ward Line subsidiary. I shipped as quartermaster (man who steers), though I rated only as ordinary seaman. I took her out through the Portland drawbridge —it was sixteen below when we sailed—and into New York.

Somewhere along the line I had picked up an infection in the second joint of my right index finger. Now it swelled to double its size and the pain became severe. When I went to the Marine Infirmary at South Ferry I was greeted with cheers by the staff, for I was the first patient in a month who didn't have gonorrhea, at that time an occupational disease of seamen.

The young doctor in charge looked at my finger with great interest and announced that amputation was indicated. That was enough for me. I got out of there quickly, was paid off the *Lake Govan* and returned to Worcester, where my uncle, Dr. Lemuel F. Woodward, prescribed a course of hot soaks in disinfectant. This treatment saved the finger, though in a permanently bowed state. This I found to be an aid in putting spin on my curve when I returned to semipro ball.

I found on my return to Worcester that my career had been laid out for me by my mother. All I had to do was to drop in at the Worcester *Evening Gazette* and accept the job she had arranged for me.

Ultimately, I called on the city editor and got the job. Never, from that time until I retired on April 1, 1962, was I willfully out of the newspaper business. Without willing it, I spent one year free-lancing and one as editor of a magazine called *Sports Illustrated*, not to be confused with the current journal.

The two-year hiatus was forced on me by Mrs. Helen Rogers Reid, mother superior at the New York *Herald Tribune*, who decided that I was not subservient enough for her and ordered George Cornish, the managing editor, to fire me. Mrs. Reid is one of the two most determined women I have ever encountered. The other was my mother, who I am sure could have outslugged the *Trib*'s Boadicea at catchweights.

While Mrs. R. merely liquidated an established sports

editor who also had scored as a war correspondent, my
mother worked miracles. By the force of her presence she
rendered scot-free two people who had been convicted of
homicide.

The first was a nineteen-year-old housemaid who had
smothered her new-born illegitimate with a pillow. My
mother sat down in the governor's office and wouldn't get
out until she got a full pardon for the girl. Then she
tracked down the baby's daddy and made him marry her.

The second was a middle-aged Italian who had got into
a fight with a friend and stabbed him through the top of
the aorta. Mother ran into this fellow at the prison hospital
for tubercular felons where she visited weekly as one of
her good works.

She pointed out to the probation board that the man
was essentially good and kind, even though he had put a
few minor scratches on earlier enemies; also that he longed
for sunny Italy and that he would have a better chance
there of getting over his tuberculosis. The probation board
ultimately saw that it would have no chance to undertake
any other work until my mother's knifer had been de-
ported. It acceded.

My mother was born in Negaunee, Michigan, April 7
or 8, 1869. She could not remember the exact date. She
was called Stella and was the second child of the Michigan
state geologist, Major Thomas Benton Brooks, who cam-
paigned in the Civil War with the New York volunteer
engineers. Her mother was Hannah Hulse, who died when
my mother was small.

The major moved to Germany and my mother was
brought up in Bavaria, principally in Munich, where her
father was teaching and studying geology. Three other
children were born in Germany and when their mother

and the elder son died, my mother took charge of the family. In the course of a few years the family had become virtually German and the Teutonization was complete when my grandfather married a German woman named Marta Geisler.

My mother couldn't speak English until she was well grown but learned it fast when the family moved back to America and took up residence in a house on the bank of the Hudson on the outskirts of Newburgh. Ultimately she spoke German and English equally well and without an accent in either language.

My mother was the world's most beautiful woman, a fact which probably increased her powers of persuasion. When persuasion failed she became a Panzer corps and rode over the opposition. She was a German in everything but birth, capable of great kindness but imperious and essentially snobbish. When she was getting her murderers off, she did not think of herself as a woman who was helping fellowmen, rather as a Junkerin acting for the good of the peasants.

My sisters and I were required to speak German at meals for some years until my mother was kidded out of it by my father, who insisted on joining in with egregious bursts of bilingualism. My father was superior in mental agility and always offered a fluid front when issues began to be drawn. He was devoted to Mother but he conned her shamelessly and preserved a life of his own about which she knew nothing.

My own attitude was the same, though, having a trace of my mother's Panzer spirit, I frequently fought with her.

She bulldozed my three sisters scandalously and thwarted them by her strange European convictions. No young girl should have a large mirror. No young girl should be told she was pretty. It would lead to vanity. No child, boy or girl, was ever to be allowed in the house until four o'clock whatever the weather. He must stay out and breathe the fresh air. Children should not eat pies, cake, doughnuts or other fried things, though they might have a little *Kaffeekuchen* for Sunday breakfast. This item was wrestled up by a series of Irish cooks who also manufactured the New England Sunday breakfast staples such as fish balls and fried mush. For some reason the last two items were not considered "fried things."

The girls had a miserable life. They were always ashamed of the weird "practical" clothes they were forced to wear. They were always being told they couldn't play with certain children for one reason or another. If by some mischance they were invited to an evening party, they couldn't go because they would get home too late.

How the girls survived it and became the women they are now I cannot conceive. Except for Stella, known as Brooksie, who came along late, their young lives were not joyous.

Hildegard, the oldest next to me, developed a quiet stoicism and passive resistance. It was obvious early that she was a gifted artist, so she was able to light out for Boston at a comparatively early age to study in the museum school.

Katharine became too tough for my mother to handle and too bright not to recognize some of the parental precepts as guff. She entered high school at eleven and was held back two years before she went on to Bryn Mawr and Virginia Medical, where she and another girl were the first female graduates.

The educational holdback imposed on Katharine was a

good thing, no doubt, for she went to a Washington school and lived with Aunt Hildegard, my mother's brilliant sister. The latter was a successful novelist under the aegis of Henry Holt, but her career was ruined by a frightful case of arthritis.

Katharine interned at Bellevue and went to Worcester to practice with my uncle, who treated a large number of factory accidents. She quickly got sick of this and went back to New York to intern in pediatrics. Then she turned to psychiatry. Now she is head of pediatric psychiatry at Lenox Hill and wife of a retired engineer.

Being a Freudian, she could not have been wholly influenced in her choice of career by two close antecedents. Her great-grandfather Woodward was first president of the American Psychiatric Society and founder of what used to be called the Hartford (Conn.) Retreat. The late Dr. Adolf Meyer, of Johns Hopkins Phipps Clinic, married Mary, another of my mother's sisters.

Stella, or Brooksie, my own third sister, followed a less distinctive course. She got married young, is now widowed and works in the public library at Worcester. She inherited my mother's blond good looks. Incidentally, if I may be pardoned a paternal brag, so did my own daughter Ellen and two of my grandchildren. The good looks of my daughter Mary and the rest of my grandchildren are attributable to Ricie, my wife, and her Irish antecedents.

From what I have told you about my mother you can see why I knew there was a job for me at the Worcester *Evening Gazette* if she said so. In getting it for me she apparently had followed a less direct method than usual.

In the course of off-watches and duty aboard ship when in port, I wrote a sheaf of letters addressed to my mother but meant for the whole family. They were about the French countryside, the seaports, the people and the less lurid aspects of a sailor's life.

My mother kept the letters in order and ultimately called John Nelson, a veteran reporter, and asked if he would like to print them in the *Gazette*. The Worcester papers at that time would print any intelligence coming from a Worcester boy who was anywhere near the war. So, in spite of the fact that the letters had been censored by me as I wrote them and therefore lacked any touches that might have redeemed them, a solid page of my writing appeared in the *Gazette*.

My mother's next move was to brace the city editor. She told him that she was Mrs. Rufus Stanley Woodward whose son Stanley had written the brilliant piece about the war which had appeared in the *Gazette*. She asked if the city editor would like to hire Stanley when he got back from the war.

Nick Skerrett—that was the city editor's name—probably had a dozen guys coming back from the war whom he had to place but he was a gallant Irishman. So to oblige a lady he said "yes" and my newspaper career was launched.

ON JANUARY 7, 1919, I STARTED TO BE A reporter. I didn't undertake the job with much enthusiasm. I knew nothing whatever about the traditions and practices of the daily newspaper. About ten o'clock I walked up the splintered wooden steps which led from the street directly to the second-floor editorial room of the *Gazette* and was directed to a big tough-looking man who wore a felt hat pulled down over his round steel glasses.

"Where have you been?" said Skerrett. "This is no time to come to work."

I explained that I had not been told what time to come to work and would show up henceforth at the time he designated.

"Be here at quarter of eight every morning. . . . Can you type?"

"No."

"Learn to type by tomorrow. I won't accept handwritten copy after today."

He then gave me my assignments: the Armory, still occupied by the wartime Home Guard, and the railroads. He showed me my desk and turned me loose with no instructions on how to do anything and without presenting me to any of the busy people I saw in the city room.

I went to the Armory and the freight office of the Boston & Albany Railroad where I knew a guy named Tommy O'Connor and returned in a couple of hours with two items: (a) Company A was planning a smoker; (b) the B. & A. had declared an embargo on some unimportant class of merchandise.

I wrote these stories—at that time I thought of them as "articles"—with a pencil. Then I turned to the pressing job of learning to type.

The machine that unfolded from my desk was a blind-writer. The keys worked under the roller and you had to lift it up to see what you had written. Over and over I tapped out, "Now is the time for all good men to come to the aid of the party." This is what a girl who sat next to me told me to write. It was before the era of "The quick brown fox jumped over the lazy dog."

By five thirty everyone had left the editorial office except a man who was typing sheet after sheet at high speed. I envied his proficiency as I plugged away. I finally quit at eleven o'clock, confident that I could type my "articles."

Skerrett didn't speak to me for a week, but I started to make friends with some of the younger staff members. Meanwhile I was turning in small items from the Armory and the freight office. They were carefully typed, virtually letter perfect. I didn't yet know that newspaper copy is habitually corrected with a pencil.

Skerrett didn't comment on my output, but some of it, in radically changed form, got into the paper. Each morning when I reported for work there would be two or three clippings on my desk. They would be the stories carried by the *Telegram*, morning paper, on the fields I was covering.

One morning there was a clipping about a minor derailment and across it was scrawled, "See Skerrett."

Skerrett let me stand twenty minutes beside his desk, then he said, "Why didn't we have that railroad story?"

"I just didn't hear about it, Mr. Skerrett."

"Well, God damn it, you start hearing about things. You start getting on the ball or I'll kick you out of here so fast you won't hit the stairs. . . . That accident happened at one o'clock, three hours before our last edition.

What were you doing all day, hanging around a gin mill?
Now get out and get some news."

This was the first attack Skerrett made on me. There
were dozens more. When the *Post*, which was the other
afternoon paper, or the *Telegram* had an item I didn't
have, he would jump on me with both feet, often without
a thread of justification.

Suppose the *Telegram* had a story that had obviously
developed within its own time (after four P.M.), I should
have known about it in advance.

Skerrett would get red and shout, pound his big fist on
the desk to emphasize points of journalistic law. You got
the idea that nothing was as important as the story, any
story; that a reporter must not only come back with
routine facts but should get into such a position that no
fact could escape him. Skerrett wrote his creed in the assignment book one day.

"A man who gets what he is sent for is a reporter. A
man who gets what he is sent for and something more is a
good reporter. A man who does not get what he is sent
for is a goddamned nuisance and will be fired."

After six weeks with the *Gazette* I was as frightened
of Skerrett as if he were a mathematics professor or a
boatswain. And I never got over being frightened of him
in his mood of righteous or unrighteous anger during the
three years I worked for him. My indoctrination into the
newspaper business was based on terror. It was a real job
of brainwashing.

Skerrett did not reveal the secrets of journalism to me.
I got better tips on how to do things from old Billy Larkin,
kindly head of the copy desk, and from Phil Ronayne,
Jim Haberlin, and George Witham, older reporters. But
Skerrett convinced me that the newspaper business was

the most important thing in the world and to this day I
remain convinced.

In his way Skerrett was a teacher of method. He
wouldn't tell you how to do anything, but if you did it
wrong he would tear you to pieces. This made you aware
of the wrong things, or the things that Skerrett thought
were wrong. Wrongest of all was not getting a picture
when sent after one.

I have committed felonies to get pictures. I have broken
into houses and stolen them off the piano. I have imper-
sonated cops. Skerrett was so much more terrible than
any outside retribution that I had no fear except of failure.
Covering a hammer murder in which a man killed his wife
and five children, I walked in among the bodies and took
every picture in the house so there wouldn't be any left
when the opposition representative got there. The cops
had left a guard at the door, but I bluffed him with my
reporter's badge.

After a long time I discovered Skerrett was two men.
The first was the savage city editor; the second was a
pleasant man with a bright sense of humor and a gift for
telling Irish dialect stories. The second personality he hid
from his staff until he decided that each in turn was an
indoctrinated newspaper man. I didn't see the pleasant
Skerrett until I had worked many months for the other
one. By then prohibition was in effect.

Then one day he came up to me at my desk and said,
"Do you ever take a drink, Stanley?"

"Yes, Mr. Skerrett, sometimes."

"Nick," he said. "My name is Nick. . . . Well, let's
go."

We walked through to Front Street and halfway to
Union Station, then turned into an inconspicuous doorway

marked "Sterling Hotel." The lobby, which was up one flight, was deserted except for an old boy who was sweeping the carpet.

"Where do we go, Jeremiah, ye spalpeen?" asked Skerrett.

"Room three and bad cess to you, Nicholas."

It was a small bedroom with a white iron bed, a rocking chair, and a washstand with a white china pitcher, basin, and slop jar, standard equipment in the pre-room-and-bath days. Skerrett removed his coat but not his hat, sat on the bed and motioned me to the chair. Jeremiah came in carrying a pint of Green River and two glasses.

"Thank you, Jeremiah. Will you have one?"

"I will not and no thanks to me. I am only the slave of that lawbreaker, Jerry Sullivan. That will be five dollars."

It turned out that both the owner and the man of all work of the Sterling Hotel were named Jeremiah Sullivan, but the owner who lived in and took the night watch was known as Jerry, he being more convivial.

Such things Skerrett explained to me as we knocked over the pint with chasers out of the white water pitcher. We ordered another pint and Skerrett started talking about Worcester and its newspapers from the days of the old *Spy*. He talked about people alive and dead and particularly about one Peleg Murray, a state plainclothes policeman who had all the characteristics of a Keystone cop. He fascinated Skerrett.

"The boys used to make a club out of Peleg's office," said Skerrett. "And the way they'd kid him was scandalous. One spring a woman's body was discovered out by Sterling reservoir and it made quite a story for a week. The lady couldn't be identified, and inasmuch as there were no signs of violence, the papers lost interest in it.

"Not Peleg. It was the only decent murder he'd had for a long time and by gum he was going to solve it. The boys started leaving clues for him. One day he found a bread knife sticking in a tree; another, there was evidence of a mysterious horseman. This clue had been arranged by obtaining a truckload of manure from the city stables and spot-piling it around the murder scene. There was enough manure for a cavalry troop.

"Other clues appeared and each time Peleg would call a press conference and make known his deductions. Finally everyone got tired of it and nobody would listen to him."

As time went on Skerrett and I made other visits to the Sterling and other oases. Sometimes Joe DeWolf, the managing editor, would come along too. He was nearly as good a newspaperman as Skerrett, but his forte was make-up rather than production of the news. From him I learned how to handle a story inside the office and the mysteries of the composing room.

In the course of a couple of years I covered everything on the paper including courts and city hall. The first decent assignment I had was the Protestant undertakers. They carried on a coy practice of not notifying the papers when a leading citizen died and had to be checked three times a day. The Catholics and Jews gave us no worry. They would call us the minute a prominent citizen cooled off.

My next job was covering police. This also included the district court which sat every morning and the fire departments. It was far too much for one man to do and ultimately Skerrett gave me an associate, a boy named Jack O'Brien who had just come back from the war with the twenty-sixth (Yankee) division.

O'Brien was smart though inexperienced and being Irish

he made more of a hit with the cops than I did. We worked well together and developed a system under which one would cover the police court while the other went out to investigate one or more of the late stories which had appeared in short form in the *Telegram*. With freedom and time to work on one story, each of us turned up some good ones.

One night a lady dropped off a man at the City Hospital who was full of bullets and barely alive. She said she found him beside the road and hurried away before anyone could question her. O'Brien and I found her and persuaded her to tell the police. The man recovered and she married him after she had spent a year in jail.

The Worcester cops caught a minor yegg who had helped rob the house of a former member of the diplomatic corps in Pomfret, Connecticut. It was no ordinary robbery, for the victim was a man who had spent a matter of millions picking up art and curios around the Mediterranean and in the Near East.

The Worcester cops had a sketchy list of what had been taken, just enough to set off O'Brien and me. We got hold of the diplomat and he reluctantly gave us a detailed description of his losses. We opened him up by telling him that the Worcester police were on the point of recovering everything and we'd like to have a list to check against items recovered. We didn't wait. The next afternoon's paper had the whole business with the following lead under an eight-column Railroad Gothic head.

"A gold scarab from the tomb of Ptolemy II attached to a priceless lapis lazuli rosary, blessed by Pope Clement VII and thought to have been worked by Benvenuto Cellini, is today the cynosure of the local and state police."

I confess to having written this chunk of Iowa No. 13

yellow dent and I hereby absolve O'Brien. It tickled Skerrett who asked me daily for a month if there was anything new on the "lazooly" story.

O'Brien and I finally came up against a story which stumped us as well as the official investigators. The body of a young man was found in the firebox of an engine in the Boston & Maine roundhouse at the north end of town. The man lived a quarter of a mile from the scene of his death and was known to be a steady, sensible fellow who went to work every day.

There was no indication that he had been wedged into the firebox by assailants. There were no marks on his body except burns, not even any serious burns, for, though the fire was burning, it had been banked for the night and was cold on top. The door was partly open.

The medical examiner said death was caused by gas poisoning, which indicated that the man was alive when he entered the firebox. The inquest found that death was accidental. This was manifestly silly but no sillier than verdicts of murder or suicide would have been under the revealed circumstance.

O'Brien and I were sure it was murder but we couldn't find anybody who seemed to have a reason for killing the man. We spent weeks of our own time trying to find new facts. We suggested the body be exhumed for examination of the stomach and blood vessels. Our theory was that the man was either poisoned or drugged and then was slid gently into the firebox.

When exhumation was ruled out we turned to psychiatry. We found a doctor at the State Hospital who said that under certain circumstances of derangement a man might crawl into a live firebox. The circumstances didn't seem to fit our man and we dropped the story.

Until I worked on the *Gazette* I thought of Worcester as a dull place. Now I found it full of fascination. I had had a parochial bringing up. I was sent to a private school for the grammar grades, didn't know any kids who didn't live on the West Side until my first year in Classical High. There I met them from all over in school and through playing against and with them in baseball. It seems there was a dearth of catchers in town and being one and, most important, having the catcher's equipment, I was in high demand.

But the town wasn't fully revealed to me until I worked on the paper and mixed in all the various activities, such as murders, robberies, strikes, symphony concerts, crap games, court trials, politics, and society.

Skerrett gave me the job of reviewing the burlesque show. We got a new one every week. Early in my career he sent me to cover the concert of young Jascha Heifetz playing in Mechanics Hall with the Boston Symphony. I asked Heifetz in the Blue Room what his encores had been and neither he nor the accompanist could remember. "Valse Bluette" was the only one I recognized.

I covered labor for a year and discovered for the first time that capital is not always right. I hung around the Labor Temple and got some good tips from the boys who were then known as business agents. A particular friend who was head of the Machinists gave me a scoop that rocked the city one afternoon. He said:

"The gas workers are going to strike. Don't say where you got it."

It turned out to be true and it was a great story because almost everyone in Worcester was dependent on gas for cooking. I got another scoop on a strike at Grattan & Knight Co., then the largest leather mill in the country. It was here that I saw a most unpleasant and galling sight—police beating up pickets for no reason I could understand.

The most joyous strike I recall was at the Diamond Tack Co., a small mill run by a cheerful Irishman named Pat Somers. He had five employees who were ordered out by their national organization. Mr. Somers invited them into the office to drink home brew and play pinochle. When a national officer came and insisted they establish a picket line he took his turn with the strikers.

The greatest literary figure who ever came out of Worcester was Robert Benchley—with all due respect to the historian, George Bancroft. Close behind Benchley comes S. N. Behrman, who was born on Providence Hill and wrote for *The New Yorker* about the Jewish residents of this area.

Another native of Worcester was Schofield Thayer, editor and—I believe—angel of *The Dial*. His mother, Mrs. Ed Thayer, rode around Worcester behind a pair of bobtailed horses and mourned that Schofield was throwing away his poor dear father's money.

The hard core of Worcester society was, and is still, I hear, about as hard core as you can get, little if at all behind the Beacon Hill-Brookline mob of Boston. You are born into Worcester society. You can marry into it. Otherwise, at least in the old days, you were out. Nowadays, I understand, some consideration is being given to gold.

But the top social stratum remained isolated and snobbish. The same might be said of various other sectional groups: the Irish of Vernon Hill, the Negroes of John and Pink streets, the Jews of Providence Hill, the Italians of Shrewsbury Street and the Swedes of Belmont Hill, Greendale, and various other localities.

The original Swedes came to work in the steel mills of

Washburn & Moen. Thousands of relatives and friends followed until in my day the Swedes outnumbered all other racial groups. It was said that half the inhabitants of the city were Swedes—a term which included small minorities of Norwegians, Finns, and Danes—or descendants of Swedes. The mayor, Pehr G. Holmes, was a native of Sweden.

Naturally the newspapers bore the city's Swedishness constantly in mind. Our own set aside one page and carried an eight-column stereo banner, "Swedish News—Social Activities, Churches, Clubs."

We had a girl named Hilda Johnson who covered nothing but Swedish news and wrote three or four columns daily about her people. She was the office beauty, though not on lines you'd expect, for she had flashing black eyes and dark-brown hair which she braided and coiled on top of her head. She was bold and brassy and loud on the telephone as she pried items out of her news sources.

Once she interrupted a Skerrett tirade by kissing the boss smack on the mouth, a maneuver which rendered our dragon pink and speechless. She had a husband, it was reported, and repulsed advances by the staff with competence and finality.

We gave no special treatment to other nationals. Whatever they did went in the general news. There was little commingling of groups and intercommunication lacked the careful politesse of present usage; it was likely, in fact, to be downright insulting. As a picaresque thirteen-year-old catcher for various groups, I was frequently addressed from the sidelines as: you goddamned Willie Boy, You (*sic*) Mick, Sheeny, or Square Head.

I worked only for the Greendale Swedes. The Belmont Hill subdivision had a living-in catcher, a rugged burr-headed Viking named Holmgren who had little skill but overpowered the ball by force of arms.

I played no ball around Worcester from the time my father grounded me in high school until my first summer on the *Gazette* when John McQueeny, the sports editor, got me a job pitching for West Brookfield, a semipro team. I had become a pitcher in college. The first game I worked was the Fourth of July extravaganza against North Brookfield on enemy terrain. I was beaten, 2-1.

I fired a chest-high fast ball to the first hitter and he hammered it over the left-fielder's head for three bases. Obviously I had underestimated the class of the opposition and things looked extremely black. I got out of the first mess by throwing nothing but curve balls. Carefully wasting the fast ball and throwing curves for strikes, I went along well after that and might have won except for a couple of errors in one of the middle innings.

I spent all summer with West Brookfield, pitching either Saturday or Sunday, relieving the other day. This netted ten dollars a game, or twenty dollars a week. This was a fortune for a reporter who was making what I shall call a modest salary.

We played in a series of tough mill towns and usually had to put up with a great deal of unfavorable comment from the crowd. We must have played home games some of the time but I can't remember them. I was seldom bothered by the riding but a fan in Rochdale finally got my combination.

He was sitting in the top row of the third-base bleachers and every time I came to the point of delivering the ball he would scream, "Let me pitch, Woody."

I spotted him early in the game and considered throwing the ball at his head, which would have certainly started a riot. This plan seemed more and more logical each inning, but in the sixth our guys whaled the ball for six runs, thus sewing up the game. After that my friend kept quiet.

The next year McQueeny got me a job in Upton, Massachusetts, on a first-class team that included half a dozen Holy Cross players. Backed by these titans I didn't lose a game. Still the season was a dead loss.

The team was operated by a high school teacher who seemed to me to be thoroughly trustworthy. After the first game, he suggested that I leave my money with him until the end of the season and then collect it all at once.

Thinking of the red cigarshaped Model T on which I wished to make a down payment, I agreed. Unfortunately along about Labor Day my leader skipped with the town blonde and the ball-club funds, leaving a couple of teammates and me with nothing to show for the summer.

My third summer in Worcester I was less impoverished, having been promoted to assistant city editor and raised to thirty-five dollars a week, so I played with an amateur team representing the Kiwanis Club. We had a couple of former minor leaguers and some high school players and we were much too good for most of the teams we played. We began to be quite proud of ourselves.

In late September Holyoke challenged us to play for the New England Kiwanis championship and we hastened to accept. We went to the Connecticut River city looking for another pushover. Even the fact that our catcher, a forty-year-old pro who did most of our long hitting, was unable to make the trip, did not seem serious. The catcher's wife was having a baby any minute and he refused to leave town.

I began to suspect trouble when we went on the field

for pregame practice. The Holyoke Kiwanians were tall, fast, and brimming with professional moves. The true danger was revealed when I saw among the enemy one Skip Dowd, a Worcester man whom I knew to be the regular left-fielder of the Toronto International League Club.

It developed that the Holyoke Kiwanis, having no ball club, had gone out and hired one. It wasn't really necessary to spend that much money to wallop us. I was the only pitcher on our roster and had to go the full nine innings. One ball that Skip Dowd hit cleared the left-field fence and went into the river. It was what later became known as a "tape-measure" home run.

My promotion to assistant city editor was due principally to the fact that Skerrett's health was failing and he could not work full time. Shortly before George F. Booth had sold our paper to its morning rival, the Worcester *Telegram*, and we had moved into the *Telegram* plant. It had a bad effect on all of us, particularly Skerrett, who had spent twenty years fighting the paper with which he was now united.

For some reason not revealed, Skerrett didn't wear his hat in the new office. Perhaps the big new boss made him leave it in the coatroom. It was revealed to us that our Dragon was virtually hairless. His glowers were out of focus now that he no longer directed them under the low brim of his hat.

Actually, the shock of the merger must have been serious to Nick and it wasn't long before his health started to fail. When he didn't come in I sat in his place and I must say the letdown in staff activity was spectacular. When he was there I did rewrite, covered stories, and took hold wherever I was needed. When Miss Alice Gwendolyn

Albee had one of her sick headaches I got out the women's page. Occasionally I batted for McQueeny on the sports page, which had to be locked up at eleven A.M.

At other times I worked on the copy desk under direction of Joe DeWolf, who taught me to write heads, a baffling art which involves epitomizing the story with a limited number of letters. DeWolf and some of our other deskmen were wizards. I was helpless for a time but then it started to come to me and I began to think like a head writer—in short words.

Learning the copy desk made me a complete, if elementary, newspaperman. When I quit the *Gazette*, the best job that was offered me was in the copyreading department and I had just about enough experience to take it.

The only sports-writing job I ever did for the *Gazette* was the Holy Cross-Boston College football game of 1921 in Braves Field, Boston. I went there as assistant to Mc-Queeny and wound up writing the story.

I had one of the original Corona portable typewriters, a tiny machine with a double shift for caps and figures and screws which had to be tightened or loosened to reverse the ribbon. In those preradio and TV days the big evening papers got out a Saturday football extra with running stories on all the important games. The Boston *Transcript* would be on the street with a pretty complete football edition at six o'clock every Saturday night.

I don't remember that the *Gazette* ever got out a football extra on any other occasion, though like all evening papers with any pretensions, we had extras for each day of the World Series.

The *Gazette*'s Boston College-Holy Cross extra was one to end all extras. I wrote nearly a page about the game as it unfolded. McQueeny wanted to see the action so he decided he would observe through his field glasses and call off the plays to me and my Corona.

It was a nasty afternoon and the northeast gale was driving snow and sleet into the old Braves Field press box, which was located on the grandstand roof at the west end of the field. Holy Cross was the underdog, but that never has meant much when these rivals play each other.

Everyone in the press box looked like a snowman before the first quarter was over but McQueeny and I didn't mind it at all for we were avowed Holy Cross fans—he, in fact, was a graduate—and our team started early to macerate the Eagles of Boston.

McQueeny started to dictate the story to me but finally decided to limit himself to the facts of the case and let me embellish them. He would say, "Riopel made seven left side."

On my snowy if faithful Corona this would emerge as, "Starting like a rocket, Hop Riopel slashed inside left tackle and charged to a first down on the Boston 33."

As the score mounted and Holy Cross started to turn the game into a rout I became more and more lyrical, stopping occasionally to reverse the ribbon on the abused Corona. Nobody ever wrote a longer or more excited running story. When the game was over I wanted to launch into a thousand-word lead to tack on the front. McQueeny quashed this. "Just flash them the score," he said. "They want to get the extra on the street."

This was the first out-of-town assignment with expense account I had had, except for one as errand boy for a couple of older reporters who were covering the police strike in Boston. I considered the football story, which was anonymous, to be real big stuff, particularly when Skerrett complimented me on it.

I responded by asking for a raise, and the reluctance of the management to come across started me thinking seriously about leaving the paper. The biggest influence in getting me out of Worcester was the late Cliff Epstein.

He was the best reporter the *Gazette* had in my time. He appeared during the summer and started writing pieces which had a literary quality as well as all essential facts, better stuff by far than we were used to seeing in our sheet.

Epstein was a quiet, inscrutable kind of character and a thoroughly indoctrinated newspaperman. He laughed at me for the bromides I habitually used and for my florid phraseology. I got mad at him at first. Then I saw I could learn from him and we became friends. Finally I moved out of the family mansion and roomed with him in a lodging house on South Main Street.

To this fellow the *Gazette* was a whistle-stop newspaper and he was admittedly biding his time until he could get into a bigger and better one. He had his name in with the Fernald Newspaper Agency, a nationally known outfit which got jobs for reporters, charging one week's pay per job.

Fernald sent Cliff an offer every three or four weeks but for a time nothing suited him. I had more than six months of association with him before he finally took a job on the Detroit *News*. I recognized his superiority and listened to him even when he tore to pieces my masterpiece, the story of the Holy Cross-Boston College game.

The day he went to Detroit, I moved back to my father's house. Epstein was a sensation from the start on the *News*. Soon he was covering many of the top stories and he made a national reputation with his work on the Loeb-Leopold trial in Chicago.

I saw him only once after he left Worcester, though I tried to reach him every time I was in Detroit. Finally I got him on the telephone and called on him at the *News*. We didn't find much to talk about. I could see he was busy and left after a few minutes.

After Epstein left Worcester, I was thoroughly discontented on the *Gazette*. Skerrett wasn't able to get me a raise and secretly advised me to leave. So I put my name on Fernald's list of job applicants and started casting around in other areas.

I called on George F. Booth, former owner of the *Gazette* and he gave me a letter to Robert Lincoln O'Brien, editor of the Boston *Herald*. I called on him and he said there might be an opening for a copyreader and make-up man.

Through Billy Dyer, collector of Internal Revenue in Worcester, I heard there might be an opening on the same paper in sports. At that stage I wasn't very keen about sports but Billy took my case into his own hands and telephoned Burt Whitman, sports editor of the *Herald*. He, as well as Ed Cunningham and Billy Mullins of his staff, were graduates of the Worcester *Telegram*.

I had had an offer from the Springfield *Union* through Fernald but I had heard nothing from Mr. O'Brien. The Springfield money was weak so I accepted a job at fifty-five dollars a week as copyreader and make-up man on the *Herald* sports staff. Two days after I went to work I received a letter from Mr. O'Brien, forwarded from Worcester, which offered me a similar job on the main news desk in the next room.

During my three years on the *Gazette* I saw very little of my father. Whether or not I was living at home I seldom got there for dinner and when I was living there I was out of the house before seven o'clock. We saved Saturday night for each other and generally attended the men's dinner and poker game at the Boat Club. He wasn't too pleased that I was about to mix newspaper work and sports or, surprising to state, that I was moving out of Worcester, apparently for good.

"Now that you are becoming a sports writer, Stan," he said, "it appears the only practical thing I've ever done for you was to teach you to score a ball game."

7 WHEN I MOVED TO BOSTON IN 1922, BABE
Ruth was three years gone from the town
after pitching the Red Sox to victory over
Chicago in the World Series of 1918 and
winning the home run championship with
twenty-nine in 1919. Man o' War was in his second year
of retirement. Bobby Jones was a year away from his first
U.S. golf championship and the story of Francis Ouimet's
victory over Vardon and Ray was still being told with
some freshness. The United States had held the Davis Cup
three years and was to hold it four more before succumb-
ing to France. Jack Dempsey was the world boxing champion. Professional hockey had not come to the eastern
United States and basketball was being played only in
dance halls and minor gymnasiums—where, in my opinion, it should have stayed.

Boston was a good place for a newspaperman to get his
start in sports because it had everything that was going
except a running horse track. There were two ball clubs,
though they were both sinking out of sight. Harvard and
Boston College were big-time football teams. Three or
four boxing clubs operated in the city and there were
others on the outskirts. Everyone was building golf
courses, for the spectacular victory of Ouimet, a Boston
boy, had spurred the town's interest in the game. The
Boston Athletic Association, then at the top of its prestige,
was sponsoring a winter track meet as well as the annual
marathon on Patriots' Day. The Charles River was alive
with eight-oared crews. Harvard, M.I.T., and sundry
school and club crews raced over the mile and three-
quarters course which ended at West Boston Bridge.

Each August the National Tennis Doubles championship was played at Longwood Cricket Club and thou-

sands turned out to watch the Bills, Tilden and Johnston, also Vinny Richards, Richard Norris Williams, the Boston pride, and the rising Frenchmen. Yachting flourished. So did amateur hockey and amateur and semiprofessional baseball. There were dog shows, horse shows, Grand Circuit trotting on the old Readville track and two half-mile tracks for amateur light harness devotees. The Revere Beach bike track (now consigned to the dogs) ran all summer with a weekly motor-paced race as the feature.

There were other things which made good stories. The Wheel About the Hub was a ride around the edges of Boston on high-wheelers in which dauntless old-timers annually participated. Another top event was the annual hurling match on Boston Common between the Irish born in Ireland and those born in Boston. Three or four ambulances always were drawn up on Charles Street for this event, whose motto was: "Play a 'gintleman's' game but get your man."

This reminded me of a speech made by Coach Frank Cavanaugh to the Boston College football squad on the opening day of practice. He assembled the boys in the bleachers on the shady side of the old field and harangued them as follows: "Men of Boston, there is only one way to play this game and that is to the uttermost limits of respectability."

That's the way the Bostonians played it from the schoolboy ranks up. Harvard—which beat Oregon in the 1920 Rose Bowl—never started to slip until politeness reared its ugly head on Soldiers Field. This was shortly after I came to town.

There was hardly a Bostonian over seven who didn't have some avid sporting interest and in many, like Doc

Kendall who launched the Boston Terrier breed and
George V. Brown, wheel-horse of the B.A.A., it was all-
consuming. You could get in plenty of trouble if you left
out of the paper such important events as the Union Boat
Club squash tennis tournament or the West End *boccie*
championship.

When I first went to Boston the radio was feeble and
people actually got athletic results out of the paper. Most
editors were aware of the pull of sports and the sports
extra was an institution. On Saturday afternoon the evening papers would be on the street before six o'clock with
all the football scores and running stories of games most
interesting to people of the Boston area. The *Transcript*
got out some of the best football papers I've ever seen.

At that time there were eight newspapers in Boston, not
counting the *Christian Science Monitor*, whose field was
worldwide rather than local, and Hearst's *Advertiser*
which published only on Sunday. The morning papers
were the *Herald, Globe, Post*, and Hearst's tabloid
Record. In the afternoon there were the *Evening Globe*,
Traveler, Transcript, and *American*.

All except the *Post, Record*, and *American* could be
expected to support the Republican candidate in any election. My own paper, I soon convinced myself, would
have backed an anthropoid ape against Andy Jackson. The
Post made an effort to appeal to the Irish. The *Globe*
aimed at the northern New Englanders and there wasn't a
barn-raising or a strawberry festival in New Hampshire
or Vermont which didn't get in the paper.

In sports the *Transcript* was outstanding, authoritative
in all fields with such writers as George Carens, Linde
Fowler, Bob Harron—currently assistant to the president
of Columbia University—Duke Lake and Ed Schrift-

gieser. The *Herald* was comparable, with Burt Whitman (sports editor), Ed Cunningham, Larry Paton, Bill Mullins, Tom McCabe, and Billy Hamilton. Whitman, Cunningham, and Mullins were from Worcester. The man I succeeded as copyreader was Bernie Austin. He conducted a weekly trotting column for the *Herald* and left to edit a trotting magazine. He continued to write his column for about a year. After that I was called on to take over.

Nick Flatley of the *American* was one of the best sports writers of my Boston days. Bill Cunningham kept the *Post* afloat with a writing gift which either charmed or enraged the readers and either way kept them coming back for more.

In the main, however, Boston sports in those days were written by hacks, some of whom appeared to sell their columns by the line.

I left Worcester in the late afternoon to go to work in Boston. The early afternoon I spent in the office of the *Telegram-Gazette* listening to a farewell lecture by Nick Skerrett. I am sure he considered only my welfare but he didn't approve of the move I was making.

"Sports? . . . No good . . ." He said, "You'll forget what you know about the English language. . . . The Boston *Herald* is not the right paper for you. The *Post*, there's a paper."

Skerrett scrubbed his bald dome with the palm of his hand. He missed his hat. "The *Post* doesn't pussyfoot like the *Herald*. When it gets a good story it plays it to the limit regardless of whom it hurts. . . . Do you know that the managing editor is required to write a letter to Grozier, the owner, every night, explaining why he selected his lead story. The letter is on Grozier's desk in Cambridge next morning.

"Going to the *Herald* sports desk may be the worst move you could make. You ought to be on the *Post* city staff. If you say the word I'll call up Eddie Dunn [city editor] and ask him to take you on. What do you say?"

If Skerrett had lectured me a week earlier I might have given in. But I couldn't go back on my promise to Whitman to be at work that night at six o'clock so I said, "No thanks, I'm committed, Nick."

"O.K.," said Skerrett, slapping the desk with his open hand. That's it. . . . Good luck."

There is no doubt I had learned more from Skerrett than I ever learned in any other three-year period. At that stage of my life I was impressed by tough people and he was the toughest. He also was one of the pleasantest companions of my life, outranked only by my father.

Skerrett was a newspaper snob. He didn't think people who didn't work on newspapers were much account. He stated his credo several times when we were relaxing in the Sterling Hotel or some such dive. "The American newspaper is the greatest institution in the world."

This is one he never wrote in the assignment book for general consumption like the one about the difference between a reporter and a goddamned nuisance or the one about Genesis which read as follows: "The creation of Heaven and Earth is told in 10 words in the Bible. It is a good story, well reported. Be concise! Be accurate!"

Two hours later I was meeting the boys in the *Herald* Sports Department and had acquired the nickname "Polack," given me on the spot by Bill Mullins, who insisted I looked Polish. Finer sensibilities were not spared in the *Herald* Sports. Mullins himself was known as "Hook" because he had a big nose. Hamilton was "Egg" because he was even balder than Skerrett. The name "Polack" stayed with me as long as I was in Boston. I got so I liked it, though I had no generic claim. It made me feel rugged.

I was soon launched on a copyreading job it took me three years to escape. The first night Ed Cunningham helped me. After that I was on my own. Whitman apparently judged me competent and after that the content and make-up of the Boston *Herald* Sports Department was strictly my business.

My salary was set at fifty-five dollars a week by contract between the *Herald* and Newswriters Local No. 1, a branch, briefly active, of the International Typographical Union. That's what I got for a six-day week. In Worcester I had belonged to Local 2, which was incontinently quashed after the treasurer skipped with the union funds.

When I got to Boston Local 1 was about to go down the drain. The contract with the *Herald* did not specify that overtime should be paid so I soon found I was working seven days a week at straight time. My boss had no other man who was both qualified and willing to do the work and keep the hours which were required of me.

The job started at six thirty and lasted until three A.M. It consisted of editing all the copy, writing all the heads, selecting and cropping the pictures, taking late stuff on the telephone and making up three editions, the first of which was scheduled to clear the composing room at twelve twenty-five.

It was a lonely job, for no member of the sports staff could be expected to be around after midnight and frequently all hands were gone by seven o'clock. Sometimes the boys would leave me with the "Bob Dunbar" column to write in addition to all my other work. Bob was a fake. He didn't exist. But his column, a compendium of paragraphs by the staff, has run seventy-five years. Bob was regarded as such a weighty authority by the Boston readers that his mail was always heavy.

In the day of Robert Lincoln O'Brien, the Boston *Herald* had a couple of weird quirks. There was a rule barring the split infinitive as there is on most papers. But the Boston *Herald* split infinitive was different from the regular product. Divided verb forms of any kind were looked upon as split infinitives on the *Herald*. It was considered just as heinous to write "Yale had utterly routed Harvard" as it was to say "Yale proceeded to utterly rout Harvard." The way Mr. O'Brien's subeditors wanted you to express this thought was: "Yale had routed Harvard utterly."

Some strange sentences came from this interpretation of the split infinitive proscription and some able staff writers who had an ear for euphony, or even scansion, were seriously jarred by the massing of verb forms by the subeditors.

Another rule was that the *Herald* should be classified to the last item, meaning that all stories and items in a particular field must be grouped together. This wasn't too bad, but some fiend in human form had contrived a system of finish rule variance which was devised for the obvious purpose of driving the make-up man crazy.

If the lead story in a category, say "baseball," were to be followed by a related item with a two-line head, the two stories must be separated by a "home rule," a special *Herald* rule, or line, which was five ems in length. If the big story were followed by a related story with a one-line head, then the stories must be separated by a three-em dash. If the big story were followed by an unrelated story with any kind of a head, then the separating agent must be a full rule, nine ems. The column width then was twelve ems. Now it's eleven.

We had two or three people on the main copy desk who specialized in catching mistakes in rules. One of them would come chasing into the sports department waving a paper that was open to a sports page. "Woodward," he would scream, "you have a home rule over a one-line head."

Except for the inanities of the system of rules I liked the close classification of news which the *Herald* required. I found it a help in making up the paper.

With this system the make-up printer was given a pattern to follow and could put a page together virtually without editorial aid. Each lead story would be slugged with the name of the category, i.e., "baseball" and items in that field would be slugged "add-baseball." Other stories would be slugged add-racing, add-auto, add-soccer, add-track, add-boxing.

The leads would be marked on the page dummies, which would also tell the printer where to put such things as cuts and racing charts. All the editor needed to do was to appear twenty minutes before an edition, cut a few items to fill the remaining holes, scan the overset to make sure nothing important was left out, and let her go.

I always revised the pages twice, three or more items if some exceptional story broke. The regular second edition went at one thirty-five A.M., and I could generally get out for my lunch between papers. The final edition went in just before three o'clock and after that there generally was a game of fantan, which was very popular at the *Herald*.

I usually got to bed by five thirty and the only way I could participate in any normal activity was by sacrificing sleep. I was a trout fisherman in those days and another fellow and I would leave for the stream in the western part of the state when we finished work, figuring on making the first cast as the sun came up. We were generally home by noon and able to get a few hours' sleep before returning to the shop.

I played golf in those days and this involved another sleeping technique. There was a couch in the ladies' restroom and, inasmuch as no ladies worked at night, it was available with limitations. I would go to sleep there about three thirty and get out just before eight o'clock. Hap Myers, lobster watchman (midnight to nine thirty) for the *Traveler*, our evening edition, would jostle me on sighting the first female.

This was my procedure on golf days when an office foursome played the Belmont Hill course. Here we had an in and could use the course until one P.M. through the intercession of Freddie Corcoran, who was then caddy master. This is the same man who became adjudicator of professional golf and personal manager of Ted Williams, the mercurial Boston ball player. We also played other courses through contacts with the pro or caddy master. None of us belonged to a club.

I kept my golf clubs hanging on a peg in the sports department, and when they were finally stolen I quit the game forever. I am sure the other men in the department were delighted when they could count me out. I was a long hitter without semblance of control, and I couldn't see the ball unless it happened to go straight. My glasses only focused dead ahead. As a result I was forever looking for balls and nobody, including me, had any fun.

I missed sleep entirely on occasion and kept going the next night on coffee and whiskey. Once I missed through a weird estival idiocy concocted by Sailor Burton, a staff man, with the connivance of Hap Myers of the lobster watch. The Sailor decided that O'Brien, the office cat, should be taken to his summer home on Cape Cod. Burton said a free-lancing former member of the staff was willing to house O'Brien as a pet for his children.

From appearances O'Brien would make a pet only for Boris Karloff. He had lost an eye and an ear on alternate sides in the desperate battle for alley favors and was the most villainous looking carnivore I had ever seen. He lived on rats, garbage from the Hotel Avery across the street, and milk the janitor sometimes brought him.

I was leery of the deal but Sailor Burton painted a beautiful picture.

"We'll get to Joe's place [cottage of the former staff member] just in time for a nice breakfast with whiskey. If we leave before five we should be back in Boston by noon. With nobody on the road we ought to fly down there."

It developed that Myers had been unable to get off from the lobster watch so the Sailor and I had to help him clean up his work. His job was to pick up type from the *Herald* for use in the first edition of the *Traveler* which went to press at ten A.M.

We had to update the stories by writing new heads and leads, mark the proofs, and send the whole business back to the composing room.

The *Herald* would say: "Two masked men held up the filling station at Brighton Avenue and Lucas Street last night and escaped with $300 after tying up the attendant."

Our rewrite would be: "Police are searching for two bandits who robbed the filling station," etc.

We had to handle fifty or sixty stories for the *Traveler*'s first edition, which in those days was nothing but the *Her-*

ald rewarmed. We finished about six o'clock and looked around for O'Brien. It was another hour before we got on the road.

The Sailor and Hap got in the front seat, leaving me as custodian of O'Brien. We had to keep the windows closed to be sure he would stay in the car. I tried the head-scratching "nicekitty" routine on him and he growled like a leopard.

At Plymouth I had to open a window. The car was hot. O'Brien immediately escaped, raking me down the fore-arm as he jumped for the open window. It took us an hour to run him down.

We arrived at Joe's cottage in a definite after-breakfast chill. Joe, his wife, and the three little girls shrank away from O'Brien. The Sailor put him in the kitchen as a temporary measure.

Finding no breakfast, we decided to push off but Joe detained me on the front porch. "For God's sake, Woodward, take this horrible monster away with you and drop him in the canal!"

"I can't do that, Joe, the Sailor loves the cat. He'd dive in after him. . . . Look, just open the kitchen door after we go and I'm sure you'll never see O'Brien again. . . . So long."

When I got back to the car there were Sailor and Hap propped against each other and snoring gently in the back seat. So I drove home, arriving an hour and a half before it was time for me to go back to work.

O'Brien? . . . Joe and his family learned to love him. He spent several happy years with them and is now buried, I understand, in a cat cemetery near Hyannis.

The second summer I was on the *Herald* the boss decided to move me to the writing staff and hired a fellow named Dick Turner from Chester, Pennsylvania, to succeed me on the desk. This didn't mean I was completely free of night work, because I had to train Turner first and after that I had to work in his place one day a week when he took his day off.

Up to that point I had written almost nothing for the paper, just my weekly trotting column and a few high school games which I covered on my own time. Now I became a regular staff member and wrote under my name every day. My assignments were not important. I covered polo and whippet-racing in the North Shore paradise of the rich, auto racing, grand circuit trotting, and an occasional ball game.

The change of hours gave me time to fall in love with the landlady of the lodging house in which I lived. She was a beautiful young widow with two little girls. Eventually we were married and it lasted eight years. She divorced me after I left for New York. For me, it was a happy experience, a good part of the time.

8 THE FIRST BIG FOOTBALL ASSIGNMENT I CAN
remember doing for the *Herald* was the
Cornell-Pennsylvania football game of 1922
Thanksgiving Day at Philadelphia. That
was the unbeatable Cornell team which
had in the backfield both Eddie Kaw, an all-American,
and George Pfann, who should have been. He made it
later.

I had never seen football as well played. Gil Dobie was
Cornell's coach, and his offensive method was to mass
single-wing power, particularly off the tackles. Pfann
made more of an impression on me than Kaw. He was,
and still is, a comparatively small man but the rugged
Pennsylvania tacklers bounced off him. Penn put up a
series of strong goal-line stands and came out of it with a
creditable defeat, 9-0.

The next year I saw one of Rockne's good Notre Dame
teams beat Princeton, 25-2, at Palmer Stadium, Princeton.
Before the game Rockne had been interviewed by the
Princetonian, student paper, and I read the great man's
words sitting on a campus bench the day of the game. As
closely as I can remember Rockne was quoted as follows:

"Our little team cannot expect to do much against
Princeton's big aggregation but I feel that our boys will
benefit from their contact with Princeton men."

Benefit from contact! . . . I'll say they did. When the
whistle blew they started knocking the Princetonians in
all directions and there was no letup in the ground-gaining
of Crowley, Layden, and Bergman until Rockne called off
the dogs in the second half.

That was the year before the Four Horsemen. Dutch
Bergman, a senior, was playing ahead of Miller. The other
three Horsemen were in place: Stuhldreher at quarter-

back, Crowley at lefthalf, and Layden at full.

I was close to participant football at that time and I spotted some things which no one told me about. Notre Dame's attack was like the Dartmouth offense I had played against, a shift from T formation in either direction and an immediate take-off, so rapid that the move from the T was almost continuous.

The only weakside play was the fullback through guard. Rockne never had a weakside attack until comparatively late in his career, when the rules committee insisted that there must be a one-second pause after a shift.

Bob Fisher, who succeeded Percy D. Haughton as Harvard football coach after World War I, carried on like the old master for a few years. In 1919 his team was undefeated, winning eight games and tying Princeton. Then it traveled to the Rose Bowl and defeated Oregon, 7-6.

By 1923, however, Harvard had hit the skids and the cry-baby era had set in. A large hospital had been set up at the field and the most minuscular hurts were X-rayed, kneaded, bandaged and whirl-bathed until the heroes started thinking of themselves as patients, not players.

I was sent out to cover Harvard practice as soon as I was sprung from the desk. I also helped Burt Whitman cover the big games but I didn't get around to writing a Harvard-Yale lead for several years.

Covering Harvard during the late Fisher era was a horror. The players didn't wear numbers and there was no roof on the press box. The press was barred from the field and also from the coach's office in the field house. The only way you could get any information was to tag along with Coach Fisher as he walked between the dressing quarters and the practice field.

He was neither informative nor polite. At that time the Harvard thinking seemed to be that there was something not quite nice about talking to the press. Even assistant managers were as rude as they dared to be. They discovered early that they could get status credits for insulting the reporters.

Needless to say, the press box on Saturday was supplementary cheering section for the team which was playing against Harvard. When "little" Holy Cross beat the Crimson we felt like conducting a snake dance.

Even the discomfort of the notorious roofless games, at Harvard in 1923 and at Yale the year after, was minimized for reporters who had to work in a couple of cloudbursts by the thought that the Crimson forces were taking a couple of very satisfactory beatings.

When Arnold Horween, captain of the Rose Bowl team, succeeded Fisher in 1926, things started to improve. He was a rich boy from Chicago. He had played pro football for the fun of it, not needing the money. He was tough, and also smart enough to see no sense in the indignities Harvard piled on the press.

Both Harvard and Yale put roofs on their press boxes but the newspaper men had to declare war to get an upstairs gents' room. The maneuver which won this war for the press was mass urination on the customers below.

Bo McMillin had made a tremendous hit in Boston when he played against Harvard for the Praying Colonels of Centre College. Subsequently Bo played some pro football then turned to coaching, first at Centenary College, later at Geneva. Boston College beat Harvard to the punch by booking Bo's first vehicle. Boston liked Bo and turned out in flattering force to see his Centenary Gentlemen.

This riled Fred Moore, a stony-faced Harvard graduate manager, and when Bo moved to Geneva, he hurried to book the McMillin cast for the opening game of 1926. He did not know that Bo had moved in a complete football team comprising what he called "my own li'l boys." There were several linemen who had played unobtrusively for Centre. There was Cal Hubbard, 265-pounder who had played for Centenary and later played for Green Bay and the Giants, and finished his career as an American League umpire.

There was also the slam-bang peripatetic halfback, Mack Fleniken, whose intercollegiate career was said to have involved prior stop-offs which were not in the public domain.

Cornell had booked Geneva for the Saturday before its game with Harvard, and Gilmour Dobie put up such a scream over Geneva's cast of characters that he shamed Bo into withholding some of the more flagrantly traveled operatives.

The Dobie protest enabled Cornell to win by the skin of its teeth (6-0). Harvard made no protest and took on the whole Geneva aggregation. The result was cataclysmic for Harvard and satisfactory to the press which wrongheadedly persevered in wishing to see a slaughter of the red shirts.

Geneva employed an offense which Harvard had never seen before. It was heavily unbalanced with five linemen on one side of center. The two outside men were the ends and they were spaced out from the end of the line and from each other.

The 265-pound Hubbard, whose speed matched his size, played the inside end position and when the ball was passed he would crash into the Harvard player immediately inside him and fold the whole Crimson line into a pleat. Fleniken then would follow a corps of blockers through an immense hole.

Looking back, it is difficult to understand how Harvard held the score to 16-7, for Geneva was on the move all afternoon. Watching the slaughter, I started to giggle and couldn't stop. The only other athletic event which affected me this way was the second Louis-Schmeling fight in which Joe put away the German in the first round.

The break in athletic relations between Harvard and Princeton started after their 1926 football game and wasn't patched up until 1934. Various loud if unofficial spokesmen for Harvard insisted that Princeton played dirty football. The accusations finally were incorporated in a magazine article by Wynant Hubbard, a former Harvard player, who declared that Al Miller, 210-pound Harvard halfback, came out of a Princeton game with the imprint of a seal ring on his nose.

Horween had nothing to do with the break-up. He was trying to convince the Harvard heroes that they were tough enough to play anybody and before he was through they actually were. In addition to propping the sagging morale, Horween should be given credit for being one of the few coaches who had the nerve to try new offensive measures. Ninety-five percent of the coaches at this stage of the game were copying either Pop Warner or Knute Rockne.

Horween based his attack on something later known as the option play. It is generally supposed that this maneuver was first shown by Don Faurot, of Missouri, when he coached the Iowa Sea Hawks during the second war, but Horween was ahead of him by fifteen years.

Faurot may well have reinvented it, but it had been

used in British rugby and in Canadian football before any-body thought of it in the United States. I saw the Cambridge University team use it against a pick-up American team in the thirties. Recent inquiries indicate the British had been using it as long as anyone can remember.

Horween actually got it from Canada. In the spring of 1926, soon after he had contracted to coach Harvard, he invited "Shag" Shaughnessy to come to Soldiers Field to teach "lateral passing" to the new Harvard coaching staff. Shaughnessy, an old Notre Damer who later became president of the International Baseball League, at that time was coach of all sports at McGill University, Montreal.

Horween had worked out an ingenious new offense in which the optional end run and keeper combination was the key play. What he wanted from Shaughnessy was a quick, accurate method of passing the ball from the fullback, who was the original carrier, to the halfback, who executed the end run at the option of the fullback.

They arrived at a two-hand basketball snap-pass off the shoulder. It traveled like a bullet and was easy to control. Except for the fact that the fullback rather than the quarterback was the first ball-handler and the method of passing was superior to anything later developed, the play was an exact forerunner of the split-T option. The latter play was engineered by the quarterback, who ran either way, faked or passed off to the halfback.

Horween's alignment was a balanced-line short kick-formation with the fullback and halfback four yards deep behind the guards and the blocking back generally on one wing or the other. On the option his assignment was the defensive halfback on the threatened side. If he was on the left and the play was going right he would start before the ball was passed so that he could get to his man. The deep back generally was the passer-kicker, Barry Wood.

For the option, going right, the ball would be passed to the fullback on the left who would run at the defensive left end. The halfback would start wider. The fullback took his cue from the enemy end. If the end came in to tackle him, he would shoot the ball to his partner outside. If the end went for the outside man, the fullback would fake the pass and run off tackle. If the end played it in the middle, either play would probably go.

During Horween's regime Harvard had two pairs of backs who were expert in running the option. The first comprised Art French and Dave Guarnaccia, the second Eddie Mayes and Charley Devens who will be better remembered as a pitcher for the New York Yankees. The French-Guarnaccia combination was perhaps the more effective because either man could fill either roll. This eliminated most of the giveaways.

Horween left Harvard at the end of the 1930 season, having beaten Yale the last three years straight. The option play went with him and I didn't see it again until the war when Don Faurot used it as part of the Iowa Sea Hawks split-T attack.

I regret sincerely that I didn't give Horween credit at the time for having the nerve to do something new when most of the other coaches were sticking to established patterns. Horween's record overall wasn't arresting, but he coached interesting football. He also eradicated the latter-day Fisher cry-baby influence and they say he did something toward reestablishing the series with Princeton, though it didn't occur until four years after he had gone. Incidentally, he did something for Harvard's dreadful public relations.

In my days in Boston two football games were surefire

sellouts. One was the Harvard-Yale; the other the Boston College-Holy Cross which then was played in Braves Field. The latter game involved a personal rivalry between the two coaches, Major Frank W. Cavanaugh of Boston College and Cleo A. O'Donnell of Holy Cross. Cav was forever needling Cleo, who almost never answered back. Both were from Worcester and both had large families. Two of Cleo's sons, Ken and Cleo, Jr., were elected captain of football at Harvard.

I met Cav the second winter I was in Worcester when one of my duties was to get the closing New York stock prices from J. S. Bache & Co. in the Slater Building. It was difficult because I did not know the board positions or the stock symbols. I was progressing slowly one day when a big man in a derby hat started calling off the quotations. After that he helped me whenever he was there.

Cav hung out in off season either in the brokerage office or in the courthouse. He was a member of the Massachusetts bar but never practiced. He was always on the sidelines, however, when an interesting case was on the docket.

He was sitting in on a murder trial one day when Edward Esty, our slightly pompous district attorney, called his star witness, a seven-year-old girl named Mary Lee. Mr. Esty did not seem to realize the child's age nor sense that she was frightened. He addressed her sternly, "What is your name?"

She looked around in panic and finally said in a small voice, "Mary."

"Please state your surname and your given name. It is Mary Lee, is it not?"

"Yes," she said almost inaudibly.

"Now, Mary Lee, state whether or not on the evening

of February the third, nineteen hundred and twenty-one, you were at the corner of Gates Lane and Main Street."

The little girl looked around wildly for help. Cav leaned over the shoulder of a pal in front and said in a loud stage whisper, "A battle of wits."

Cav professed to believe that the theory that Cleo and he were enemies was important to the financial success of the Boston-Holy Cross game but the stories he told about his vis-à-vis were mostly friendly and almost all compounded in the fertile Cavanaugh brain. One of his favorites, which apparently had no basis in fact, involved Cleo and a gatekeeper.

Half an hour before one of the annual games Cleo walked out the gate to watch the big crowd come in. He was stopped by the gatekeeper when he tried to go back.

"Where's your ticket?"

"I don't need a ticket. I'm Cleo O'Donnell."

"I don't care if you're Cleopatra. You've got to have a ticket."

There was some sort of a ceremony before one of the games and Cav and Cleo were required to meet in the middle of the field. When the oratory was over Cleo stuck out his hand and said, "May the best team win, Cav."

Cav, severe in his black overcoat and iron hat, assumed a parade ground brace and put his right hand behind his back. "Not here, Cleo, in front of all these people. . . . We are enemies. . . . Remember? . . . Incidentally, may the better team win."

THE BOSTON HERALD GENERALLY MOBBED
the Boston College-Holy Cross game, meaning we covered it with six or seven men.
We had a color writer, a note writer, a technical writer, an interviewer for each coach, and, of course, a lead writer. This extensive coverage was in part due to the importance of the game but principally to the fact that it was played either on the fifth Saturday of November or the first one of December and so came at a time when we had little for our men to do.

Burt Whitman, my boss, believed in mobbing a good assignment when he had the men available, and I followed his lead when I became sports editor of the New York *Herald Tribune*. We always swarmed over the championship fights and the World Series unless extreme distance made it too expensive.

An important assignment on the Boston *Herald* was the Harvard-Yale boat race at New London. This occurred at a time when manpower was needed for other purposes, so Burt thought up the idea of getting as much out of one man as he did out of five or six at the final football game. We had an erroneous idea at the time that volume was superior to quality.

I covered the race alone one year, writing a normal story of two columns, and Burt was disappointed. The *Globe* sent six men including their veteran political editor who took his vacation annually so he could be present at Red Top, Harvard quarters on the Thames River, for the whole training period. Traditionally he wrote the boat-race lead. He was a violent Harvard rooter and you could hardly tell from his story that Yale had won the race.

I pointed this out to Burt but he said *no, no*, the *Globe* had beaten the stuffing out of us because it had six columns on the race to our two.

Fifty weeks later he brought up the subject again.

"The Harvard-Yale race is coming up next week," he said. "I'd like you to go down there Monday and give us a good daily story. I'd like an advance of two and a half or three columns the day of the race.

"Now about covering the race itself. . . . You had a good story last year but it was too short. We didn't look good up against all that stuff the *Globe* had. . . . Now this year I want you to let go. I want you to write a whole page. . . . I mean a whole newspaper page. . . . Eight columns."

I gasped at the enormity of the idea. The *Herald* then was printed in nonpareil on a twelve-em column. This meant that he was asking me to write approximately ten thousand words on a one-day spot story. He looked out of the window and kept on talking.

"The *Globe* now has four men staying in its own cottage on the Red Top grounds and they'll probably send three or four more. I may be able to send Lindsay [our newest recruit] down to help you the last couple of days."

New London was the same jolly old town. I found my friend Coddington Billings Pendleton in his usual place behind the desk of the Hotel Mohican. The old gray-brown headwaiter smiled out of the double doors of the dining room and Harold, the bootlegger, waved from across the lobby. Early conditions seemed favorable for the great endurance test.

The daily stories were easy. The day before the race Steele Lindsay, my aide, woke me up at ten o'clock. He had been coxswain at the University of Washington and was full of rowing science and tradition. He wanted me to go up-river with him immediately to study the form of the crews.

I sent him off by himself and ordered up my breakfast. I was comparatively green in the sports business but I had learned a few principles. One was that a man can defeat himself if he gets out of his pajamas before six P.M., the day before any important athletic event.

The New York and Boston papers came with my breakfast and I read them restfully as I ate. Then I wrote my advance story and sent it by messenger to Western Union. It was 10 to 1 there wouldn't be any news at this late date but I could check later by phone to find out if anything untoward had happened. I lit a cigarette and started to figure how we were going to get up ten thousand words on a very ordinary boat race the next day.

To begin with the freshman and junior varsity races were scheduled in the morning. That would be a good job for Lindsay. He would get a chance to cover some competitive rowing and I wouldn't have to get up until noon.

I sent downstairs for the estimable *Day*, New London's evening paper, and found, as I expected, that it had a formidable list of yachts which had either already arrived in the harbor or were about to. So I wrote a lead on some of the more celebrated craft and pasted the *Day*'s yacht list on the bottom. That gave me a column or two and a half in aggregate, considering Lindsay's projected piece on the preliminary races.

I considered a separate race-day color story which I could have written out of my head without difficulty but turned down the idea on the theory we could handle the color in other ways. The race was late in the day so both Lindsay and I could get up a column of notes in the early part of the afternoon. If we wrote two columns of notes it would leave about four for my overall lead on the varsity race.

I planned to do my big story in my room, banishing Lindsay to the Western Union office to write some kind of a lead note. Coddington Billings Pendleton was providing me with an off-duty bellhop for my special assistant. His duties would be simple but important. Each time I finished two pages he was to run them to the Western Union office. On his return to the room he was to mix me a two-ounce Tom Collins. Sugar, lemons, gin, a knife, a spoon, a high glass, and a bucket of ice already were set up. The ice would need replacement on race day.

This was still the day before about five thirty P.M., and I was still in my pajamas. I called Mr. Pendleton and asked him to send up the bellhop for a trial run.

The boy's name was Conrad, which I took as a good omen. He was fast and clever in all his moves. The trial Tom Collins was good—and strong. He made the run to the Western Union in two and a half minutes. I called Ed Nourie, the manager, as Conrad left the room and he called me back when my speedster got there.

Conrad made the return trip under light restraint in 2:38 and immediately seized the gin bottle and poised it over a clean glass. Every move was a picture.

"Hold it, son. . . . How old are you?"

"Twenty-three, sir."

"Do you want a drink?"

"Yes, sir."

I explained to Conrad that he could not have a drink on race day until I had hit the tenth page of the story. After that he was off bounds. He was to get ten dollars for the job. This sum might win sneers from a present-day hopper but it was good money for New London in the twenties.

"If by chance I am unconscious when the job's over,

take the money out of my pants, Con."

The arrangements for race day had been completed and only the literary and sportive phases remained to be carried out.

It was now evening and I decided to get dressed for the day. As I was lacing my shoes Lindsay rapped on the door. He had watched the Yale crew and was full of expertism. He wanted to write a story to go with my advance. Of course it was too late but an idea struck me.

"Go ahead and write your story, Steele. Put in all that stuff about the strokes per minute and whether the boys are clearing their puddles. . . . You know . . . I'm going to the Western Union and I'll take it for you. But hurry up."

The story was just what I had hoped it would be, an appreciation of the Yale crew which wasn't necessarily limited in time to the day before the race. With a little editing it could be transformed into part of our coverage of the race itself, and because Yale was absolutely certain to clobber Harvard, I marked it as follows: "Boston *Herald* Saturday night press—Slug EXPERT—By Steele Lindsay, former Washington coxswain."

Then I put it in my pocket.

With Lindsay's expertism I now had, in hand or in prospect, approximately five columns of race coverage. If I could drag the lead out to four columns we would have a column more than the boss had ordered and would be dead sure to outmanure the *Globe*.

I avoided thinking about the formidable lead story. Better to roll with it and do it freehand. However, I was sure the race was going to be a stinker and that I would get no dramatic lift out of developments. This was one of those stretches when Yale won every year. This race in particular didn't look like a contest.

Things went pretty well on race day. Lindsay wrote a good—by which I mean long—story on the preliminaries. I showed up for breakfast at lunch time and then we both worked industriously on notes describing the costumes and the behavior of the big happy race-going throng, the special window decorations of the local stores, episodes involving drunks. We lifted what we could out of the New York papers and the helpful New London *Day*. By three thirty we had enough. By four I had persuaded Ed Nourie to start sending our stuff at the night press rate which is cheaper. . . . Six is Western Union's arbitrary time for the rate change.

I put Lindsay's expert story in the middle of the pile. I had refrained from telling him about the change of venue on the theory that he might make some kind of a beef and want to write it over after the race. I couldn't stand for that because the decks had to be clear then for the immense diuresis which was supposed to be forthcoming from Woodward. Of course Lindsay was disappointed his story hadn't been in the morning paper.

As we sat waiting for the observation train to pull out to the starting point four miles up the river, I gave Lindsay his last instructions.

"Pick up something that will make a lead-all for the notes. You sign them at the end. Write your lead-all in the Western Union and mark it plainly so it won't get mixed up with any of the other stuff. You're finished as soon as you do that. Go back to Boston if you want to or have dinner or get drunk—but don't come near my room."

The race was as expected. It started half an hour late. Yale won by six lengths and nothing out of the ordinary happened. I jumped off the observation train as it was pulling into the station and sprinted for the hotel.

Conrad had everything in shape for the main bout. There was paper in the typewriter and the first—or launching—Collins was within easy reach. He went out to get me a couple of sandwiches.

The story came easily as is often the case when a man has thought about it enough in advance. The facts were not interesting. Yale had taken the lead at the outset, built it up to three lengths and held it easily at twenty-nine strokes to the minute. Harvard was rowing thirty-one.

Halfway down the course—off the submarine base— Harvard boosted the beat and gained a little. It was not significant. Yale pulled away and was presented with an unearned length when a Harvard rower caught half a crab just before the finish at the railroad bridge.

Considering the lack of drama, I felt a moment of panic. I took a big slug and settled down to hammer the typewriter at a route-going pace, letting the gin write the story.

I husbanded the few facts I had. I would come to a place where it appeared logical to let go of one of them. But I'd say to myself, "*No, no*, it's too early. . . . Suggest it but hold it back a page or two."

Conrad did not miss a beat. He made such time between the hotel and the Western Union that his absences were hardly discernible. I sent him off with the ninth page, breaking the two-page rhythm, and called Ed Nourie on the phone to see how the copy was moving.

"We're right up with you, Polack," he said. . . . "Say this is a powerful piece you're writing. . . . Here's your guy now with another take. . . . Say, can this be right? It says here 'As the leading eight went by the ketch *Co-manche* her Yale complement swarmed up her rigging like lascars on an X-E-B-E-C?'"

"Dead wrong, Ed, but let it go."

To myself I said, "Better skip the next gin."

From there it was downhill. On page 19 I suddenly found myself finished. I wrote "30" on the last sheet, shuffled over to the bed, and passed out for seven hours. . . . Then I went back to sleep for several more. It must have been noon when Conrad knocked on the door. He brought the paper and a telegram.

I seized the paper in fear but was soon reassured. The brief part of the story which was on the first sports page was clear and almost austerely factual. Soon after it jumped inside it started to flow and ripple. I was fascinated and marveled I had written it.

"What happened, Conrad?"

"Nothing much. You just sat down and drank nine drinks and pounded the typewriter. Then you fell on the bed. I pulled off your pants and shoes and put that sheet over you. . . . I took my ten out of your pants."

The telegram from the boss was as follows: "Wonderful story. Great coverage all around. Lindsay expert piece excellent. Beat *Globe* hollow. Congratulations.—Burt"

"What do you know, the boss is happy. . . . Give me my pants. . . . I'm going to feed you another ten."

10 I STAYED IN BOSTON EIGHT YEARS, during which I covered a wide variety of sports assignments, left sports—I thought for good—but returned to the field when the New York *Herald Tribune* offered me forty-five dollars a week more than I was making as top reporter on the Boston *Herald* city staff.

I had something of an attachment for Boston and it was a wrench to leave it though I never wholly approved of the town. The most influential people who live there are the Irish and the Brahmins. Both are formidable. Chub Peabody, the present governor, and an old-timer named Tack Hardwick, both representing old New England, may have been the two toughest football players Harvard ever had. If so, the margin was slight over the Mahans, Caseys, Codys and O'Donnells who also played for Harvard.

The two groups do not associate to any extent. They are divergent in politics, religion, and most other ways, but they are very much alike and they have an unavowed admiration for each other which boils down to the standards of toughness each sets for itself.

Boston has a warped moral outlook and it is common to rate individuals by false standards. You hear things like this: "He's a hell of a guy. His uncle is police commissioner."

If you listen to the conversations of hack drivers, bartenders, and other men-about-town, you will conclude that no politician or policeman ever does anything he is not illicitly paid for doing. It is hard to say that this is wholly unjustified, at least as to some, if the miasma arising from the town is carefully sniffed.

Boston has an underlying viciousness which I have never sensed in any other town. Three times I have seen outcrops and they were very ugly.

The first was the savage uprising which occurred when the police went on strike in 1919. Mobs roved the streets, smashing store windows, slugging peaceable pedestrians, and committing every known crime including murder. One night I saw a big crap game at the corner of Boylston and Tremont. It wasn't that the participants wanted to shoot craps. It was that they had an urge to demonstrate the rule of lawlessness.

There was practically no control. A few newly discharged soldiers in tin hats rode rubber-shod horses on the sidewalks, apparently with the idea of breaking up mobs who were pillaging the store windows. A pile of bricks, stacked for use on a construction job in Scollay Square, made handy window smashers. The brick throwing was indiscriminate and the throwers were breaking them in half on the curb stone and shying them into the crowd.

In the middle of the square there was one old police sergeant, perhaps a year or two away from retirement, who had not joined the strikers. Nightstick in hand, he backed against the subway kiosk and faced a crowd of a thousand unspeakable mugs.

Suddenly he charged, cracking the nearest heads. I was afraid he would be killed but the rioters gave way before him, and finally poured down Hanover Street in wild and unreasoned flight. Three or four soldiers on police horses took up the chase and one segment of the mob was broken up.

Those who saw Boston during the police strike had trouble figuring out how Calvin Coolidge gained the proper impetus out of it to win the vice-presidential nomination on the Republican ticket with Harding. His refusal to call out the home guard left Boston undefended until Mayor Andy Peters forced him to act. Part of the persuasion, according to Boston lore, was a punch on the nose on the steps of the State House.

The second outcrop of viciousness was at a hockey game on Christmas Eve in Boston Garden. The Boston Bruins and Detroit Red Wings had been on the verge of warfare throughout the game, and the crowd blamed a Detroit player named Ebbie Goodfellow. This inaptly named character may not have been a troublemaker but he certainly was one who took no guff from anyone and he did nothing to spread peace and good will.

As soon as the game was over a fight started. It might have been controlled by the referees, coaches, and traditionally cooler heads, except that the police saw fit to mix in. A dozen of them climbed onto the ice and tried to stop the fight. A couple of hundred people followed and the fighting became general. The cops whose opening gambit had been to lay restraining hands on the players now started swinging their war clubs at the customers. No one except those on skates could keep on his feet, and numerous cops and citizens plunged to the ice and rolled around in the snowy scum trying to choke each other.

At this point the idiot who operated the canned music remembered it was Christmas Eve and put on "Silent Night" without any effect on the mayhem below. A few of the less pugilistic Detroit players attempted to leave the scene but were punched and mauled as they tried to get out through the dressing-room aisle by a reserve detachment of Boston hoodlums.

The brawl spilled out into the big entrance lobby and new combatants joined in. By now the fans were fighting each other as well as the cops and hockey players. The appearance of the riot squad was marked by intensified fighting and the substitution on the loud speaker of "O, Little Town of Bethlehem" for "Silent Night."

The hockey players finally entered their dressing rooms and half an hour later the police pushed the last of the combatants out into the street.

My first reaction to the hockey riot was that it was funny. Then I recalled the viciousness of the police strike riots and it lost much of its uproarious timbre. The third outbreak of Boston mugsterism was considerably worse.

During my years in Boston there was no big-time horse-racing, for pari-mutuel betting had not been legalized in Massachusetts. The rest of the New England states also had been successful in avoiding this plague of locusts. But after I had been in New York a few years and had hardened myself so that I could enter a race track without losing my lunch, I decided to go back to the Hub of Civilization to see how the sport was conducted there.

It was the summer of 1945 and I had just returned from my second tour of war correspondence, this one with the navy's fast Carrier Force in the Pacific. I reached the racing scene in a cab through the new Sumner traffic tunnel to East Boston and found that Suffolk Downs had the usual posh clubhouse facilities and the usual racing crowd, i.e., the scum of the earth.

The feature was the Fifty-thousand-dollar Massachusetts Handicap and when rusty gray First Fiddle won it for the second straight year under Johnny Longden, it made a good little story. I was busy writing it before and during the eighth race. I was brought up short by a tremendous booing.

What had happened was that the stewards, after having

abstained from penalizing a single horse during the meeting, had announced the disqualification of the winning
favorite in the eighth race, on which about half the people
in the park had bet their money.

After a few minutes of booing a short stocky man
crossed the track and went up the steps to the stewards'
stand, a glass-enclosed crow's-nest in the infield. He got in
before anyone thought to lock the door and began to
argue with the stewards, who called the police.

Three patrolmen responded and with practically no
delay drew their blackjacks and started to beat in the skull
of the single protester in the full view of everyone in the
park.

If there had been any hope of saving the situation it had
now been blown. A rain of bottles quickly broke all the
windows in the stewards' stand. All the occupants, including the stewards, the cops, and the prisoner, now
nearly unconscious, were forced to lie on the floor to get
out of the barrage.

There was a brief letup and the cops took their man
away in a Black Maria driven through the infield. At this
juncture a lady in a purple dress climbed up in the stand
to argue with the stewards. The first thing she did was to
gash her arm on a broken window. She bled freely as she
gesticulated in support of her argument.

She was finally persuaded to leave, but when she came
across the track and the crowd got a look at the gory picture she made, it went out of control entirely, assaulting
the police, smashing everything smashable, setting fires
under the stand, kicking the bulbs out of the mutuel board
and ultimately burning up a police motorcycle on a
pyre of gasoline-soaked newspapers. The police who had
started to use strong methods to suppress the trouble now

were abject. They stood around and let people do anything they wanted to. One cop, knocked down by a bottle
thrown from close range, merely got up and wiped the
blood off his face without making any effort to seize his
assailant.

The crowd now was running wild. It smashed in all the
pari-mutuel windows, kicked in the dining-room door,
and tried to make a fire of tables and chairs.

A navy shore patrol, comprising about eight men, finally
got the crowd started home after the ninth and last race
had been called off. It was still wartime and even race-
track hoodlums drew the line at fighting the navy.

Being in the press box, which is slung under the grandstand roof, I had a fine seat, bomb proof and commanding.
I started to cover the thing like a regular racing story with
the lead on the feature race. I rewrote the lead four times
during the riot as new developments took place, finally
sending a story which the Boston *Globe*, a syndicate customer, thought good enough to use with an eight-column
head on page 1. The other Boston papers flunked the riot
entirely. They had mere racing stories with short paragraphs which said that "disorderly conduct" followed disqualification of the winner of the eighth race. . . . Disorderly conduct! . . . That's like calling murder a foible!

Before I left Boston I had covered all the sports in the
spectrum. The shift of Bill Mullins, the *Herald*'s general
assignment man, to full-time coverage of golf and later to
politics, left a whole line-up of sports for me to take over.
Hockey was one of the biggest, even before the Bruins
launched the professional game in the winter of 1924-
1925, one year before it came to New York. I inherited
tennis just at the time it became most important on the
international scene, before and during the challenge of

France for the Davis Cup.

Boxing I worked on sporadically as aide to Billy Hamilton, our large bald and good-natured fight writer. Billy was no literary ace, having launched himself as a sports writer from the very apron of the ring. By dropping around to the newspaper offices to publicize fighters whom he managed, he got to know all the boys in the business and finally worked himself into a job on the *Herald*. I didn't know Hammy when he was a fight manager, but he had some good battlers, including Matty Baldwin and Honey Mellody. They say he could have licked any of them. I saw him in action once or twice and I can say that I have never seen a more formidable man. It took a great deal to get Hammy into a fight, for he was kindhearted and so good-natured that any old friend could drop around and hit him for ten dollars.

His prose was adequate for ordinary fight coverage, but the boss insisted on backing him up, or, rather, superseding him when a big fight came around. I didn't like the idea of taking a job away from an old pal but occasionally it became a matter of necessity. I would get a peremptory order to go to New York or somewhere to cover a fight. Under such circumstances, Hammy would go along too and write an "expert" story.

In addition to hockey, tennis, and boxing, I was called on to do a number of other assignments and when I wasn't busy on a spot news job Whitman would send me to interview people. One of the interviews I remember in particular was with George Owen, Harvard's great all-around athlete, on the night he turned professional with the Boston Bruins hockey team. As everyone knows, practically all hockey players come from Canada, but George was supposed to be a local boy without Canadian taint. I called him up the afternoon of the game and he invited me to dinner at the University Club. I started in to set the plan for the interview.

"There have only been a few American pros, George," I said, "and you are the first one who comes from Boston. Everybody will be rooting for you because we all think that you are just as good as any player born in Canada."

"That's all very well," said George, "but there is something wrong." He fiddled with his knife and fork, drawing lines on the tablecloth. They might well have been diagrams of hockey plays.

"What do you mean there's something wrong?"

"Well, you see," said George, "though I hate to spoil your story I was born in Canada. . . ."

It developed that George's father, later a celebrated naval architect, was working in Canada as a young engineer when George was born. George had no Canadian ancestors and left the Dominion when he was three months old, but the fact that he was born there tends to make me believe that Canada exerts some weird influence toward hockey on babies born within its boundaries.

Burt Whitman himself was our first-string baseball writer. When Ed Cunningham left us to become secretary of the Boston Braves, the second-string baseball job fell to me. It wasn't much of a job because the Boston ball clubs were at their absolute nadir while I worked in the town. The only year the Red Sox didn't finish last between 1922 and 1930 was 1926 when they finished seventh. The Braves were hardly better. They finished last in the National League in 1922, 1924, 1929 and seventh in 1923, 1926, 1927, and 1928. They rose to fifth in 1925 and to sixth in 1930. There was scant excuse to send a man on the road with such dismal representation in the big leagues, but we would occasionally cover an out-of-town series if one of the clubs developed a winning streak. In 1923 the boss decided that the Red Sox were going to be improved under the management of Frank Chance and ordered me to go to Philadelphia to cover the opening series.

"What does this mean, Burt, am I going to follow the Red Sox around the circuit?"

"That's my plan but we will have to see how they do."

The next day in Philly, John (Pincus) Quinn, the veteran spitball pitcher who was supposed to work the opener was out of sorts in his room and couldn't go to the park. The Red Sox got beaten 7-1 and I got a wire from Whitman to come home at once. However, the morning of the one game I covered something developed that is perhaps of interest. We were staying at the Hotel Benjamin Franklin and so was Holy Cross College which was at the tail end of its southern trip, stopping over in Philadelphia to practice in the Phillies' ball park on its way to play Princeton. I met Jack Barry, the coach, in the lobby and he invited me to watch his team work out in the morning. I went out to the park with the team and hung on a strap in the trolley car between Owen Carroll, the great pitcher, and Doc Gautreau, the second baseman who later played for the Braves. On the way out to the park the Doctor, always a great conversationalist, brought up a matter that was bothering him.

"They have a new paper up at the college called the *Tomahawk*," he said. "They are trying to get a name for Holy Cross teams and I am afraid they are going to call us 'The Chiefs' to go with the name of the newspaper. It is a lousy name and we would like you to help us get a better one. Ownie and I think 'Crusaders' would be a good name —what do you think of that?"

"I think it's great, Doc. Let's call the teams that."

So I started calling Holy Cross the "Crusaders" in the Boston *Herald* and they have been called that ever since. I disclaim credit for the name. It originated either with Gautreau or Carroll.

Incidentally the Holy Cross-Princeton game the next day turned out to be one of the greatest of all time. Princeton beat the Crusaders 2-0. It was one of two games Carroll lost in his whole college career. The winning pitcher was Charlie Caldwell, who later pitched for the Giants and coached the Williams and Princeton football teams. He held Holy Cross to three hits, had a no-hit game up to the seventh.

I went along covering sports until the spring of 1930 when the managing editor called me in and told me that he wanted me to go back on the city staff.

"You are doing a good job for us, Woodward," he said, "and I would like to spread you around in the paper. I want you to think up your own assignments, bring in a feature every day you can. Sometimes the city editor will ask for your services to cover a spot news story, but in the main you will be on your own. Burt Whitman can also call on your services when he has a job he thinks you can cover better than anyone else."

This was fine with me, but the money was a little bit unsatisfactory. I did not consider the raise they gave me commensurate with the fine, new, and supposedly important job. In those days money was a constant trial—I mean the lack of it. Having married a family which included a wife who wanted everything "nice," I was always up against it for money and not infrequently my pay was garnisheed.

So while I was delighted to have a job with such varied

possibilities I started thinking that it was beginning to be time to move again. The Boston pay scale did not suit my requirements. However, for a while I threw myself into the job and forgot pay.

If it hadn't happened that the son of the chief editorial writer of the New York *Herald Tribune* jumped or was pushed off the roof of the Harvard *Crimson* building, things might not have developed so fast. Jeff Parsons, Jr., was the jumper or pushee—and if he jumped it's 10-1 that he did it on a bet because he's that kind of a guy. He had no morbid introspection. He was lying in traction with a broken leg in Stillman Infirmary, hospital for Harvard University, when his old man, the chief editorial writer, called from New York to ask about his health. The old man said, incidentally, that Grantland Rice had quit the paper and that Bill Hanna was about to be retired because of ill health.

The *Tribune*, said Jeff Parsons, Sr., would have to get a football writer before fall and was looking over a few people in Boston, none of whom was I. Jeff Parsons, Jr., told his father that the persons he was looking over were undistinguished and that the guy he should get was Rufus S. Woodward of the *Herald*. This was strictly on the basis of palship because Jeff, Jr., and I had been on a couple of benders prior to his removal to Stillman Infirmary.

However, young Jeff's plea for Woodward apparently attracted attention in New York because he asked me to come and see him. I found him stretched out in great boredom. Knowing him in Europe and America later, I now realize that if he hadn't been bored and in need of a project, I might never have seen New York City. As it was, we had a nice talk and he told me something about the New York *Herald Tribune* and gave me an idea of how much money I could ask for. I suggested I write to the managing editor. He said not to do that, to let him handle it and sooner or later the managing editor would telephone me.

I didn't like this idea because I was in a virtual rage to leave Boston by then. My homework was in a mess and my money was inadequate.

I've always made bad deals for myself unless good ones were forced on me, so I had the sense to talk to a friend about the New York possibility. He was Arthur Graves Sampson, a man who went to the heart of all matters and generally came up with the right answer. A short time before he had asked me to get him a job in the *Herald* sports department. Mullins had been moved from golf to politics and the golf writer's job was open. Sampson liked golf and wanted it, but he already had two jobs; he was football coach at Tufts College and he had an insurance agency. The money that would be forthcoming at the *Herald* could not have interested him, but he planned to keep the other jobs in addition.

I suggested Sampson to Burt Whitman and he said "no." Two or three days later he came around and said, "You know, it might not be bad to hire Sampson. He is a smart guy and he could make us a good football writer in addition to his golf." The result was that Sampson got the job. So you might say that he was under a small obligation to me. I asked him what he thought about my going to New York and he said, "Great if you get the right deal." I said that I had been advised that I could get 135 dollars a week in New York, which was 45 dollars more than I was then making.

He said, "All right, hold out for that. They'll call you up pretty soon and make you a smaller offer. Don't listen to it. I want your promise that you won't go to New York until you submit the proposition they give you to me. You're an easy mark and I'm going to protect you."

As Sampson said, the *Herald Tribune*'s sports editor called me up not long after and offered me one hundred dollars a week, then fairly important money. I said it was insufficient and that I couldn't possibly leave Boston for anything like that. Sampson commended me for my forbearance. He knew how anxious I was to go to New York.

All summer I waited for another call from the *Herald Tribune*. In August I told Sampson I was going to call them up and say I was ready to come. "Don't you do it," said Sampson. "They'll give you what you want if you wait."

So I devoted myself to my new job and forgot about the *Herald Tribune*. There were many good stories in the summer of 1930. One of the best that I can remember was the naval battle between two coast guard boats. Each thought the other was a rum runner and both opened fire; three men were killed before they found out they were wrong. I covered the hearing in the coast guard station at Gloucester, where the gory details of the unfortunate battle were brought out.

A lady named Mrs. Peabody, top Prohibitionist in Massachusetts, gave me an interview in which she skinned alive such political powers as Governor Al Smith of New York and Congressman Piatt Andrew, who represented her own district. The latter had abandoned the standards of Prohibition that week and had turned to rum and the open saloon, or so I gathered from the statement he gave the papers.

I also covered the reenactment of the battle of Concord

and Lexington and was present in the bilge of the original U.S.S. *Constitution* during her reconditioning when the mainmast was stepped. I put a dime under the mast as it dropped into place. I got involved in a chase after Boston's police vice-squad leader, who had taken it on the lam without accounting for important money.

I uncovered another local story of considerable interest which involved the front doors of Mr. Beano Breen. He operated a little joint and the cops kept battering down his doors.

The evidence to close up Beano never was forthcoming and he kept replacing the doors. In the end he contributed fifty or more and the story became nationwide.

It got to be August and I was getting nervous, but Sampson wouldn't let me call the *Herald Tribune*.

"Just hold your horses," he said, "they can't start the football season with the staff they have now so they'll have to get you or somebody. I think they've got their eye on you and I'm sure your best plan is to wait." So I waited.

Late in August the sports editor called again and repeated the hundred-dollar offer. I was now thoroughly indoctrinated by Sampson and said "no" without a qualm.

By now Sampson had accepted another job. He had agreed to be chief assistant to Lou Little, new coach of the Columbia football team, and was planning to spend the autumn in New York himself. Through some necromancy he was also able to hang on to his job as golf editor of the Boston *Herald*. For me the break finally came around September first when Armstead R. Holcombe, managing editor of the New York *Herald Tribune*, called me and asked a leading question. "How much money do you want to work for us?" I told him and he said "yes" and when could I come. I said in two weeks.

I told Burt Whitman that I was going to New York in two weeks and he said, "Hell, go now. You're no good to me if you are just going to stay around that long." The boys gave me a new typewriter as a going-away present. Somehow or other I raised the fare to New York and entered the big town with one suit and a holey pair of extra pants. Those were the days of two-pants suits.

11 NEW YORK ON SEPTEMBER 7, 1930, was not the town it is now but was lively if you knew where to go and living was cheap. That's the only reason I was able to make it for I had arranged to send my family in Boston seventy-five dollars a week. The chances of supplementing my two-pants suit were not rosy at the outset.

I gave off an aura of genteel poverty when I dropped in at the *Herald Tribune* to go to work. The first man I saw was the late Cas Adams, who at that time was acting as assistant to the sports editor, the late Floyd Taylor. Adams greeted me pleasantly and said he would put me on the payroll as of then. Then he said something that practically flattened me— "There is nothing for you to do today. Call me up in a few days and I'll let you know if there is anything then."

For me this was new procedure. In the places I had worked, the boss never failed to find something for a reporter to do. I didn't know what to make of it or where to go. I called up Sampson at the Wentworth Hotel where we were supposed to live, but he had gone out. He probably was at morning football practice at Columbia so I left my bag and typewriter in the office, asked directions from Adams, and headed for Baker Field, West 218 Street and Broadway. For the next few days I spent most of my time at Baker Field hanging around the sidelines during practice and eating with the Columbia players at the training table. Lou Little, whom I knew only slightly, though he came from the same county in Massachusetts, treated me hospitably and let me sit in at the coaches' meetings.

It turned out that Sampson had engaged us a parlor,

bedroom, and bath in the Hotel Wentworth on West Forty-sixth Street off Sixth Avenue. This pad was operated by Nate Tufts, former district attorney of Middlesex County, Massachusetts, who had fallen into bad times and had turned up in New York as a hotel operator.

When Sampson and I entered the premises at about seven thirty the first night there was a big stir in the lobby and a vital, dark looking gentleman was the center of it. It turned out that he was Tullio Carminati, star of *Strictly Dishonorable*, then the hottest play on Broadway. It was in its second year then and ultimately ran 567 performances. That was the play in which Eddie McNamara played the Irish cop and set the pattern for all theatrical Irish cops of the future.

A few days later I called up Adams at the *Tribune* and he said that I was to take off on a football trip. My first assignment was the St. John's University team which was encamped at Mattituck, Long Island. Then I was to go to Farmingdale, where Chick Meehan was coaching New York University, and so on, for a week or so. I had heard about the accessibility of Long Island and the fact that trains ran every fifteen minutes so I did not worry about my first assignment until the next day. Then I went up to the window in the Long Island station and said, "A ticket to Mattituck, please."

The ticket seller looked at me quizzically. "Did you want to go today?"

When I told him "yes" he explained that it was impossible unless I went to a point fifteen miles from Mattituck and hired a car to go the rest of the way. There was only one through train a day.

I thought if I was going to go by car I might as well start from Penn Station. Having drawn some expense money, I felt rich. So I went out on Seventh Avenue, got in a taxi, and said to the driver, "Mattituck, Long Island, please."

He looked at me blankly and said, "Where in the hell is that?" We got a road map from another driver and finally found it. It was almost down to Orient Point, a matter of ninety-five miles as far as we could make out. So we started. I was half asleep in the back seat as we rolled through the beautiful countryside, then much less heavily populated then it is now, when the driver slammed on the brakes and the car careened toward the ditch.

"What's the matter?" I said.

The driver was gazing off to the right, "Holy jeez, there's a cow!"

Ray Lynch, the coach of St. John's University football team, and his assistant, Eddie Dooley, a former quarterback of Dartmouth and later congressman from Westchester, received me hospitably. They helped me in every way to get a good story about St. John's, a team I had never heard of until that day. St. John's played football only for a few years but is still known for its strong basketball team, for Joe Lapchick, and for various educational assets. From St. John's I called up Chick Meehan and he offered to send a car over for me in the morning. This sort of lavish treatment was out of my ken. I told him that I would take the train and arrive under my own power. This involved getting up a five o'clock, but I was not then inured to a life of ease.

When I got back from my trip I found there was very little to do during the week. In fact, all I was supposed to do was to keep in touch with the office so that they wouldn't have to look for me to give me my assignments. I decided it would be a good idea to meet my boss so I went into the office in the early evening to see him.

Floyd Taylor had been put in the Sports Department to straighten out a hideous mess. The management decided that it needed a man on the job who would keep a firm hand on the rather mercurial staff, systematize the assignments, watch the money, and straighten out the writing and copyreading. Taylor was a good editor but he went into sports with great unwillingness. He knew nothing about it, as I soon discovered in talking to him, and hoped that he would soon be returned to the city side of the paper.

I discovered that the work I was to do wouldn't really begin until competition started in football and it would be all right to amuse myself during the interim. So here I was in New York without companions and without any program. I decided the best thing I could do was to learn the geography of the city. So the next day I walked west on Forty-second Street to Twelfth Avenue. Then I turned north and walked around the upper half of Manhattan, staying as close to the water as I could. This involved walking through Inwood Park and took me by the Columbia field where I saw the football players running around in practice. I continued down the speedway and then along the East River through a waste expanse without housing developments or the Franklin D. Roosevelt Drive. The East Side was solid tenements in midtown, practically nothing like it is today.

The next day I walked around the lower half of the Island, a longer trek, I discovered, due to the huge bulge into the East River of the lower East Side where streets with strange names wound and twisted east of the avenues A, B, C, D, etc. I continued around the curve of the island into South Street, stopping now and then to look at the ships.

I dropped into the South Street Sailors' Home where I once lived for a week when I was waiting to move from the *Amphion* to the *Pawnee*. The bars we had known during the war were all closed so I continued around through the Battery and up West Street, where I looked in at the *World-Telegram* and found no one I knew. It was a long haul uptown from there, but ultimately I made it back to the end of East Forty-second Street and the office. The next few days I devised a series of zigzag courses which cut through the city. In this way I found most of the landmarks I had heard about.

In addition to my walking tours I spent a good deal of time at Baker Field with my roommate, Sampson, and Coach Lou Little. I had followed the career of the coach since I was in high school, when he played for Worcester Academy. His wanderings then led him to Vermont where he played a year or two, Trinity College of Hartford, where he was in residence during the spring term but skipped before football started, University of Pennsylvania, where he played a couple of years, United States Army, in which he was a combat infantry captain, the Frankfort Yellow Jackets where he coached and played right tackle, Georgetown where he coached, and finally, Columbia.

Lou's football team operated in mortal terror of their roaring boss. He was a strange kind of coach. He made himself heard all over Baker Field, but when trouble came to one of his players, he was kind and considerate. He insisted that his players dress neatly, shave every day, and get a haircut once every two weeks. He sent a man-

ager around collecting the scholastic standing of each
player each week. Those who showed signs of delin-
quency were called together evenings in a study hall, over
which one of the assistant coaches presided.

Except for Ralph Hewitt, a real football player from
Lawrence, Massachusetts, Lou had practically nothing out
of which to form a team the first year. He redeemed the
season to some extent by beating Cornell with the aid of a
fifty-yard drop kick by Hewitt and an inspired performance by Bill McDuffie. The latter was told to cover
Bart Viviano, Cornell's great fullback. His instructions
were to tackle Viviano on every play. McDuffie brought
such devotion to the task that Viviano had his worst day
as a ground-gainer. McDuffie was black and blue from
head to foot but was able to play the following week after
a series of hot soaks.

The night of the Cornell game I went with Lou and
Arthur Sampson to call on Gil Dobie, the Cornell coach,
in the Hotel Pennsylvania. He was hospitable but he took
some of the joy out of the occasion for Little and Sampson
by his characterization of the game. "Just a couple of
lousy football teams mulling around," he said.

Lou's teams were better each year and in 1933 he beat
everybody but Princeton. The season was over and I
invited Lou and his wife Loretta to come to dinner with
Ricie, my new wife, and me in our railroad flat on East
Fifty-second Street.

Loretta showed up without Lou. "He'll be here later,"
she said. "Something has happened which made it necessary for him to talk to Dave Smyth." The latter was
chairman of the Columbia football committee, a devoted
Columbia adherent and a first-class guy. Why did Lou
have to see him?

Loretta was excited and anxious to talk but obviously under orders not to. I wormed the story out of her. Columbia had been invited by Stanford to play in the Rose Bowl at Pasadena, California.

I went out to the drugstore, theoretically to get some Seltzer, and called the office. I told Daley the story and he wouldn't believe it.

"Who's the authority for this story?" he asked.

"I won't tell you my source, George, you'll have to take it on my authority. I assure you it's all right."

When Lou arrived I told him our office had the story and he at once telephoned Bill Corum of the *Journal-American*, who was a particular friend. I didn't mind at all because Corum worked for an evening paper and couldn't get the news into the paper until the *Tribune* was on the street.

Daley didn't have much faith in the story for he under-played it with a small two-column head. It was a cold scoop and it made a sensation and forced the other morning papers into a late rewrite job.

The next day the Columbia committee, comprising faculty members and graduates, met at the University and accepted the invitation. Among those who were hanging around the lobby waiting for the decision was a big sophomore named Al Barrabas. No other football player was there. The interest of Barrabas was prophetic for his part in the game that was played and won January 1, 1934, was the lead.

Lou Little started with customary zeal to get ready to play Stanford, at the same time moaning pathetically over Columbia's prospective inability to hold the Stanford score down. The poor old Columbians scrimmaged end-lessly in a Bronx armory and left before Christmas by special train to complete practice at Tucson, Arizona. I went with the team, as did Gallico, Corum, and a few other newspaper men. Captain Thompson, sports editor of the *Times,* was still enraged by the *Herald Tribune*'s scoop and wouldn't send anyone.

The trip was by stages, with daytime stopovers for practice in St. Louis, Dallas, and El Paso. In the last town the fears expressed by Little for his team seemed justified, for a pick-up team comprising a nucleus from Texas School of Mines, abetted by others home for the holidays, gave Columbia a good beating in scrimmage. At the very end the New Yorkers redeemed themselves slightly by pulling off a play known as KF-79 with a substitute named Maniaci carrying the ball.

The play in question was a fake reverse by the fullback in which all the faking which made it work was conducted after he had taken off around end. Columbia employed an unbalanced single-wing formation with Cliff Montgomery, the quarterback, in the tail position and Barrabas, the regular fullback, close beside him.

On KF-79 Montgomery whirled and handed the ball to Barrabas who hid it behind his body with both hands and started around the weak side end. Montgomery then executed another spin and faked to Ed Brominski, the wingback who made a realistic run off-tackle without the ball. The Columbia blockers acted as if it were a real tackle play.

It was effective because of Montgomery's superb ball-handling and his ability to execute the double spin.

At Tucson, Little drove the team hard in 90-degree heat. He moved to the scene of the game two days before with his team in excellent condition and apparently ready to play the game of its life.

When the team arrived in Los Angeles a small group of graduates, and an aging beauty they had chosen as Columbia's queen, were waiting on the platform. Little got off the train with a roar that frightened the half-grown lion (Columbia mascot) the graduates also had brought on a leash. He kicked the lion in the slats and led his players to a waiting bus without speaking to any of the adoring graduates or even to Miss Columbia. The lion took off down the platform dragging the leash-holder.

The weather was "unusual." It rained and rained. The fire departments of Pasadena, Los Angeles, and the surrounding towns were commandeered to pump the water off the field.

There was some doubt that the big dam in the Arroyo Seco, dry gulch where the Rose Bowl is located, would hold.

The day of the game it was still pouring. But the fire engines had the field free of water except around the edges and a mat of brown Bermuda grass was visible.

The trainers had put long cleats on all Columbia's shoes, but changed them to regular cleats when Herb Kopf, assistant coach, discovered that the tangle of Bermuda grass made good footing. This decision may have had a great deal to do with Columbia's victory. Stanford in long cleats was consistently outrun.

At that time Columbia played a strange defense. All members of the six-man line, guards, tackles, and ends played on four points and did not use their hands. They aimed their heads at the enemy's chest and hit him with their foreheads. The result of this billygoat maneuver generally was to make several little piles in the enemy backfield and strip the carrier of interference. The two linebackers, Al Ciampa and Newt Wilder, at center, and

Bill Nevel at fullback made practically all the tackles. This defense kept Stanford within bounds throughout the game, though it had to make one stand on its own 5-yard line when Little took extra time out to substitute and incurred a penalty.

As everyone knows, Columbia won the game, 6-0, and Barrabas scored a touchdown with the end run known as KF-79. A successful pass from Montgomery to Tony Matal had advanced the ball to Sanford's 26-yard line.

Late the night of the game I was in the car with the Littles, a fellow named Bob Moore, and Ralph Hewitt, the old halfback, en route to the home of some movie actor in Beverly Hills. He was giving a wing-ding for the Columbia team. We found the house and as we got out of the car Little saw one of his players, a third-string full-back, sitting in the window with a highball in his hand.

"Wait, driver," he said. "I'm going back to the hotel. I won't go anywhere where my players are drinking."

Loretta argued feebly but was overruled, and we drove all the way back to Pasadena. That's the way it was all the way back across the continent. We stopped at Denver, then Chicago for an alumni banquet. Little kept strict reins on the players and lectured them daily on the need for getting right back to work on their studies when the team reached New York. I can guarantee that Columbia had less fun winning the Rose Bowl championship than any previous or subsequent victor.

12 WHEN I FIRST CAME TO NEW YORK the Empire State Building was being completed on the site of the old Waldorf Astoria at Thirty-fourth Street and Fifth Avenue. The West Side elevated highway was in prospect but had not been started and neither had the Pulaski Skyway in New Jersey. To drive a car from New York to Princeton was a major problem. The route carried you through many narrow streets in New Jersey cities before you got clear sailing on Route 1. My first winter I got a ride there to cover a basketball game and didn't get home until 3 A.M.

This was Prohibition and a great deal of New York's life was lived out of the public gaze. I don't know how many speakeasies there were in the town but there must have been twenty thousand. In spite of the supposed efforts to enforce the noble experiment, many of them operated with scant effort at deception. A couple of breweries also operated and pretty good beer was available for twenty-five cents a glass in the rougher type saloons.

As far as I could make out, some members of the New York Police Force were not interested in the enforcement of Prohibition, leaving this grim chore to federal agents, many of whom were saving the prices of country mansions and steam yachts out of the graft they were getting.

A man's standing in New York's society depended largely on how many speakeasies he could get into. I made a fetish of collecting cards and somewhere at home I have a drawer full, each one representing a place that is gone forever and a group of shadowy characters who have faded into the distant past.

The best eating places in New York at that time were speakeasies and the prices weren't too bad, nothing like as high as they have been recently. In the Basques, a neat little place on West Fortieth Street, dinner was $1.50 and drinks were sixty cents and seventy-five cents. It is no longer possible to get in New York as good a Martini cocktail as was served in the Basques.

The *Herald Tribune* staff hung out in Bleeck's, almost next door on West Fortieth Street. This place is still running under new management and is known as the Artists and Writers Restaurant. In the old days entrance was gained through the warehouse where the Metropolitan Opera scenery is stored. Guests rapped on an unobtrusive side door in the warehouse corridor and were admitted through what is now the ladies' toilet. New guests were required to be introduced by a member and to write their names and birthdays in a book. Until they were known they had to cite the proper birthday to gain access.

In those days there was no street entrance and a small one-armed restaurant occupied the area where the front door is now. Between the one-arm and the speakeasy was a double partition where Bleeck stored all his booze. Late at night after all the customers had gone, he and Henry Schiffgen, a nice guy who got off a German boat one day and forgot to go back to "Der Vaterland," would get out the next day's liquor supply. Henry would let himself down into the hollow partition and hand up the bottles to Bleeck. Once or twice a month Bleeck would restock; the new supplies were wheeled in through the warehouse and the ladies' toilet-to-be on hand trucks.

In those days the bar was in the back and was presided over by a series of characters including Harry McCormick, a gentleman with an acid tongue, and an old Alaskan named Fred and later by Henry Schiffgen himself.

In those days practically nobody on the *Herald Tribune* came to work entirely sober. It was not considered fashionable. Everybody patronized Bleeck's—from Ogden Reid, president and editor, to those copy boys who could spend seventy-five cents for a drink out of the fifteen dollars a week the *Tribune* paid them.

Though drinks were expensive, judged on a pre-Prohibition basis, they were full value. The highballs were two ounces and the cocktails, served in something that would now be known as a "king-size" glass, were undiluted. When the day bartender came in he would spend an hour bottling his Martinis and Manhattans at the ratio of about 5 to 1. He would then put them in the ice trough to chill and when the customers were served, the drinks would be poured out of the icy bottles. In other words, there was no taint of dilution. They were 5 to 1 gin and vermouth, period. There was great democracy in the bar. Mr. Reid used to have drinks with copy boys and reporters, always paying the tab. He also entertained distinguished people, like Prajadhipok, King of Siam. He brought the King in one noon and said to Harry McCormick, "Harry, I want you to meet the King of Siam."

Harry was mixing a rum cocktail. He put it down on the bar, gazed at Mr. Reid's companion and said, "Who, that black little son of a bitch?"

The clientele of Bleeck's included some of the top figures in the newspaper business. Stanley Walker, city editor of the *Herald Tribune*, was the leading customer and last word in such arguments as developed. Among the other habitués were Lucius Beebe, perennially best-dressed man and bon vivant, Wolcott Gibbs, Corey Ford, Dick Watts, John O'Reilly, Ned McIntyre, Dick Maney,

Charley Washburn, Nunnally Johnson, Joel Sayer, St. Clair McKelway, Miss Tallulah Bankhead, and Don Skene. The principal activity in Bleeck's, besides drinking, was the match game, a contest in which each participant tried to guess the exact number of matches hidden in two or more hands including his own. Each man was a possible three. Championships were held in this and Bruce Pinter held the title for most of two winters. In the big multiple-handed games drinks were the usual stake but occasionally big money was on the line. Stanley Walker was reputed to have lost the advance his publisher paid him for *Mrs. Astor's Horse* in a one-night session.

Life was peaceful in Bleeck's and I can only remember a couple of violent interludes, one of which petered out. The only time punches were actually exchanged was the night Jack Kirkland, author of the stage adaption of Erskine Caldwell's *Tobacco Road*, floored drama critic Dick Watts as they stood at the bar. Kirkland had opened an unfortunate adaptation of John Steinbeck's *Tortilla Flat*. Watts had been honest but vicious in his newspaper criticism. The fight involved almost everybody in the bar, Watts being a regular and Kirkland an outsider. The latter caught numerous punches of various voltages and the last one knocked him out the door.

A strange character known as Doc Clifford, an undertaker from Newport, Rhode Island, made his New York headquarters in Bleeck's. He was originally introduced to the place by W. O. McGeehan, *Herald Tribune* columnist, who referred to him frequently as the "Merry Mortician." Clifford made himself unpopular occasionally by getting out a tape measure and measuring the regulars at the bar for coffins.

One night he cleaned out the place with another dodge.

Jack Johnston, the horticulture editor of the *Tribune*, was bragging about how he had punched a Jersey racketeer on the chin. The "Merry Mortician" went to one of two telephones and called up Johnston, who answered the call in the next booth. Speaking in a gruff, quiet voice, the mortician said, "Johnston? . . . We're coming over to get you. I'm giving you fair warning." Johnston went back to the bar and had two more Martinis and started telling again about his conquest of the Jersey gangster. The "Merry Mortician" went back to the telephone booth and called him again. This time Johnston was frightened. When you come right down to it, the Petunia Mob was no match for the Jersey beer gang. So Johnston called up the precinct police station and demanded protection. Twenty minutes later the police banged on the door and a dozen cops filed in with rifles and submachine guns. The sergeant in charge posted his men around the premises, then threw all the customers out the door.

It is reported that the police finally went home about five o'clock, but Jack Bleeck was pretty sore when he looked at the night's sad receipts. He never forgave the "Merry Mortician."

I am writing this material without considering chronology. Much of it happened in the old warehouse days and some of it after Prohibition was repealed when the place became a membership club for a while, then opened on the street and let in the girls.

At the time of the 1939 Papal election, a bunch of us were sitting at a table and Cas Adams, a member in good standing of the Catholic Church, was telling us about the possibilities.

"It will have to be an Italian," he said. "The cardinals won't pick anybody else, of that you can be sure."

Various arguments developed. There were those who maintained that an American might be elected and the German waiters had a candidate who looked good to them. The most prominent man in the race was Cardinal Pacelli, who ultimately became Pope Pius XII, but at the moment of the argument everything was moot. Somebody said the Papal secretary of state had never been made Pope and, therefore, Cardinal Pacelli, who held this office, was a bad bet.

Somebody got out a copy of the *Journal-American*, which had pictures of all the cardinals on one page. So many bets were offered that Adams and I hit on the idea of making book on the election. Without knowing anything about it we quoted odds against all the cardinals.

To attract special groups of bettors we quoted odds on combinations like the Irish-American entry, this designed to attract the bartenders, and the German-American entry, to attract the waiters. In no time at all it got to be a pretty big thing and Adams and I sold a third of the pool to Irving Marsh.

For four or five days bettors came in from all over town looking for us and we finally got much too much money in hand, considering the fact we had no idea what we were doing and did not know how much we could lose. We had held Pacelli at 3-1 but the money flowed in on it so freely that we backed him off to even money. The last night before the cardinals assembled a priest came in and bet ten dollars at this figure. That was the tip-off. We sensed that Pacelli was going to win and we made him 1-3, which virtually shut off the betting. As it turned out, we came out almost exactly even; in fact, we were even when I gave a squawking customer twelve dollars out of my pocket which he claimed we owed him.

Right in the middle of the pool's activity, a stranger wandered in and announced that he could name all the popes from St. Peter through Pius XI, who had just died in the year 1939. He took all bets. Somebody went upstairs for the *Almanac* and checked him on each name. Without stumbling once, he recited 262 names beginning with St. Peter and including such obscure ones as St. Eleutherius, St. Zozimus, and St. Deusdedit, and not overlooking Benedict IX, who held the job three times.

The Papal pool had a brief return before the election of John XXIII, but it wasn't as big.

Various election pools were run and Stanley Walker once organized something known as the Ghoul Pool. He got a copy boy to take down the names of one hundred men over seventy-five years old and he sold them for one dollar apiece. The first man who got a dead one received one hundred dollars. This was quite popular for a time but was discontinued, or so it is reported, because it horrified Mrs. Reid, the mother superior.

In the days of Walker, the *Herald Tribune* was a lively place and a really good newspaper, even though much of its business was carried on in a gin mill. Walker undoubtedly was the man who brought the *Tribune* up to the status it enjoyed before the war, and it was a blow when he left to join Hearst.

The Sports Department was a queer organization. It included a great many top men, including McGeehan, the daily columnist, Harry Cross, Bill McBeth, Richards Vidmer, Don Skene, Everett Morris, Bill Taylor, and Adams, who was the greatest phrasemaker of all.

I have been credited with inventing the name "Ivy League" but actually Adams suggested it. We were sitting around the office one day when Adams started talking about the Ivy colleges. I immediately stole the term and converted it into Ivy League, meaning a rather indefinite group of polite universities of the east. It wasn't formulated into an actual league until many years afterward.

Floyd Taylor, the sports editor, became a very good friend of mine later on. He was conscientious and thorough, but he ran the Sports Department like a school-teacher and worked himself to the bone, chasing commas and reporters. Every little while McGeehan would disappear for several days. After a week one of the staff members, generally McBeth or Cross, would volunteer to go out and find him. After another week the one who didn't go would volunteer to go out and find McGeehan and Cross or McGeehan and McBeth. After a third week someone would call Cross's brother in Naugautuck, Connecticut, and he would come down and bring them all in.

McGeehan was so irregular with his column that he was paid by the day; one hundred dollars when he wrote, nothing when he didn't. Not knowing the arrangement at the time, some of us wrote thousands of dollars worth of unpaid work to cover up McGeehan.

When McGeehan was on the wagon, he was severe in his criticism of drinkers. He would stay off the hooch a month or two at a time. But ultimately, some of his pals like Colonel Tillinghast l'Hommedieu Houston, coowner of the Yankees, would come to town and the period of abstinence would end.

The *Herald Tribune* was in a period of prosperity and the Sports Department was given a tremendous allotment of space. This our editor filled by covering almost every little thing from Dartmouth College south. We were smothered under summaries of freshman and junior varsity games. The cost of composition and wire tolls must have been stupendous. Moreover, the regular writers were sometimes crowded out of the paper on account of this mass of trivia. I recall going to New Brunswick, New Jersey, to cover a swimming meet and coming home to discover that my story had been cut to one sentence and the summary. Unfortunately, the copy desk had neglected to take my name off it so it read as follows:

By Stanley Woodward

New Brunswick, N.J., Feb. 26—Rutgers defeated Fordham in swimming today, 52 to 37; the summary.

This kind of paper was what the bigwigs wanted and Floyd Taylor did his best to please them, knowing it was nonsense. He couldn't stand it long, however, and finally left to become assistant city editor at the *World-Telegram.* There was a period of a week when I acted as sports editor pro tem. During my tenure I let things go, knowing nothing could be done about it. That Saturday I covered a boat race at Annapolis. The next Monday morning Arthur Draper, one of the big editors, called me into his office and said truculently, "Why didn't we have the Harvard freshman rugby game?"

I went up virtually in smoke. I held my fire for a minute and then said, "I don't know why we didn't have the Harvard freshman rugby game, but I am damn sure that not having it was a good thing for the newspaper. If we could throw out a thousand pieces like it we might start to get together a sports department that amounted to something."

"Stanley, Stanley," said Mr. Draper, trying to mollify me. "We are trying to get out a complete newspaper." My tenure as sports editor ended therewith.

The next thing I knew George Daley had come in to

take the job. For years George had been sports editor of the *Evening World* which, with its great morning counterpart, had ceased publication in late February, 1931. Daley had moved to the *Telegram,* nominal purchaser, for a few months and then had been let out. He was on the loose and in a state of moderate desperation when our editorial board picked him up for its sports editor. He was over sixty years old and his relief must have been intense when the *Tribune* signed him.

Actually, George wasn't a bad sports editor for the *Herald Tribune* at that particular stage. The depression was beginning to bite into the newspaper's income and it was time to end the spending spree. George was used to the low-budget operation of an evening newspaper and when he started to cut expenses, the bigwigs thought they had found a wizard. It had never occurred to them to eliminate such immortal items as the summary of the Harvard freshman rugby game.

From the standpoint of an experienced reporter, which was what I considered myself at this juncture, George was pretty hard to take. He was given to homilies about newspaper procedure and nearly drove us crazy by detailing the ABC's of our profession to us. He did not understand that all he had to say was go and cover this and the men would do it. He gave each man a lecture with his assignment, telling him what to look for and ending by urging him to get "that evening paper touch" into the story.

He was a nice old boy with silvery hair, always neat in a blue suit and bow tie. He was effusive whenever he met a big editor in the hall and terribly wounded when one of his staff men committed the unforgivable sin of getting drunk. His greatest trial was William (Bunk) McBeth, who fell into many days of temptation while covering racing. George used to lecture him endlessly whenever he fell by the board.

One night Bunk was just able to walk, and George called him over to his desk. He talked to him in a fatherly manner for almost half an hour. Bunk stood there swaying and saying nothing. After a while George indicated he was finished and Bunk walked three paces to the copy desk and said in a loud voice, "What was that old son of a bitch saying?"

In the winter when there was no racing, Bunk sometimes covered the amateur hockey in the Garden on Sunday afternoon. Mrs. McBeth frequently accompanied him, but one day he took his little daughter. Immediately they met a friend of Bunk's who sat with them. After the first period the friend suggested that they go out and get a drink, but Bunk refused.

"If the old lady were here, I'd go with you," said Bunk, "and find some way to get out, but to fool the kid wouldn't be sporting. No sir, no drink."

The stories about Bunk are so numerous and have been so mangled that little remains which may be offered with assurance. Once he is reported to have gone to Chicago to cover the races and to have been provided with a ghost writer by the considerate management. After a couple of days he complained to Western Union.

"I've been reading my stuff in the paper," he said, "and if it doesn't improve, I'm going to change to Postal." It is necessary for modern readers to explain that Postal Telegraph was Western Union's rival in the long dead past.

McBeth, to give him his due, was an excellent reporter. If you want to get the facts of the World Series baseball strike when the Red Sox and Cubs refused to come to bat, you will find Bunk's was the best story. The same may be said of his story of Man o' War's only defeat by the filly called Upset. Set down clearly in his lead are all the facts that have stood up through the years, principally that Man o' War was boxed on the rail, pulled to the outside and had to go too wide and too far to close with his conqueror.

Harry Cross was a great newspaper man with a gift of epigrams. It was he who said, "Work is the curse of the drinking classes." He also announced, "Racing is the backbone of the national poverty."

When Harry put his teeth into a story, nobody could do a better job, but he was sentimental and easily offended and the pomposity of George Daley was a little hard for him to take, particularly so because he was almost as old as George and had behind him a much more distinguished career. Harry fell off the wagon on numerous occasions. One night I received a call from Bill Taylor's wife in Port Washington that Harry was spending all his money at the Yacht Club and was getting in bad shape.

It was a Friday and he was due to cover a Princeton game the next day. I asked Ann Taylor to take him up to her house which was next door to my own. I got there just as Harry was demanding release and a case of champagne. I took him to my house and gave him a slug that knocked him cold and put him to bed. The next morning I heard the victrola playing "I've Got Rings on My Fingers and Bells on My Toes," Blanche Ring's rendition of a great old song. I went downstairs and Harry was there in his underwear. He was crying bitterly and had finished seven bottles of beer. Without saying anything to him, I called a fellow he lived with and got him over to take Harry away. Poor old Harry was so happy in his sadness that he didn't notice anything wrong until the jailer arrived. He put on his pants and walked down the front steps, announcing, "I come out of the hills to give myself up."

The head man and the model for us all in the writing department was McGeehan, who, in my own opinion, topped all the great sport columnists of his day; by whom I mean Damon Runyon, Westbrook Pegler, Grantland Rice, Heywood Broun, etc. He was a Philippine War veteran and well along in his career when I first met him. He was a pleasant gentleman with a head of gray hair who walked around the office between paragraphs rolling cigarettes out of Bull Durham and brown paper. He came to the office in the morning and spent three or four hours on each column. He had a plain style which employed exact words and he coined original names for the things he wrote about. Boxing, for instance, was "the manly art of modified murder." Primo Carnera was the "the tall tower of Gorgonzola," and the three New York boxing commissioners headed by William Muldoon were the "Three Dumb Dukes." McGeehan's humorous style masked a keen grasp of sports value. He declared that Tunney would beat Dempsey long before it happened.

He came in the office one summer day and offered the boys a parlay: "You can get any odds you ask for on this one," he said, "and it will come through. Tunney will beat Dempsey and René Lacoste will beat Bill Tilden." Of course, both happened. A bookmaker would probably have laid 50-1 against the double result.

McGeehan regarded Daley with tolerant disinterest, never speaking to him if he could help it. Daley had enough sense to avoid giving McGeehan lectures but not enough to refrain from fawning on him. This McGeehan couldn't stand. Daley got the idea it was up to him to protect McGeehan against himself and sometimes formulated little plans to keep him on the straight path. Once there was a football dinner at the Harvard Club and McGeehan announced he was going to go. Daley told me to go too and see that McGeehan got home. At three o'clock the next morning McGeehan left me at my own front door and my new wife, a tolerant girl, had to come down from our apartment to get me up to bed.

I had been divorced a short time after I came to New York and made a unique arrangement with my former wife. I gave her an allowance for more than a year and then gave her all the property I had in the world except my personal things, which consisted of a few clothes and a typewriter. So I made a new start after I was thirty-five years old and my new girl, who was known as Ricie, enabled me to get over my difficulties.

She was an assistant buyer at James McCreery's department store. When I was crippled by my payments to my former family and by a depression cut of 19 percent which the *Herald Tribune* inflicted on its employees, she came to the rescue. We were married early in my New York career and rented a railroad apartment at 405 East Fifty-second Street. This was the whole second floor of a brownstone and the rent was seventy-five dollars a month.

The next year I made a plea of poverty to the landlord and he reduced it to sixty-five dollars. I suppose now it would cost 250 dollars. It had a big living room with a fireplace, one large bedroom, one small bedroom, kitchen and bath and two windowless rooms in the middle. I used one as a writing room and the other we turned into a dressing room and closet by putting up a pipe rack. We turned the apartment around and slept in the front so that we could have the outlook from a big room in the back.

The kitchen and bathroom both were off this living room, which was a little unusual, but we had a nice little back-yard with grass and a couple of ailanthus trees. After we got over being disturbed by the street noises in the bed-room it was ideal.

We had a rare guy named Dick Aylward for a super-intendent and there was nothing he wouldn't do for Ricie. She also made a friend of the man who kept the Cordial Shop, i.e., bootlegging establishment, in the basement and he did us a great many favors—such as bringing us gin out of hours, accepting packages from the department stores when we were out, and shutting our windows if he thought it was going to rain. My wife loved it there and I often think that I was crazy to move to the suburbs even after we had started to have children.

My salary was cut from 135 dollars to 110 dollars early in my *Herald Tribune* career. But the depression had ad-vantages for salaried people and we were very prosperous despite my salary cut and the fact that my wife had quit her job. At that time you could buy pork chops for fifteen cents a pound in the Third Avenue markets. Hamburger steak was fifteen cents a pound and other things were priced accordingly. The Cordial Shop sold gin for around seventy-five cents a fifth, but if you really wanted to economize you could buy a gallon of grain alcohol at the corner drugstore and make your own with the addition of juniper, glycerine drops, and water. You cut the alcohol by fifty percent so that you got two gallons of gin for five dollars. As far as I could see, it was just as good as any gin you can get now and just about one eighth the price.

People drank more during Prohibition but it cost less. The swankiest gin mills in town didn't charge more than one dollar a drink and in most of them the tab was either sixty cents or seventy-five cents, or slightly less than it is now.

In spite of my prosperity, the pay cut rankled and when I got what looked like a good offer from the *Daily News*, I was much interested. Paul Gallico was the sports editor then. He called in Henry McLemore and me and suggested we join his sports staff. I don't know what he offered Henry but his offer to me equaled my original salary in New York without the pay cut. Paul seemed to think that we could come to terms at once. Then he reconsidered and said, "I'd better let you know whether or not everything is all right in a few days. But I'm sure it is."

I went back to the *Herald Tribune* and resigned.

The *Herald Tribune* accepted the resignation with apparent equanimity and nobody commented to me as I worked out the first week of my two weeks' notice. I hadn't heard a word from Gallico since seeing him in his office so I called him up.

"Oh," he said, "I'm sorry. That fell through. They are going to make me take three men off the city staff. I hope we can get together later on."

I went back to the *Herald Tribune* with the idea of trying to reinstate myself on the staff. Then I said to myself, "Hold everything. Don't hurry . . ." I went home and talked to my wife. I told her I did not think that the *Herald Tribune* would let me go without opening some sort of conversation and asked her if she were game enough to stick it out with me and refrain from telling the *Tribune* that the *News* job had evaporated.

It was a rhetorical question—she was game enough for anything, as I later found out.

The difficulty was that I had to leave on a baseball trip with the Yankees. First stop, an exhibition game in Nor-

folk. The telephone started while I was in the Norfolk
Hotel—minor executives started calling me up. That night
we moved from Norfolk to Washington by boat and I
won eighty dollars in a crap game enroute. In Washington
calls became more frequent and finally I was called by
Bill Haskell, who was Mr. Reid's personal assistant. He
asked me what it would take to keep me on the *Tribune*
and I said that I wanted restoration of my pay cut. He
said, I'll ask Mr. Reid and send you a night letter. Next
morning I got the night letter and it was as I asked. I sent
back the following wire—"Not wholly pleased with conditions at *Trib* but talk of money soothes. I agree to stay
with you if my pay cut is restored."

George Daley may have been a nuisance to his staff and
a fatuous old man but the sports section was improving
under his fuddy-duddy direction. He had cut out all the
silly items about freshman rugby, etc., and was playing
important stories more fully. He had certain favoritisms
and they were a little hard to take. Horse-racing was the
most important thing in the world and Herbert Bayard
Swope was a great god. To me he was only the man who
let the *World* die. I neither liked him nor his sport.

The thing that pleased the bigwigs about Daley was the
fact he saved the paper's money. He ended the college
correspondent racket which sometimes earned an outland
student as much as a staff man would get. The correspondents scraped up anything they could find and sent it
in by telegraph. Daley cut thousands off the cost of operating the paper by cutting out the trivialities and so saving the correspondents' fee and the telegraph tolls. If he
had been content to sit tight and keep his rather puerile
stuff out of the paper, he might have got a reputation as
a great sports editor. But he insisted on writing two col-

umns a week. Vanity was his weakness, and though it didn't bring him down, it made everyone laugh at him.

George was a right thinker from way back and he attempted to police the thoughts of his men as well as their actions. He once got hold of my wife and asked her if she wouldn't do something to turn me away from Communism. By "communism" he probably meant minor rebellion when he attempted to lecture me on how to cover an assignment. I tried to be nice to the old gentleman but I often slipped and said something rude. So I was a Communist. However, the work of covering sports went on uninterrupted. I had a crack at about everything—hockey, baseball, rowing, tennis, golf, and horse-racing.

13

IN 1935 DALEY SENT ME SOUTH with the Brooklyn Dodgers, then managed by Casey Stengel. The training site was Orlando and I was able to get a little house there so that I could take my wife and my year-old daughter, Ellen. It was a very pleasant spring and Mr. Stengel, in his 1935 form, was a most pleasant companion. However, the nuttiness which clings to the Dodgers was much in evidence and strange happenings were a dime a dozen.

The wife of a rookie left-hand pitcher lost all the family funds in a slot machine at the Orange Court Hotel and was so ashamed of herself that she took a bottle full of sleeping bills. A doctor, who happened to be in the hotel, saved her life with a stomach pump. Soon after this a rattlesnake was killed in center field. A Dodger rookie stopped an exhibition game and came to the bench for a baseball bat; he then slew the reptile in view of all the customers and fired its remains over the fence with the bat. It developed the rookie was an old rattlesnake hunter from the morasses of South Carolina. It was further discovered that there was a whole colony of rattlesnakes under the clubhouse and that Babe Hamburger, Dodger general factotum, had made friends of them.

We were covering a game between Detroit and the Dodgers one day when there was a shot behind the press box. We turned around and saw a colored lady waving a pistol. A man, who turned out to be her husband, was lying on the ground. The shooting was only an expression of love. The husband was a night elevator operator in one of the hotels and had refrained from going home after work. He just hung around with the boys and then went to the ball game. The lady headed him off at the

bleacher gate and shot him through the stomach, fortunately missing all the essential plumbing. The episode
turned out happily. The couple made up and the lady
spent only a week in jail. It was discovered that the husband was a promising singer and a collection was taken up
to send him to New York for vocal lessons. It is assumed
that his life companion went with him after being frisked
for weapons.

When the Dodgers started on the road at the end of the
training camp, it became necessary for me to send my wife
and child home with the car. The drive was too long for
Ricie and child so I drove them to Jacksonville and put
them on the boat, which then ran between Miami, Jacksonville, and New York. The trip to Jacksonville will live
long in memory. The day before, I ate a few interesting-
looking beans which were growing on a bush in the front
yard. That night and for three days after I was terribly
sick. It turned out that I had eaten castor beans, which, in
the raw state, are a potent poison.

The next year we went with the Yankees to St. Peters-
burg and so I was in on the beginning of one of the great
baseball careers of the century, that of young Joe DiMag-
gio. He arrived in camp the first day and was subjected to
a mass interview by the assembled baseball writers. He
was a diffident, hatchet-faced kid who seemed to lack confidence and assertiveness. But when he got on the ball
field, there was a remarkable transformation. You could
look at him and say to yourself, "There's a great ball
player," without any chance of making a mistake. Everything he did was just right. His throwing arm was fluid
power. Without any apparent effort he could rifle the ball
home on one hop from deep center field. From the first
day he patrolled the outfield like a hawk and when he

came to bat, a series of line drives rippled off his bat.

Up from San Francisco at the age of twenty, young Joe never showed any reason for doubt that he would be the Yankee centerfielder from the start of his big league career or that he would hit .300.

As a matter of fact, Joe did not start the season for the Yankees, but that was due to a clubhouse booboo by the trainer who burned one of Joe's feet with some sort of a therapeutic baker. The damage was so severe that Joe missed the balance of the training season and the first two weeks of competition.

The manager of the Yankees was Joe McCarthy, who was the only big league manager who thought Woodward could pitch. He asked me if I would like to work out with the team and suggested that I get down early every morning and pitch to the hitters while the regular batting practice pitchers were warming up. As long as we were in St. Pete, I was there on the dot of nine o'clock.

I borrowed a shirt from Lou Gehrig and tried to put on a pair of his pants. They were three inches too small around the waist and I had to use a pair belonging to Pat Malone, a veteran pitcher who was finishing his career with the Yanks. I was then forty-one years old and it was the first time I had ever pitched to big league hitters. I survived it without damage, even though a couple of drives whistled by close to my ears.

After the training season I made every effort to get loose from the ball club, for I hated the daily grind of baseball and, in particular, the long western trips. Ricie, Ellen, and I had moved to a little house in Port Washington and I resented the necessity of being absent for two or three weeks at a lick.

Daley kept me with the Dodgers until well into the

summer of 1935. For a while this wasn't too bad, for Stengel, by the exercise of some magic, got the club away from the post with an amazing rush and they were at the top of the league until they started to sag in June. Win or lose, Stengel was a good companion. Frequently on the road a writer would find a note in his box on returning to the hotel after the game.

The message would be, "Mr. Stengel is pouring in room 806."

I had a high regard for his ability as a manager after a couple of months with the Dodgers and admired him, particularly, for a coup he tried to pull one day in Pittsburgh. One afternoon the Dodgers were opposed by Cy Blanton, who had the most amazing screwball in baseball. It was known as "the butterfly." Blanton was right-handed and the screwball would duck away from a left-hand hitter as if it were on string. So Stengel sent in an entire line-up of right-handed hitters. It didn't work because Cy also had a curve and the Dodgers of that era were renowned whiffers—at curves. But anyway, he tried something that no other manager in my experience ever had tried.

Stengel was also capable of blaming himself for something that went wrong rather than trying to pin it on one of his coaches. That spring in Orlando the maestro had been fooled by a Detroit centerfielder named Jo Jo White. Casey was made to look extremely foolish but instead of hiding behind an alibi, he talked about his own mystification in detail. White's play was one of the cleverest I have ever seen in baseball.

The score was tied in the last of the ninth inning. There was one out and the Dodgers had a man on third, where Casey was coaching. The batter hit a long fly to center and White settled under it. It was obvious that the man on third would have plenty of time to tag up and score the winning run. But before the ball got to White he made a fake catch and throw. Casey shouted "go!" and the runner tore in from third. Then White made the actual catch and the runner had to go back to the bag. The ball was in the infield before he could start again for the plate and the run was lost when the next hitter went out.

Casey told the story with gusto as he poured in room 806 that night. He was unchanged in triumph or disaster. He was just as good a guy when the Dodgers were knocking them stiff in the early part of the 1935 season as he was in the late stages when they were slowly gravitating toward position No. 8.

It was just after this decline started that I came closest to murdering a copyreader. On one occasion at Ebbets Field, the Dodgers were taking a beating and Casey was walking back and forth in the dugout glowering at his heroes. I wrote a preliminary paragraph giving the essential facts of the game. Then, paraphrasing Milton's description of Satan in "Paradise Lost," I added, "Field Marshal Casey von Stengel viewed the proceedings from under the low roof of the dugout, but under brows of dauntless courage and considerate pride, awaiting revenge."

The copyreader made it "High courage and considerable pride."

In the fall of 1935 I went to the Polo Grounds to watch a few professional football games. I had a low opinion of professional football, for, in earlier games I had seen, there seemed to be very little hard hitting and the ball carrier generally wound up standing on his feet in the arms of two or three opposing behemoths. But in one game in the fall of 1935 the Giants looked like a real football team and

I was impressed.

After the game I encountered Tim Mara, owner of the club, in the dressing room. Tim was an old-time book-maker in the days before pari-mutels. I knew his word was as good as a contract. So when I got the oral assurance of his team's services for an All-Star game the next September, I was sure of my ground. Arch Ward, sports editor of the Chicago *Tribune*, had started an All-Star game matching new college graduates with a professional team, a few years earlier. My idea was to cooperate with Ward and bring his All-Stars to New York after they had played in Chicago. The *Herald Tribune* had a legitimate and particularly worthy charity in its Fresh Air Fund which provided country vacations for thousands of New York children.

My idea in trying to organize the game was to get myself something important to do. The *Herald Tribune* staff was large and, unless I wanted to settle down and be a baseball writer forever, assignments were rather scarce and many of them were unimportant and uninteresting.

I started working on the All-Star game as soon as the football season was over. The first thing to do was to persuade the paper to take it on. George Daley was enthusiastic about it and immediately dashed off in all directions to talk to the bigwigs and implant the conviction that it was his idea. When the business of hard negotiating with the bosses ultimately fell on me, I found that a lot of damage had been done by George's misrepresentations.

The *Tribune* had never undertaken a promotion of this sort and didn't like to risk the money. Wilbur Forrest, one of the main editors, lived near me in Long Island and I undertook to drive him to work every day, talking to him about the All-Star game en route. His resistance was unyielding. I finally went to Tim Mara and told him that I thought I had to give up the game. When I told him that the chief difficulty was the *Tribune*'s reluctance to put up the money, he said, "Hell, I'll underwrite it. Don't let money worry you."

In view of Tim's reliability I knew I now had a solid contract but it was hard to convince my bosses that an honest bookmaker's word was a contract. They wanted me to get a written agreement out of Mara. This I ultimately had to do at the cost of offending Tim. For years he had been keeping the faith of his clients, sometimes paying out thousands on a contract made by a word or a nod.

The next thing was to get the cooperation of Ward, who was very jealous of his All-Star brainchild. However, he was in a little trouble with a group of rivals who wished to move in on his racket. Each year Christy Walsh, a syndicate newspaper man, picked an All-America football team. The next year he planned to insist that each man he selected for either his first or second team must agree to play in an All-Star game in New York, presumably against the Giants. The Hearst papers were supposed to be cooperating with Ward. I talked to Bill Corum and he told me that Walsh and he had an agreement for the game and that he had already contacted Mara about the Giants.

I knew he couldn't get the Giants unless I released them, but Ward had never heard of my proposition and was in a state of desperation. He was going around the country signing up football players for next fall at 250 dollars apiece, which was high money for All-Star participation at that time. I met Ward in the Hotel Astor and told him I had the Giants for an All-Star game and would like to cooperate with him. He seemed to be impressed but there were long negotiations before he would agree to let us have his players.

I had to go to Chicago and have a midnight supper with all the bigwigs of the Chicago *Tribune*. I never knew the exact reason for this; apparently they wanted to see if I was trustworthy, or perhaps Ward wanted to get their approval of the Chicago *Tribune*'s participation in the New York plan. Ultimately, we got the details straightened out.

Mara had been after me for some time to decide definitely to have the game under *Tribune* Fresh Air Fund auspices or to release him so that he could make a contract with Walsh and the Hearst people. Now I was able to assure him that we would promote the game, and soon after our attorneys drew a contract which he signed.

The game finally came off on the hottest September night in the history of the New York weather bureau. The heat was so dreadful in the Polo Grounds that the coaches did not take the players in the dressing rooms between the halves, just let them lie around on the field.

The game had to be played at night and there were no adequate lights in the Polo Grounds. Horace Stoneham, lessor of the park, however, agreed to put in lights. As the game drew close it became pretty obvious that I was an amateur promoter. I scaled the house all wrong, enraging some of the early buyers who thought they had bought good seats and found out they had bad ones. Nobody wanted the upstairs seats back of the goal posts. By calling the end locations "coaches section" we ultimately got these seats moving. I signed some of the leading eastern players for one hundred dollars apiece.

When the game approached, George Daley became more and more difficult to handle. He wanted to stand behind the downstairs counter and sell tickets. Moreover, he wanted to show each customer where his seat locations were. As a result, the ticket line did not move and the rumor spread that we were out of tickets. It was a terrific mess and the fact that we came out of it with our shirts was remarkable.

I had a terrible time with the players. The ones who were getting 250 dollars in Chicago didn't like the hundred-dollar fee I was planning to pay in New York. I finally had to come up to 150 dollars apiece which made the eastern players I had signed resentful. I went to Chicago to see the game there and to bring my players home. I had a special train of six cars with a handsome All-Star sign on the tail end. It was murder rounding up the players and getting them on the train and I soon discovered that many of them had bottles. The trip to New York was uproarious. The boys did not apparently take their New York game seriously, but they were mollified when they saw their quarters at the Westchester Country Club. Still they remained hard to handle and the coaches—Bernie Bierman of Minnesota, Bo McMillan, then of Indiana, and Elmer Layden of Notre Dame would have no part of disciplining them off the field.

I finally found a good player-contact man in Cas Adams. He was so much smarter than any of the players and so quick with repartee that he anticipated their outrageous requests and made them laugh at themselves.

Still they signed checks for golf lessons, champagne, and midnight lunches—I having neglected to cut off their signing privileges—and one of the two centers we had, a boy from the midlands, went down to the Yacht Club and took a cruise on somebody's yawl for two days.

I made a mistake in neglecting to cut off the telephone

in the players' rooms and another in failing to give them complimentary tickets with the prices stamped on them. On the night of the game this caused the first sit-down strike in history. When the players got into the dressing room for the game they were rebellious because they had been unable to sell their tickets which were marked "Players Ticket, Complimentary" and had no location.

A Fordham player found out how to open the door onto Eighth Avenue and the whole mob went out half an hour before the game for a last effort at getting some money out of these tickets. A quarterback from the South came out of the door onto the field half-dressed and shouted, "Hey, Woodward, we're not going to come out."

At this point I said to hell with it and went up to my seat in the press box. At this point I did not know whether or not there would be a game. But soon after I was seated, the lights on the field were dimmed and each starting player was introduced under spotlights. Each one showed up in his assigned place and each appeared to be full of fire and ready to go. It was quite a surprise.

I had had additional trouble with the various unions I had had to engage. I had signed up the West Point Band, but I couldn't get union permission to bring it in, without which the general wouldn't send it, until I hired a stand-by band. The Electrician's Union wanted stand-by men for the loudspeaker employees who had been hired on a contract basis from a firm in Queens.

All these things were straightened out, I thought, until the introductions began. With great difficulty we had obtained the college song of each player and had written the music and had orchestrated it for the West Point Band. Owing to the fact that the band would be standing in the dark during the opening ceremony, we installed a special floodlight on the grandstand roof and employed an electrician to turn it on.

That was all he had to do, snap one switch and get a night's pay. But, when the time came, he forgot to turn on the light and so the West Point Band was silent and all the work of collecting the music and writing it out for one hundred pieces was wasted.

We had borrowed pads and helmets from Northwestern University and when we came to check after the game, we discovered that the players had stolen about half of them, which made it necessary for us to pay replacement prices. One pair of shoulder pads had been left in a taxi and the driver brought it into the *Tribune* office the next day.

In spite of all the trouble, we cleared ten thousand dollars for the *Tribune* Fresh Air Fund. The game was generally considered a success, but to me it remains the most botched-up job I ever had anything to do with. The next year I knew enough to anticipate possible difficulties. I signed my own players well in advance and engaged Andy Kerr of Colgate as the coach. I sent each player a "Bill of Rights and Obligations" which told him exactly what we would do for him and what he was supposed to do for us.

I had professional ticket sellers. I called the General Electric Company and arranged for a decent lighting system. The first lights were unsatisfactory. I moved the training site from the Westchester Country Club, which was too gay, to the Peddie School in Hightstown, New Jersey. I took no players on Ward's list, but signed the leading eastern players to exclusive contracts to work for the *Tribune*. In cases where I had to get the man I paid a bonus. The game came off in good shape but the aroma of the first one lingered and we didn't do better than forty thousand people in a fifty-thousand-seat stadium. Still, we made a good deal of money.

Moreover, the crowd was pleased with the show. The All-Stars, though somewhat delinquent defensively, ran the ball all over the field with Kerr's deceptive double-wing attack. The Giants finally won, 14-7, through the exercise of power against the All-Star line. Still, the Stars would have tied it except for a lapse by Yale's great end, Larry Kelley. Standing on the goal line unattended, he dropped a pass which hit him on the chest, a most unusual proceeding for him.

The next year the All-Stars had the most remarkable defensive line I have ever seen, comprising, on the left or poison-ivy side, Ed Franco of Fordham at guard, Tony Matissi of Pitt at tackle, and Frank Souchak of Pitt at end. At the right, or Ivy side, were Joe Nee of Harvard at guard, Charley Toll of Princeton at tackle, and Stinky Davis of Dartmouth at end. Against this front, which was backed up by Alex Wojciechowicz of Fordham, the Giants made no gain of more than six yards by running or passing. They won the game, however, on two forty-five-yard field goals by Ward Cuff.

Jock Sutherland coached the next year and the All-Stars lost again. They finally won in 1940 when Tuss Mc-Laughry of Dartmouth produced a remarkable team out of unknown players. The score was 17-7 in favor of the All-Stars. From 1936 on, the All-Star game filled all my slack time, but I was out covering this and that, i.e., baseball, football, tennis, and rowing.

In 1938 I went to Poughkeepsie ahead of time to write advance material on the Intercollegiate Regatta. There I met my old friend, Robert Fulton Paul Anthony Kelley, of the *Times*, who proposed that we collaborate and come up with something new in rowing expertism. On the third day we were there water conditions were perfect on the river and Kelley judged that all the crews would have time trials that afternoon. He suggested that we walk out on the traffic bridge over the Hudson, which is approximately one-half mile from the finish of the old four-mile course, and do some artistic spying on the crews. Kelley's idea was to spot the start of each crew with his Zeiss 7-50 glasses and leave the timing to me. We couldn't tell what crew was coming down the river when it started, but we could identify it when it got near us. The coaches were too secretive to start close to each other.

When Kelley saw the splash of the oars at the start, he would call go and I would write down the exact time in minutes and seconds. When the crew got near enough to be identified I would label it and then I would mark down the time when it stopped rowing. This way we had a good chance of being within one second of the exact time. During the afternoon we timed every varsity crew on the river and then went back to the hotel, fondly known as the "Half Nelson House," to tabulate the results.

To our great surprise, we discovered that Navy had made the best time; that Washington and California, which were the hot favorites, were third and fourth respectively behind Cornell.

Kelley wouldn't believe it. "Navy isn't that good," he said. "We'll have to throw all our figures away."

Foolishly, we did, and lived to regret it. Navy won the race with ease; Cornell was second; Washington third; California fourth. If we had had the faith to stick with our own clocking we could have called the finish exactly.

14

A FEW MONTHS BEFORE I COVERED that race at Poughkeepsie, I had been made sports editor of the *Herald Tribune*. George Daley died and the bigwigs finally settled on me, in spite of the fact they had found out about my double-dealing in the case of the *Daily News* and were still angry about it. They thought I had gotten money out of the company under false pretenses. They might have turned me down except for the fact that Al Laney went to the front and told the bosses the Sports Department would quit in a body if my rival for the job were selected. I should have known enough to fire the rival immediately after accession, but I let him stay. Later I got him moved to the general desk and from that day until he retired in 1962, he never spoke to me.

We were living in Plandome, Long Island, in 1938. By now we had a second little girl named Mary and a wonderful colored woman named Thelma Burgess who stayed with us for nearly twenty years. It was an ideal situation in many ways. The house was on an acre of ground, planted with maple and fruit trees. On one side there was a grape arbor and a patch of blue violets which bloomed spring and fall. On the other side there was a large garden planted with perennials which kept the place colorful from early spring to late fall. The house had four bathrooms and a downstairs lavatory. It was slightly Edwardian in construction with a wide front porch and numerous gables, but it was wonderfully comfortable. It also had a three-car garage. We kept our Chevy in the end stall, leaving two stalls for roller skating. There was a paneled study facing the garden in which I observed my bird-feeding station in the daytime and sat with my wife in the evening.

Not knowing what the bigwigs had in mind about filling the sports editorship, I was in a highly nervous state and was launching into my third highball in the study one night when Grafton Wilcox, the managing editor, called me on the telephone.

"Hello, Woodward? . . . I'd like to see you about this job. Will you be in tomorrow afternoon?"

"How long are you going to be there, Mr. Wilcox?"

"I'll be here until midnight but tomorrow's time enough."

I looked at the clock. It was twenty after ten and there was a train at ten thirty.

I executed a quarter-mile dash to the station and caught it. When I got to the paper, Mr. Wilcox seemed surprised to see me but he came through with the job of sports editor, which I held, with two years out for war correspondence, until 1948. Some of my pals were still around after Wilcox and I got through talking and we all went down to Bleeck's to celebrate. As a result, I didn't get home until three thirty A.M. and Mama, though pleased about my new job, was a little put out by my lateness and my stumbling gait.

I was back in the office at eleven o'clock the next day and home again about three the following morning. This was not a popular procedure, particularly when I kept it up for a month. In justification of myself, I can say that I worked most of the time on the new job. I wanted to be around all the time while the paper was operating; though I came home late and loaded, I had been busy practically all the time in the editorial and composing room. My devotion to the job ultimately reawakened Ricie to the advantages of living in New York and, after a summer in Europe, we moved to the West Side in an area known as the steam-heated ghetto.

George Daley had made a record as the most economical sports editor the *Tribune* ever had and I set out to beat it. I adopted as a motto: "It is impossible to outcrap the *Times*. Let's not try."

My own theory was that there are four sports which are of paramount importance to a newspaper: baseball, horseracing, boxing, and football. Other sports rose to prominence on occasion and faded to nothing when they were out of their active period. This could be said of tennis, golf, and yachting. There are some sports that are of comparatively little interest to the readers but are important to the paper because of their advertising connections. Among these are skiing, again yachting, horse and dog shows.

Skiing bothered me to death until I devised a chart for Snow Reports that solved all the difficulties. This covered all skiable areas, and after describing conditions in detail by a system of symbols, it gave the name of the observer in each area. This was a wonderful safety valve. If people went to a resort and discovered that conditions were not as reported, they would find the observer there as a handy whipping boy and would not blame the *Herald Tribune*.

We had two very good men on yachting—Taylor and Morris—and so tended to overplay this field. Incidentally, Taylor had won the Pulitzer prize with his series on the America's Cup in 1935. Arthur (Red) Patterson doubled in baseball and dogs until he left us to become a baseball executive.

To have an efficient staff you had to double up on a number of men. The baseball writers, for instance, all covered football.

Morris was one of our best football writers as well as

our second man on yachts and our leading expert on basketball. Al Laney, who came to us in the thirties, after nine years as night editor of the Paris *Herald,* was a great tennis man and filled in during the off season with various odd jobs and features. It was he who charmed the clientele with competent stories about the National Horse Show. His "Forgotten Man" series was one of the best we ever had in the paper, rising to a pinnacle in two stories he wrote about Sam Langford, the old, blind Negro fighter.

It was easy to cover these things fully and still save money by chopping coverage of items dear to Daley's heart, like the Union-Hamilton football game. George had been quarterback for Union and insisted on a column story every time these old, if obscure, rivals came together. Union College had such a proprietary interest in the *Tribune* when I took over that Daley's correspondent felt he had carte blanche to send in anything. This made it necessary to fire him.

I also got rid of all other correspondents who were not in key positions. Those I kept I put on small salaries and required they query before filing. In general they filed only on order from the office.

It is wonderful how much a move like this will save. After the first month my expenses were appreciably below Daley's. Being proud of my ability to save money, I was startled when Bill Robinson, the publisher, indicated to me I was on the wrong course.

We were standing at Bleeck's bar one day and I was bragging a little about what a noteworthy saver I had become. Robinson gave a loud snort.

"Listen, Stanley," he said, "no sports editor ever made a reputation by saving money."

This started me thinking about how different newspaper men had made their reputations. Bennett sent Stanley to Africa in search of Livingston. Somebody else sent Nellie Bly around the world, and somebody sent Richard Harding Davis to Cuba during the Spanish-American War. All these expeditions were expensive and all resulted in great renown for the organizations which financed them. Robinson was right; I must change my philosophy. If I didn't I would be remembered as that stupid old fellow who was tight with expense money.

So without going hog-wild I decided to try to make a few coups with the excellent staff I had at my disposal. We started sending men out of town to cover crucial baseball series. We staffed important football games in the South and West. Whenever anything important was going on, there was our man. It made a great hit and it drove the respected *Times* into a slow revolving fit.

We were just getting started on the new policy when the bugle blew and the prewar drafts began. Then, while we were covering the football game between the Giants and Brooklyn Dodgers at the Polo Grounds, we heard about Pearl Harbor. There was no announcement on the loudspeaker that the island base had been bombed, merely a succession of calls over the loudspeaker for Colonel William Donovan to call a downtown number. We got the bulletin in the Press Box and the rest of the day seemed futile.

I was there backing up the football writer with a column of notes and a clubhouse story. I didn't get much enthusiasm into it. It seemed trivial. The fact is I lost my enthusiasm for sports that afternoon and did not regain it until the war was over.

Our boys started leaving. We lost eight or ten of them within the next year. Among them, Richards Vidmer,

who had acted as columnist since the death of Bill McGeehan five years before; Bill Taylor; Everett Morris; Bobby
Cooke, a promising young baseball writer; Harold Rosen-
thal; Dynah Davis; Arthur McKen; Arthur Glass; and
others.

Our department was reduced to half its size. I asked to
be sent out as a war correspondent but nobody paid any
attention to me. I was supposed to stay in there and operate the Sports Department.

It was a difficult assignment. In addition to the loss of
able reporters, our copy desk was decimated. Glass, Mc-
Ken, and Davis were its strongest men. We also had no
columnist. I undertook this job and also went back to my
old trade of copyreader.

I was busy in the office and busy at home. I've neglected
to state that we were now operating a dairy farm on the
road between Princeton, New Jersey, and Somerville.
We had the beginning of a herd of Guernsey cattle and
also a dozen shoats and three hundred chickens. We were
trying to bring up the burned-up farmland. This we did
by plowing under soy beans and rye and spreading hun-
dreds of tons of chicken manure, which we hauled seven
miles from Hopewell.

The man who had previously been on our farm was a
battery chicken raiser. When we first saw the place there
were seven thousand young chickens in the barn and, incidentally, about fourteen thousand rats all over the place.
The chickens were kept in cages and fed all they would
eat. In this way my predecessor on the farm raised them
to broiler-size in about ten weeks.

When I moved into the farm, he transferred his chickens to a brick building he had built in Hopewell. The
town authorities soon told him he would have to do some-

thing about the disposal of what we shall call the residue. I decided that it would be very good for our farm. So we went over there three times a week with our tractor and manure spreader and put it on our fields, starting with the permanent pasture.

This was, and still is, the most beautiful farm I have ever seen. The house and farm buildings were set back 150 yards from the Princeton-Somerville road with a lovely live stream between. A long lane led past the house to the other buildings; they included a barn capable of handling one hundred tons of baled hay with a cow stable on the lower floor. This was joined to a small milk house by a breezeway.

There also was a garage with two horse stalls and a machinery shed attached. There was a silo and a low building which we used, at one time or another, for pigs, calves, and chickens. While we were there, we built an open shed for winter occupancy by our livestock, a 20 × 20 house for the hens, a brooder house, a corn crib, and a small fortress for the bull.

Leroy Burgess, son of Thelma, was our original farmhand. He didn't know anything about farming, but he agreed to work an apprenticeship on the Rutgers University farm in New Brunswick. I made a deal with professor Bill Skelley of Rutgers that I would pay Leroy and supply his room and board in New Brunswick while he was learning. Bill was to let him off Sunday and Monday so he could come over to the farm and help me get the place organized. I took only one day off, but I wrote my column at home on Sunday and so had most of the day to myself.

The first year we bought two cows and three hundred day-old chicks. We also bought a dozen young Duroc

pigs from Bill Skelley. The pig herd was immediately sup-
plemented by the Football Writers' Association of New
York, which sent me eleven more, via Skelley, as a gift
because I was the retiring president of their association.

We made butter out of the cream from our milk and
fed the skimmed milk to the pigs. We bought a supplementary ration until our first crop of corn came in that
fall. It was the only feed I ever bought for my animals,
with the exception of a supplementary dairy ration and
mash for the hens. We raised everything, including most
of our own food. Sugar and salt were practically the only
items we had to buy. We had half a dozen freezing lockers
in Princeton Junction, and we generally had them full of
beef, pork, chickens, vegetables, and fruit.

We had a large vegetable garden which we cultivated
with a tractor. In that part of New Jersey corn is planted
in rows forty inches apart. Our corn planter was set for
that width and so was the cultivator on our tractor. So
when we planted our vegetable garden, we carefully measured every twenty feet to be sure the rows were exactly
forty inches apart. Then when we came back from the
fields, after cultivating corn, we could run through the
garden with the tractor.

The soil in this part of New Jersey is Penn Shale. It is
good soil for corn, alfalfa, and most field crops, but you
can't grow potatoes in it that get to be bigger than wal-
nuts. When we started living on the farm, my wife and I
spent a day taking soil samples. We set out with a shovel
early one morning and dug holes at each corner of each
field and in the middle. We then took slices from each hole
and mixed them in a paper bag.

We took the samples to Rutgers and had them analyzed
for nutrients and acid-alkaline balance. The results were

discouraging. The nutrients were insufficient and the *ph* was down in most cases to five. This meant we had to buy about forty tons of lime to get started. We also bought enough 5-10-10 fertilizer to spread three hundred pounds per acre on the fields we planned to cultivate.

In view of the fact that I hadn't worked on a farm since I was ten years old, when I weeded vegetables and milked cows on my grandfather's place at New Windsor, New York, it may be unclear how I knew enough to do these things and also why I was farming at all.

The impetus toward the farm came from two sources: from a child's book called *Farmer Boy*, which my seven-year-old daughter got out of the library, and from the great golfer Gene Sarazen, who had a big dairy farm in Brookfield, Connecticut. I read *Farmer Boy* and found it fascinating, though somewhat lacking in exact information.

I visited Sarazen at his farm and was greatly impressed. Almost immediately after, Gene and I, along with Governor Harold Hoffman of New Jersey, were speakers at an athletic dinner at the Pittsburgh A.A. Sarazen and I talked farming all the way to Pittsburgh and back and Governor Hoffman joined in between Trenton and Pittsburgh.

The governor agreed to send a state agricultural expert to view the farm I proposed to buy. The expert met me at the farm and took me to see Henry Jeffers, an agricultural genius who ran the Walker-Gordon milk-production business in Plainsboro, one station north of Princeton Junction. Mr. Jeffers knew every farm in the area. He easily identified my place from the description I gave and advised me that it would be safe to pay between 17,000 and 18,000 dollars. I got it for 17,500 dollars.

Leroy Burgess turned out to be a good farmer and a willing worker; but the place got to be too much for him and me, and we brought in a friend of his named Isaac White from Blackshear, Georgia. Ike was a lanky, handsome Negro boy who had many skills. He was one of the best milkers I have ever seen and was a superior substitute on Leroy's days off. It was a happy combination; but with a war going on, the boys got restive and one after another they left me to join the army. Leroy was decorated for his work with the Red Ball Express.

The first winter on the farm, Ricie, my wife, agreed to go to Rutgers six days a week, ten hours a day, to undertake the short course in dairy farming. In the middle of winter she left in our little truck before daylight and got home after dark. She stuck with it and made a wonderful contribution to the farm. The knowledge she acquired and the textbooks she brought home prevented us from making many mistakes and gave us some knowledge of cattle diseases and obstetrics.

Ricie was a game girl and also self-sacrificing. She wanted very much to fix up the beautiful old house as it should be fixed, but postponed the remodeling until we had the essential repairs and additions to the farm buildings. The kids enjoyed the farm from the beginning and contributed some little jobs.

Ricie and I apparently had solved the problem of where to bring up the kids. In addition to Ricie's loneliness when we were living at Plandome, there had been an ugly problem that we had to face. When our oldest child was about ready to go to school, we discovered that Plandome was "restricted." This meant that we would not send our children to school in the area. We moved back to New York and took an apartment in a building which was "restricted" in reverse.

We moved to Brooklyn Heights where we found normal and pleasant conditions and that's where we were living when we bought the farm. We bought it in the spring, but didn't get it into full operation until midsummer, though we planted a corn crop after liming and fertilizing about twenty-five acres. We added about two hundred pounds of fertilizer in the corn planter and the result was tremendous.

When I put in the corn I told Bill Drake, the local builder who was making our essential repairs, that I wanted him to build a forty-foot corn crib for storage of the prospective crop. He said I'd never fill it, and I bet him five dollars I would. We filled it once and a half the first year, storing the excess in cribs made of snow fence.

After Leroy and Isaac left for the army, we had makeshift help for a while. Then I was able to engage the Hurley brothers, born farmers of that area. After that we were in business. They knew how to do everything. I borrowed money to buy such things as an eight-can milk cooler; a two-unit de Laval milking machine; a hammer mill which we drove with a tractor; a corn-sheller which we plugged into the electric light system; a smaller tractor to supplement our big McCormick-Deering and various other accouterments.

I tried to get a baler but found I was thirty-second on the list. However, there was a four-man baler rusting in the yard of Percy Van Zant, Hopewell machinery dealer. Nobody wanted to buy it, for the new Holland baler had come out and this was an automatic which could be operated by one man.

I pointed this out to the county agent in Somerville but he was adamant. I couldn't buy the baler because I didn't

have the priority. "This is wartime, Woodward," he said
to me.

It did not seem to me that stupidity should be justified
by warfare no matter how world-girdling. However, I refrained from saying this to the county agent; I just went
back to see Percy Van Zant. He took me out to look at the
baler and explained its workings.

"Wartime or no wartime, I can't sell this thing," he said
to me. "I'd like to move it because I've got money tied up
in it and also because it could be a great asset to this community if somebody would take it over and operate it."

He hesitated a moment and then said, "Suppose I lend
it to you . . . Incidentally, I am a little hard up for cash
now—would you be able to lend me eight hundred?"

"Well, Percy," I said, "that would benefit both of us,
wouldn't it? I'll accept the loan and I think I'll be able to
fulfill the other half of the bargain."

So I went home and got my tractor and drove it first to
the Hopewell Bank, where I borrowed 800 dollars on
20-payment notes, then to Percy Van Zant's, where I
lent Percy 800 dollars, and hitched the baler to the tractor.
It proved to be too wide for the bridge in our lane and we
had to cut down a piece of fence and build a temporary
bridge over our brook to get it on the farm.

Throughout the summer our borrowed baler ran. It
baled a good share of the hay and straw in the county. It
saved the hay crops of twenty farmers whose sons had
gone to war. It also paid for itself, for we were now in
the custom-farming business and received fifteen cents a
bale for putting up hay and three dollars an acre for straw.

It wasn't really a four-man baler in our hands, it was a
two-man, one-girl, and one-boy baler or a one-man, one-
girl and two-boys baler. We operated it with all kinds of

crews. I worked on it when I had my days off. My wife often drove the tractor and so did Betty Hurley, the wife of our junior farmer. The person who forked the hay into the hopper had to be a man, for it was heavy work. The tractor driver and the two bale-wirers could be less powerful.

We finally organized a team. The United Nations still was operating in Princeton and we engaged the twelve-year-old sons of the Swedish delegate and the Peruvian delegate. They were great boys and they worked all summer without missing a day. At the end of the baling season I told Herb Hurley, the farm boss, that I planned to divide the baling money into four parts, one for the machine, one for me, and one each for him and his younger brother Pete. He and Pete refused to take their shares.

"If you want to do it next year, that'll be all right," said Herb. "But this year we'll pay for the machine."

By this time we had forty acres of alfalfa plus clover and timothy of our own; also, a number of acres of oat straw and wheat straw. However, we did ten times more baling off the farm than we did on it including all the work for Squire Jim O'Brien, who had a large spread north of us.

The finances of farming were a great bother to me my first couple of years. Then I arrived at a plan which eliminated money. I needed supplies, which I obtained from Bill Labaw in Bellemead, New Jersey. Once when my bill had gotten up to eight hundred dollars, I suggested that he pick up my wheat crop, which I was about to combine, and credit me with it.

"If there's a balance, Bill," I said, "take it out of my corn crib."

Next day Bill had two men and a corn-sheller working

in front of our crib. A couple of days later he picked up two big loads of wheat in our field. Never thereafter did money pass between us except when we bet quarters on the bowling game in the local pub. Sometimes he would owe me a few hundred dollars. Sometimes I'd owe him. He took my wheat and corn, I took his 32 percent protein dairy ration and laying mash, and now and then a load of coal for the milk-house water heater.

Farm cash came from the dairy which took our milk away in an eight-wheel truck which swung through the barnyard every morning, from occasional sales of stock, produce, and eggs.

The eggs I sold in the offices of the New York *Herald Tribune*. Two or three times a week I would come to town with two suitcases full of eggs. I would lay them out on the copy desk in the Sports Department and mark them, "Modern eggs—60¢ a dozen." I would put an ashtray in front of the display and pick up the money and suitcases, invariably empty, before the copy desk came to work.

The whole time I was farming, nobody complained that I wasn't concentrating on my work at the *Tribune*. Newspapering remained my principal interest and I worked at it six days a week, sometimes staying in the office until two o'clock in the morning. The wartime problems around the shop were hard to solve and it was almost impossible to get men.

The copy desk was the principal problem. I hired one man after another and each proved incapable of doing the work. One admitted that his principal task had been music criticism; another that he had never written a head in his life. He had been a hot crime reporter in San Francisco.

One day a nice young fellow came in looking for a job

with a letter from his pastor. This was a new approach and I took scant interest in him until I discovered that he had only one leg. That clinched his job for him because a 4 F was worth his weight in platinum. He turned out to be a good man too, worked well on the copy desk and later covered racing. He was a real asset as a human being and was mourned by the whole staff when the damage from the same accident that cost him his leg caused his death.

Somehow we got by with men the draft had turned down and with others above military age. Ultimately I decided I could leave the column and sports editorship in the hands of Al Laney and get out and see the war. The office at last agreed and I commenced my efforts to be accredited as a war correspondent. This involved an examination of my loyalty and my personal record. After a couple of months I was accredited.

Ricie, who had backed me up in a hundred dubious enterprises, said it would be all right for me to go. She just took on all the bookkeeping which the Guernsey Cattle Club and the American Kennel Club demanded—we now had a side business in breeding and showing dachshunds.

I'll have to admit that things were much better, agriculturally, when I got back from the war than when I left. In other words, my wife, with the help of Herb Hurley, proved that I wasn't much of an asset on a farm.

15

MY ONLY EXPERIENCE IN THE United States Army had been in two pre-World War I training camps at Plattsburg and in the National Guard after the first war. I joined up then only for the purpose of playing on the regimental basketball team. I was what we then called the standing guard.

Having no genuine army experience, I did not know the old army principle of "Hurry up and wait." Consequently when I got verbal orders to report at Pier 90, North River, at eight P.M., I took them literally. I kissed my wife good-bye in the Hotel Commodore and started on my way to a stretch as war correspondent in the European theater.

The ship, which turned out to be the *Ile de France*, didn't sail that night or the next morning. We finally cleared the pier sometime in the afternoon. Between the time I got aboard and the actual sailing, thousands of soldiers came over the gangway. Each was burdened with pack, blanket roll, steel helmet, and weapon, and each was sweating fearfully in the summer heat.

It must have been brutal in the quarters these fellows occupied, for they were stacked three high all the way down to the bilge; and when a ship isn't moving the deck ventilators don't work. Of course, the air-conditioning system, which cooled the passengers in peacetime, had been ripped out as unessential when the *Ile de France* was turned from a luxury ship into a transport.

My quarters were not bad. There were twenty-eight of us in a room which formerly housed one rich first-class passenger and his wife. The pipe bunks were comfortable enough and the meals, numbering two, which were served in the late morning and late afternoon, were adequate.

It was an uneventful trip except that one afternoon I went on deck and discovered that we were heading due west. Discreet inquiries, possible for me because I was an ex-seaman, indicated that Intelligence had found a wolf-pack waiting for us and discretion indicated that the best way to avoid it was to head back toward home for a few hours and take a circuitous course around the submarines.

A couple of torpedoes into a ship like the *Ile de France* would have produced one of the most horrible disasters of the war. It would have been impossible to get ten thousand men out of the interior of the ship short of an hour.

The first land we saw was hilly northern Ireland, unbelievably green. Then we headed up the Clyde and anchored in the stream off Gourock, a Scottish port twenty-four miles west-northwest of Glasgow. The *Ile de France* was the most impressive ship in the anchorage, which was occupied by battered old British coasters, two or three wornout destroyers, and an obsolete British aircraft carrier.

At the evening meal, which happened at four o'clock, all hands were instructed to be at the unloading port, an iron door on the main deck, at five twenty the next morning. Breakfast, we were told, would be served at five o'clock; it was, too. But immediately after breakfast the principle of "Hurry up and wait" was put into operation again. We sat on our luggage at the unloading point until eleven, when a little steamer came alongside to take off the first contingent.

Within an hour I was on land in Scotland and was hurried to a train which eventually pulled out of the station at four twelve P.M. In Glasgow our whole trainload went forward to get some water out of a tap beside the tracks. The old engineer got off his locomotive and filled several hundred canteens.

"Don't push, Yanks," he said. "They can't go without me."

For some reasons we went northeast to Edinburgh before heading into England. We were in a dead blackout, and how the British railroad men handled the heavy traffic on their line without seeing it is still a mystery. We sat up in coaches through the long night.

The symptoms of daylight and the fringes of London arrived simultaneously. We crept into the city. Suddenly the train was stopped and a minute later a tremendous explosion occurred somewhere ahead of us. Nobody showed any excitement except us Americans. The railroad men waved signals to each other. We backed up five miles and started down a new stretch of track. I found out later that a buzz-bomb had hit about hundred yards ahead of the train and had torn up half a railroad yard.

I had transportation orders as far as London but when I got off the train I was on my own. It was Sunday and very early in the morning. I found a pay booth and called young Jeff Parsons, who was our newspaper's London correspondent. He told me to go to the Savoy Hotel and meet him in the office sometime that afternoon. When I got to the Savoy I found he had made arrangements for a room, and, having missed one night's sleep entirely and most of another, I turned in.

They said the buzz-bombs were thick that day but I was too far gone to be frightened even though I vaguely heard the horrible moan of the London airraid siren. I discovered later that no one in an American uniform ever went into a bomb shelter. There was no rule about it; the American army just decided that it would disregard Hitler's long-range attack.

The *Herald Tribune*'s office was in the Daily Telegraph Building on Fleet Street and just below it was the best pub in London, called the Kings and Keys. We preferred this greatly to the Cheshire Cheese where Samuel Johnson's mob used to hang out. The Cheese was moldy, not to say stuffy. Why wouldn't it be? It had been standing in the same spot for four hundred years.

The Kings and Keys was operated by a couple known as Doris and Charles. Doris was a large, not to say overblown, blonde. Charles was a snappy and thoroughly presentable man who turned out to be a boss electrician in civil life. Doris had a voice like an angel and would sing if bought sufficient double gins. Her best rendition was "Melancholy Baby," but her whole repertory was American.

Though somewhat blowsy with drink most of the time, Doris ran the place well and served good meals, if you knew enough to avoid the long-boiled vegetables. I soon found that the best bet was a slice of roast beef, a pile of lettuce with oil and vinegar and a few slices of bread.

We worked mostly at the Ministry of Information, which was out beyond Oxford Street. We had a large newsroom in one of the buildings of the University of London. The *Herald Tribune* had a full-time secretary there named Ivy. It also had a driver named Jimmy who took us around through the blackout in a big hired car.

We transmitted to the New York office mostly by telephone. The management had arranged for two fifteen-minute contract calls a night and when there was news we could run overtime.

Frank Williams, a Cockney, was the talker on the telephone calls. I couldn't even understand him when I was conversing face to face, but the girls in New York found his diction ideal, even when he put on his top speed. I listened in wonder at his orations to New York; almost never did the receiver at the other end of the line break in.

In the Fleet Street office the chief functionary was the late Miss Kay Thorp, an English girl of manifold abilities. She issued the expense money to the staff, made housing arrangements for all hands, acted as secretary to Jeff Parsons, and served tea every day at eleven A.M. and four P.M.

Our routine was to arrive in the office at eleven o'clock to look at the papers from New York, drink a cup of tea, and wait for the Kings and Keys to open at eleven thirty. Then all of us would go down for a drink and the day would get an official start.

The airraid siren went most of the time, but the English had developed a remarkably efficient tracing service. The course of each buzz-bomb was plotted and immediate danger warnings were sounded in the area lying in its path. If you heard a loud bell, you knew it was time to duck, even though the bomb might go over your head and continue for five or six miles. When you heard the engine stop, that was the time to scramble. The noise of the bombs in transit was thunderous, but they were hard to see, except at night.

Later, when the Germans started shooting rockets, there was no defense. I lay in bed one morning, full of dope, and heard rockets explode at nine o'clock, ten o'clock, and eleven. One of the explosions was so near that I could hear the building falling down. Censorship prevented reporting the exact places where the buzz-bombs and rockets hit.

I found my work rather routine and was anxious to get to the business of covering the war. Jeff Parsons, in self-defense, did his best to keep me active, for I was always bothering him. He sent me on a day's plane trip to France to see the first American airplane bases established on the continent and to fly over the scene of the heaviest fighting in Normandy. We went in over Mont-Saint-Michel, that remarkable rock on the Normandy coast, and saw the unbelievable criss-crossing of tank tracks at Saint-Lô.

After stopping at one of the new airplane bases and being briefed by a twenty-two-year-old colonel, we swung back over the beachheads where the American troops had landed and which were now active in handling supplies. The Germans were being bombed at Le Havre and we could see the flashes of the antiaircraft guns.

Jeff also sent me to Dover on the Channel which was under frequent shellfire from Cap Gris-Nez on the French coast. I was quite lame from a minor leg injury. A British naval commander apparently mistook me for a wounded man and offered me a ride as I walked up the hill from the Dover station. I explained that I was a war correspondent and was sent down there to cover the shelling and would like him to recommend a good place to stay.

"O-ho," he said. "I'll take you to the Hotel Shalimar."

This turned out to be a small and battered building on the beach front. It was the only building along the coast that was still occupied. The others had been either knocked down by shells or deserted by their usual occupants, who had sought less perilous living quarters. But the Misses Scanlon who ran the Hotel Shalimar could not be scared away by any old Germans. The hotel had been hit a dozen times.

Once when the older Miss Scanlon was cooking breakfast, a shell fragment practically carried away her hair curlers. Another time a big chunk of hot steel whistled through the dining room as the few remaining guests were having breakfast. The elevator shaft was so bent that the car would not go above the second floor.

There were only three floors and I got a room on the third. The one other occupant of my floor was a Canadian army lieutenant engaged in some mysterious work. Now that I think of it, it was the Canadian army which ultimately overran the German gun emplacements on the Channel.

As soon as the Germans started shooting at Dover and other towns along the coast, the British answered with similar blasts. The Misses Scanlon were up at all hours of the night routing out persistent sleepers when the racket began and herding them into the cellar.

The Scanlons were heroines. Winifred, the younger, was a telephone operator by profession and had been decorated by the King in Buckingham Palace for sticking to her switchboard during Dover's worst airraid.

It was a bore to sit in the cellar. However, nothing else was permitted, so I complied. After a couple of days I went back to London.

During my time in Dover I had got a fairly decent story and had made friends with the members of an American antiaircraft battery which was firing at buzz-bombs. Members of this unit were burned because the War Department declared they were not in a combat area even though they had had casualties.

They invited me to a dance in the building near Dover Castle and I observed the unique method used to acquire dancing partners. They drove army trucks around the streets of Dover. A big sign was propped up behind the driver and read as follows:

GIRLS! GIRLS! GIRLS!
BIG DANCE TONIGHT AT DOVER CASTLE.
GET IN.

When the boys spotted a willing woman they boosted her over the tailgate into the truck, and before long they had a load. There was no dearth of either women or beer when the dance began. Four barrels of beer stood in an anteroom with helmet-liners full of pretzels. An American combo furnished the music. Its featured performer was a Comanche who whaled the drums. He beat a savage rhythm.

Back in London I continued to haunt Jeff Parsons and he gave me a succession of stories to cover, none of them very exciting.

I moved around the country occasionally, visiting air bases and other military installations.

About this time Duncan Sandys, Winston Churchill's son-in-law, who was in charge of the defense of London against air attack, decided that his organization had the buzz-bombs in control and held a big press conference. There were present RAF flyers who hunted the bombs down in transit, girls who manned the British aircraft guns, and manipulators of the barrage balloons, which occasionally entangled the bomb with their cables and set it off. There were also some RAF bombers who had made numerous attacks on the German launching sites.

We interviewed some of these people and the story turned out to be pretty good. Still, it wasn't war as I saw it.

By now the Allies had entered Paris and soon Parsons

left for the continent to see what could be done about reopening our European edition.

Those left to cover the London scene were the sports editor, the radio editor (Richard L. Tobin), and the literary critic (Lewis H. Gannett). This trio was run by Gannett and Tobin with Woodward as the odd man. The result was that I got most of the good assignments. Gannett and Tobin would get into a row over which of them would cover. Neither would give in and they would resolve it by giving the job to me.

At about this time Gannett got a chance to cover the land attack on the German-held ports of Normandy and left for the continent. Tobin and I were the survivors. I deferred to him but kept insisting that I get some kind of a decent assignment. One day he came up with one.

"Go out to the Ministry of Information and see Wing Commander Budcroft of the RAF. He has something that might interest you."

Within the hour I was sitting across the desk from the wing commander. What he had to offer me was a chance to go on an airborne invasion of continental Europe. He scared me half to death by describing it as above average danger.

"You can either go in aboard a glider," he said, "or else you can fly over the invasion area in a photographic plane which will return to London before dark. Personally, if you are really looking for a story, I suggest you go in a glider."

By now I was scared almost speechless, but I managed to say almost inaudibly, "All right, I'll go in a glider."

He pledged me to secrecy about the mission and I met Tobin for dinner in a place that somehow managed to avoid the rigors of rationing. I was badly shaken by the prospect of invading Europe by glider but after three Martinis, of real American character, I began to relax.

Two days later, we assembled in the Ministry of Information to be taken to the takeoff point. There were three American reporters, two of them, Bill Boni of the Associated Press and I, had been sports writers. The other was Walter Cronkite, who attained fame as a television man after service with the United Press.

Cronkite and I were assigned to the 101st Division, Boni to the 82nd. We started out by car and stopped for lunch in a little inn where the Thousand Guineas horse race was being broadcast.

We continued on to the 101st Division headquarters which was near Windsor, about fifty miles west of London. The division was commanded by Major General Maxwell D. Taylor, later the nation's chief military man.

Upon our arrival, a sergeant took us in charge and outfitted us with combat clothing and strapped the replica of a small American flag around the upper part of our arms. I had brought my portable typewriter; the sergeant said I would not be allowed to take it with me, and he would see that it was returned to my office in London.

"You can't run carrying that thing," he said. "And you'll probably have to run."

The only baggage I had left was a musette bag containing a sweater, a roll of paper, and a carton of cigarettes. A group of young officers invited me to their quarters and I sat with them for a couple of hours before dinner. The intelligence officer, a nice fellow from Minneapolis named Paul, started to brief me on the operation when one of the other officers interrupted.

"Don't tell him a thing, Paul," he said. "If you do, he can't go off the base and I think we ought to send him to

Windsor to buy a couple of bottles."

"Hell, the general is gonna drown us in going-away booze," said Paul. "Come into the next room, Wood-ward."

There he showed me a big map with a red mark on it. "This is where we are going," he said, "Zon, Holland. The British 1st Airborne will land at Arnhem across the Rhine. The 82nd will land at Nijmegen, about halfway between us and the British. This is going to be the biggest airborne operation in history. We shall be supported by a large group of British and American planes."

General Taylor staged his preinvasion formalities and festivities with rare, dramatic effect. We assembled in the mess hall after dinner, and the general awarded all the medals won by division officers in Normandy.

To a civilian the heroism embodied in the bald citation was impressive and the modest young fellows who saluted and accepted the medals were remarkable people. It lasted quite a while for there were many medals to bestow. Then the general dismissed us and told the sergeant to open the bar. The general left to spend the rest of the evening with his ten thousand enlisted men.

I don't know what effect the proceedings had on others, but to me they turned Operation Market into the great adventure of my life. For some reason, perhaps because I knew I was going with men I admired, I became perfectly relaxed and slept through the night without waking up.

In view of the "stickiness" of the operation, Cronkite and I were urged to carry weapons. We were promised they would be delivered at the glider but someone forgot to deliver them, and before long Cronkite and I were wandering behind the German lines with our pocket knives for defense.

We took off at ten thirty the next morning, each glider towed by a C-47. We circled till they all got off the ground; then we flew straight for our objective on the continent at a height of twelve hundred feet. There were thirteen men in our glider; it was fifth in line and, incidentally, third to land, two of the four ahead of us having been shot down.

The rear of the glider was filled with cases which I feared contained ammunition. There was no copilot; but a colonel who looked capable of anything sat up front and learned to fly during the three hours we were in the air. He gave us a few thrills when Scotty, the pilot, turned the controls over to him.

Halfway across the Channel another column of gliders crossed ours at a slightly different elevation. It was the 82nd going to Nijmegen. It was a glorious sight and reassuring, too, for it gave the poor civilian a new assurance of power.

I was startled to find that I was not frightened. I thought of my personal business and once more assured myself that my life insurance was paid and my will in my desk drawer.

Death would be sudden but not painful. The suspected ammunition in the back might blow up, in which case the occupants of the glider would be vaporized. We might go down in one swift plunge but we couldn't burn up, there being no gasoline supply in a glider.

Some of the soldiers actually went to sleep. One tall corporal who wore gold-rimmed glasses put a clip in his M-1, thumped the butt on the floor, and said, "Now I'm dangerous." Then he grinned and went to sleep.

We went over the Germans, still at twelve hundred feet, and we got hit by machine-gun fire and by one big shell fragment which tore a hole in the top of our ship. It was a little scary for a few minutes, then Scotty let go the tow rope and we plunged toward the ground. This took us temporarily out of the fire.

I looked ahead and saw a big red barn directly in front of us. Scotty pulled back on the stick and skimmed over the roof. Then he landed in a pasture, tore through two barbed-wire fences, and came to a stop.

Every glider landing is a crash, for the wheels are small. This, I am told, was a good landing. The craft stood virtually on its nose, then fell down right-side up. We scrambled out and took cover, such as it was. I found a little depression where I could hide most of me. There was firing all around us.

After a minute or two the corporal next to me passed the word, "Prepare to rush." The colonel who had acted as copilot jumped up and shouted, "Follow me," and our guys began the sprints for the woods surrounding the field. There were four such sprints and I got farther and farther behind.

I was practically the only target remaining for the German army when my companions found real cover among some farm buildings. After the first rush I had thrown away my musette bag. When I joined my pals back of the barn, I discovered it had caught in my ammunition belt and was dragging on the ground. I was glad to have it.

The paratroopers who had landed before us had done a good job of establishing a perimeter around the landing area, but German self-propelled 88's were firing here and there. I watched a Mustang silence one with repeated strafing attacks.

The landing wasn't bad but there was some visible carnage. Two gliders had hit fifty feet off the ground and everybody in them was killed. There was a smashed German truck beside the road with a dead driver and a woman cut practically in two by machine-gun bullets. Apparently, an American fighter plane had stopped the truck.

We joined the general in his makeshift headquarters in the woods. Cronkite had his lightweight typewriter which strapped on his back and after he finished a story of about three hundred words, I borrowed it and sent off fifty. The Signal Corps officer sent mine to London and ignored Cronkite's. He had evidently written too much. We had been limited to fifty words. So I got credit for an undeserved global scoop on the operation.

The first objective of our division was to save the bridge over the Wilhelmina Canal just south of Zon. A paratroop unit had moved toward it, meeting some resistance. Just after we joined the general there was a muffled boom. General Taylor shook his head. "I'm afraid the boys didn't get there in time," he said.

It turned out that the Germans had rigged the bridge for destruction with a marine torpedo and had only to push a button on the bank to blow it up. Notwithstanding the destruction of the bridge, a detachment of paratroopers crawled over the wreckage in the dark and marched ten kilometers south to clear the Germans out of the city of Eindhoven, an important industrial site in South Brabant.

Cronkite and I walked into Zon in a gingerly manner over a twisting country road. We were relieved when we struck the highway and joined a company of glider infantry.

Operation Market was supposed to be a method of short-circuiting the war by getting across the Rhine. The three airborne divisions were supposed to seize and hold the road and the bridges and the British 2oth Corps was expected to come up and pour reinforcements and gunfire into Arnhem at the head of the operation.

I am no military man but something was definitely wrong. The German Intelligence was too good, the demolition too prompt, and the reinforcements, ahead and on the flank, too quickly brought up.

The English support came up too slowly. Everything stopped for three days until the British engineers were able to install a Bailey bridge to replace the one that had been blown up. Then the army moved forward; but by now the Germans were cutting the road every hour or two and the 1st Airborne was in terrible condition at Arnhem.

Its remnants finally withdrew across the Rhine, leaving about eight thousand men killed or prisoners. The two American divisions had done their work well, but the great airborne offensive had lost its significance.

Some of this information was available to me even on the scene but I had no way of communicating. I sent one dispatch via courier, a motorcycle rider who had come up with the British war correspondents who accompanied the ground forces, but he was killed on his way to Brussels. Another long dispatch was carried for me by an escaping glider pilot. This one got in.

The first night in Zon I slept on a German cot in a nunnery which had been taken over as headquarters by our general. The next day I went to Eindhoven in a jeep with Paul, the intelligence officer. We were ferried across the Wilhelmina Canal on a raft of planks which the engineers had installed as partial replacement for the blown-up bridge.

We sped to Eindhoven through two ranks of cheering

Dutchmen. They all wore the colors of the House of Orange and most of the young men had rifles or shotguns they had hidden through the German occupation.

Paul went to the telephone office in Eindhoven and I looked around. Across the square there was a long straight street stretching out into the country. As I looked down it, I saw a German rocket take off on its flight to England. It might have been five or six miles away. It was a good story but Paul forbade me to write it. Not long after, the paratroopers sneaked up on the rocket base in the night and put it permanently out of commission.

I returned to Eindhoven the third day and found Ned Russell, another *Herald Tribune* writer. I decided to stay there and hired a room on the third floor of an old wooden hotel opposite the railroad station. That evening I borrowed a candle from the proprietor and sat down in the bar to write a story.

It was just about dark when the whole sky was illuminated by flares. I hadn't been in a bombing attack before but I knew what the flares meant. The Germans were after us, no doubt to attempt to knock out the British ammunition convoy which was crawling slowly through the city.

The first bomb landed very near and broke all the windows in the bar; however, I was under a table flat on my face and didn't get hurt. The British correspondents and I retreated to the cellar and sat on the floor as the Germans dropped stick after stick on Eindhoven. The uproar was terrifying.

Through the stairs we could see that the town was burning; exploding British ammunition trucks added to the din of exploding bombs. They had caught Eindhoven without any defense. There was no antiaircraft artillery;

the only retaliation we heard was a few stuttering machine guns.

I decided to reconnoiter the cellar for a possible secondary escape route if the building should be hit. It was pitch dark and the first thing I did was to ram my face into a steampipe, knocking both lenses out of my glasses. I crawled around the coal cellar feeling for them and finally found the frame and both lenses unbroken. I felt my way back to the place where we had been sitting and spent the next half-hour fitting the lenses back into the frame. My extra glasses were in my musette bag, three floors above.

The Germans came back twice more; then there was a lull and we decided to move. All the British jumped into their jeep and took off, leaving me in front of the hotel. There was a little soldier with a motorcycle who was apparently their dispatch rider. I got on the back and we trailed the jeep through the burning city.

There was an officer accompanying the British correspondent, and when he stopped for breath, I walked up to talk to him. It seemed to me that the Germans were not bombing indiscriminately and that our best bet was to take refuge in the church which loomed above us in the square where we had stopped. I didn't think the Germans would deliberately bomb a church.

As it turned out I was right, they didn't even scare us with a near miss, though they came back twice more. Two women were praying and weeping in front of a lighted candle. A Yankee paratrooper opened the door and asked, "Any chance to borrow a blanket in here?"

The assistant pastor who had just come in from the burning city wearing a tin hat hurried to help him. Then he dragged out mattresses made of ticking and straw for us. The women recovered when the bombs stopped dropping and motioned us into the refectory for supper. They gave us everything they had, which was little.

The British quickly grabbed all the mattresses after supper, leaving me the doormat. They woke me up every ten minutes on the grounds that I was snoring. It wouldn't have been so bad, except that I didn't have any cigarettes.

At the first sign of light I got out of there and joined the paratroopers outside the church door. They had dug fox holes in the church lawn. The tall, gaunt pastor came out and shook his head sadly at the destruction of the church lawn. The corporal gave me a pack of cigarettes and I pushed off through the town.

It was a dismaying sight; whole blocks of houses had been burned out, bomb craters were everywhere, gutted buildings were still smoldering. I joined up with a paratroop patrol and they took me into a building and gave me breakfast, K ration and a can of stewed fruit. I went back to the hotel to rescue my musette bag and found everything intact including my carton of cigarettes.

Across the street some local residents were standing in a bar whose front had been blown in. I joined them and we discovered that the beer tap was still working. I raised my glass and exclaimed, "*Oranje boven*." This is a motto I had cribbed off the fireplace in the Princeton Field House. It is supposed to mean "The Orange above all." And it is the first line of the Dutch National Anthem.

My companions and I couldn't talk to each other, but they seemed to understand me in this one instance, for they smiled and downed their beer bottoms up.

I just happened to run into Ned Russell. He had joined with two British correspondents who had their own jeep and trailer. We started back up the road to Zon, which was a mistake. The Germans were making terrible trouble. They had dragged up big guns and were periodically pounding the road.

British tanks chased them out but they took up new positions and started all over again. We spent half the day trying to get up to Zon; but two thirds of the time we were lying flat in a roadside ditch as the German shells hit around us.

I got sick of it, I had had enough, and I said to the correspondent of the *Daily Express*, "Why are we going to Zon? Why the hell don't we go back and see the British army? All we're going to do here is get killed."

He said, "Righto." We ran to the jeep and the driver took off at eighty. Before long we were out of the fire and we were never so close to so much trouble again. That night we slept in a little hotel in Moll, Belgium, close to the headquarters of the 20th Corps.

A lady lieutenant, who operated a magazine for the RAF and had been illegally at the front with her staff car and driver, was on her way to Brussels. In the morning I hitchhiked a ride with her and we took off at a high rate of speed.

The lady was directing the driver by airplane map and I soon saw that she was almost wholly unaware of Belgium geography. Some of the towns through which we went gaily flew the black, yellow, and red flag of Belgium. Others were grim and silent and, inasmuch as there were still one hundred thousand Germans in Belgium and Holland, I got a little frightened. I told the lady that she should try to avoid driving through towns occupied by the Germans, and she answered, "Oh, that's all right, we can go fast."

After a while we ran out of gas, which is a court-martial offense in the British service. A Canadian lieutenant came along in the nick of time and gave us a few liters out of his tank.

We then proceeded to the RAF headquarters near Louvain where we stopped for lunch. Even in the field the British make quite a fetish of their meals. A tent had been rigged up with rugs on the ground and a bar in the corner. I made quick work of three pink gins and answered many questions about the airborne invasion.

After lunch I was horrified to find that it would be necessary for me to make a formal speech. I got by, sticking strictly to my own experiences. The RAF commander gave me an order for transportation back to London and told me to present it to the flying officer at the Brussels Airport.

The lady lieutenant took me right to the office and before long I was on my way back to England in a "Dakota," British name for a C-47, with a group of evacuated glider pilots and slightly wounded paratroopers. After some fumbling we came down through the fog on a little airfield twenty miles out of London. An hour later I was sitting at the bar of the Kings and Keys and Doris was singing "Melancholy Baby," without recompense.

The idea in coming back to England was to get near a system of communication. For a week I pounded out copy about the airborne invasion. Back in New York my stuff led the paper five days in succession. I continued to write features about the event until even Frank Williams, the talker, was sick of it.

16 THE AIRBORNE INVASION HAD BEEN set in motion September 17, 1944. I got back to the United States in late November after another stretch of work in England. I came home on the *Mauretania* with a shipload of British girls who had married American soldiers, a gay group.

They were delighted when we came into New York harbor in the thickest fog of the fall and went around assuring each other that it was worse than London. All the way across the ocean a group of them had solicited such men as there were aboard and didn't stop until we tied up at the pier. A great number were looking for a companion for a week in New York before they pushed off to join their in-laws.

I explained to one lady that my grandchildren were going to meet me at the dock, thus escaping in good order.

It was great to get back to the farm, which I found to be in spectacularly good condition. Ricie and Herb Hurley had done a great job and the baler had earned its own cost all over again. I found I could wear suits which I had discarded because they were too tight. Herb came up to the house to welcome me home and said, "Okay, you can have the rest of the day off. But tomorrow we need a man to shuck corn."

I went to town after a few days and wrote stories for a while from notes I had made in Europe. I learned a valuable lesson from the questions that were asked of me. The boys in the office wanted me to explain things which I considered routine and not worthy of comment. I thereupon determined on a plan for any future foreign reporting I might do.

The idea was to write down before I left the United

States all the topics I wanted to know about in the foreign countries to which I was going and try to satisfy the curiosity of the people at home about ordinary matters. Writing it down fixed in my mind the American point of view.

When I left for the Pacific a few months later I carried a long list of things I myself wanted to know about Hawaii and other Pacific islands. The main idea was to cover the war, but the office was always glad to get mailers for supplementary coverage.

To illustrate what I mean: the first day I reached Honolulu I went all over Pearl Harbor to get a picture of the base as it was at that time. I poked around Ford Island and climbed the water tower where a naval detachment was observing and controlling the traffic of the port.

My second trip to the war was not planned far in advance. I had expected to resume my job of sports editor and had, in fact, covered two football games, Ohio State-Michigan and Army-Navy, soon after my return from Europe. But I found I didn't like America any more. It seemed to me that there was something which blocked my communication with people I had known.

The sports writers of New York had a queer attitude. They fought to preserve all peacetime activities, citing the fallacy that the British, though much nearer the war, were carrying on their sports as usual. In vain did I write that the system in Great Britain was only to play games on Saturday afternoons and to use as participants only athletes who were home on furlough or who could get a day's pass.

The New York sports writers seemed to think that it was perfectly logical to run baseball games seven days a week and to keep everything going full blast. Whatever I

wrote had no effect; the boys kept on with their campaign to save sports. Other things disgusted me and I
found that returning soldiers and sailors thought as I did.

At this time a big noise would propel me automatically
under a table. Except when I was talking quietly with my
wife and playing with the kids, I felt out of my element,
and gradually I began to think of going back to the front.

The chance came when one of our boys was unable to
accept an assignment with the navy in the Pacific. I was
already cleared by the military and in possession of the
proper papers, so I offered my services and within two
weeks I was on my way.

In London at the Savoy you were served sausages
stuffed with sawdust and you could get your clothes
pressed or your shoes shined by ancient servitors who did
a remarkable job of filling the places of younger people.
In my room there had been three buttons, maid, valet,
and waiter, and a push on the proper bell would bring the
proper person in five minutes.

At the Hotel St. Francis in San Francisco I couldn't
even get the new shoulder patches sewed on my uniform.
They had abandoned laundry service and pressing, and
half the time they forgot to make your bed. I borrowed an
iron from a girl who traveled with me on the train and
pressed my uniform after basting on the patches.

The navy told me to be in my room each day from ten
thirty to one so that I could be called. About the fourth
day I was told to report to the Navy Transportation
Office at nine o'clock the next morning. I was there with
my seabag on my shoulder.

A bunch of us were taken to a navy base in Alameda,
where we stayed for two days, waiting for something or
other. The second night we moved to an air base where

we sat up until two o'clock in the morning waiting for our plane. Ultimately it came to the starting line, a DC-6. We took off in another hour in pitch darkness.

First thing I saw from the plane was the view immortalized by the ancient mariner. It took us twelve hours to make the island of Oahu, where the territorial customs combed through our baggage and tried to take away my Colt .45. I told the man that I was not going to let him have it. I said I had been in Europe and from that point on was not going near any other war without some kind of a gun.

The navy sent a nice young officer to meet me at the field and I found that I had been put in the Moana Hotel on Waikiki Beach. The navy had made a special arrangement with the hotel to take care of correspondents at three dollars a day doubled up.

The navy was very nice to us. We were given cards to the Officers' Club and I was invited out to dinner by my old friend Commander Tom Hamilton. Through him I got to know the commanding admiral and I was well set up in short order. However, Honolulu was strictly governed by the navy; there was a positive curfew at nine o'clock. The hotel bar was open only from noon until two thirty.

The distances were very great and the things we needed were scattered around. The cable office, for instance, was located in downtown Honolulu, which is miles from the Moana Hotel on the one hand and from Pearl Harbor and the Officers' Club on the other.

I started writing some of the stories which I had suggested to myself on my foreign reminder list, starting with a two-column description of Pearl Harbor which included interviews with a navy coxswain, an admiral, and a couple of civilian workers from the mainland.

There were routine stories to be covered at navy head-quarters, but by now the command had shifted to Guam, and Admiral Nimitz, top source of news in the Pacific, had gone there.

I visited a navy hospital on the island and found a friend, Cy Titus, who had played center on our 1940 All-Stars. He had been shot through the left arm and throat on Iwo Jima and was recovering in the hospital. He put me onto a couple of good stories; one about an airfield private who got sick of his job and stowed away with his fellow marines for the invasion of Iwo.

He had been badly wounded, but was able to tell me his story. His experience had been harrowing and he was sure that he would be court-martialed for leaving his post at the airfield without orders. As a matter of fact, nothing happened to him.

I soon discovered that I had to move on to Guam to get into the news channel so I applied for air transportation there. It was a long time coming and I ultimately asked to be sent on a jeep carrier, the *Cape Esperance*, which was due to leave immediately.

I walked aboard the *Cape Esperance* late one after-noon, saluted the colors and the officer of the deck. I didn't look at him particularly or recognize him and, therefore, was startled when he said, "Why, Stanley, you old son of a bitch. What are you doing out here?"

It was Hal Schumacher, the pitcher for the New York Giants. He was a senior-grade lieutenant and watch officer on this little carrier. He traveled back and forth across the Pacific, ferrying airplanes to the fleet at the front. He had been through some rough times, the worst of all being a typhoon which capsized several destroyers and nearly did in the *Esperance*.

It took us ten days to Guam. The captain stayed on the bridge continuously at sea and gave me his regular quarters, which included two rooms and a bath. He was tough otherwise, for he made me stand general quarters on the bridge every morning before daylight.

Inasmuch as he also wanted me to play a bastard form of rummy with him until late at night, I did most of my sleeping in the daytime. I skipped out on him one night and played poker with Schumacher, the Catholic chaplain, and a couple of other young fellows. The captain was so angry with me I thought he would throw me in irons.

When we passed the Marshall Islands, which include the island of Bikini and also serve as the site for atom bomb explosions, we had a gunnery practice.

A plane flew back and forth over us, towing a sleeve. Our guns opened up, five incher's and 40-quads. I don't recall that anyone hit it. It was the worst shooting I have ever seen. Ultimately I discovered the reason for this: the gunners were in no danger. Later when I was out where people were shooting for their lives the accuracy was uncanny.

The author of *Mr. Roberts* must have got some of his business from the *Cape Esperance*, for we carried two little palm trees which the captain was taking to Admiral Nimitz. They were on the hangar deck beside the forward elevator. One night one of them disappeared, as in *Mr. Roberts*. The thief brought it back, and from that point until we were moored at Guam, a chief petty officer with a gun belt stood watch over the shrubbery.

We stopped at Saipan and visited the Marine Chamber of Horrors, a cave on high ground where a Japanese contingent held out to the last man. There was a big pile of skeletons and skulls. Schumacher and I each took a skull on the theory we could have ashtrays, but both of us threw them away before we got back to the ship. Live Japanese were still on Saipan in small numbers, and the naval officer who took us to the cave carried a carbine.

Guam is sixty miles south of Saipan, and in between there is an island called Rota which was still occupied by the Japanese at the end of the war. You could see it on a clear day. The army bombers used this for practice missions for green crews.

Guam was hot and if you didn't spray your room every night, you were eaten by mosquitoes. I lived in a BOQ (Bachelor Officers Quarters) and paid ten dollars a week for mess, served in a big quonset hut. The Officers' Club occupied a smaller quonset.

On a hill above the group of naval buildings was the wooden house in which Admiral Nimitz lived. One of his aides invited me to walk up a mountain with the admiral one afternoon and I foolishly did it, along with an editor from *Fortune*. It was interesting to see the rugged Guamanian terrain. We were accompanied by a marine guard, as the island hadn't been fully cleared of Japanese.

We both came back with no skin on our feet and discovered that the Officers' Club was out of beer.

Japs sneaked up through the commissary to steal food at night sometimes and you weren't entirely sure you wouldn't run into one or two wherever you went.

The navy's blithe disregard of enemy stragglers was startling. As one army captain expressed it, "The navy's system is to come ashore after a beachhead has been gained, set up an officers' club and a prophylactic station, and declare the island secure."

The Guamanians were wonderful people. The pure

strain is called Chamorro but there are strong admixtures of Spanish conquistador, Yankee whaler, U.S. Marine, and Banzai warrior.

On St. Joseph's Day a bunch of us went by truck to the village of Inarajan, where we watched the festivities celebrating the day of Guam's patron saint. The only priest left on the island celebrated Mass. There was a parade through the village road which ended on the baseball field. After that two troops of Boy Scouts played a ball game.

I walked around by myself and finally got talking with a man who spoke good English. He climbed to the top of a palm tree and brought down a bamboo bucket full of tuba, palm juice which ferments as it accumulates in the bucket. It was not bad in its original state, but my new friend spoiled it by throwing in sugar.

The Guamanian houses were mostly one-room shacks on posts which were covered with sheet metal and thatched with palm fronds. The cooking was done outside. The people were happy and overwhelmed by their good fortune in having the Americans back. I can't believe they are saying, "Yankee go home," even yet.

Life on Guam during the short period I stayed there was routine. Once in a while there was a break in the boredom. One night I was borrowing the flit gun from the watch in the BOQ when I was seized by the neck and two powerful thumbs were pressed against my cervical vertebrae. I whirled around and my watch fell on the desk and was broken. It was just George Halas, coach of the Chicago Bears, and he was extending an affectionate ursine greeting. He was just back from a long tour of the South Pacific in active navy service and had seen plenty of shooting.

We had a couple of nights discussing old times over the

nice stock of bourbon which he had with him.

Occasionally there would be a poker game or a session with the dice. I had left the United States with twenty-five hundred dollars in travelers' checks and an unlimited letter of credit, several hundred dollars in office cash, and more of my own. I was, in short, for the first and only time equipped to wage successful war in either craps or poker. I waged it. I was cleaning all the boys. With supreme confidence, born of money, I was unbluffable and I lifted many a big pot. The dice behaved for me. For the first and only time in my career, I had great good fortune in putting passes together.

One night, in the room of the late John Lardner, we were sitting on the floor in our underdrawers, rolling the dice, I shot ten dollars and blew the dice. This left me in the fading position on the right and I covered all bets. John Lardner protested that I did not have the right to fade, and in the argument that followed, I withdrew from the game. I was happy to do so because I was 340 dollars ahead.

Lardner was a good friend and there was nothing acrimonious about the argument. We kept it going for about ten years until the rights and wrongs of the case were thoroughly mixed up. To be strictly honest, Lardner knew more about the rules of dice than I. But at the time I considered myself right. Now I don't know.

There was a press room where we were briefed once or twice a day on the progress of the war. I dipped into my list of possible stories and came up with a few features; one of them was a long interview with the only Guamanian priest, a young native who had received his education in the Philippines.

He told me the horrible story of the imprisonment and

murder of the other priest by the Japanese. I met him at his church in Agana on the sea coast. It had been leveled by the bombardment preceding the invasion of Guam but was being rebuilt. At this stage the roof was up and a group of workmen were building the sides out of mats, constructed of woven palm leaves.

I promised the priest I would show him my story before I sent it; but I didn't keep my promise because I left in a great hurry. However, I left him a carbon copy of the story and an envelope addressed to the New York *Herald Tribune* with an enclosure signed by me requesting the editors to make any changes the priest wanted.

One day an army air force man came into my room in the morning and asked, "Do you want to go to Tokyo in twenty minutes?"

I said no. If I were going to take any more rough stuff I needed more time to plan it.

The army then planned a reportorial excursion to Iwo Jima which it had taken over from the marines. The excuse for the trip was that a squadron of U.S. fighter planes was going to take off from Iwo two days later and strafe the streets of Tokyo. I went on this one.

It was a three-hour flight above an extremely low ceiling. We stayed at thirty-five hundred feet until we had passed Minami Iwo Jima, a cone-shaped peak which rises thirty miles north of the island. The pilot then took the plane down to the water and we flew ten feet high the rest of the way. When we landed, we actually had to go up to get over the high, black sand shore of the island.

The army engineers had built a runway which was long enough for B-29's to land, and several planes had been saved after raids on Japan through having a nearby airport. Iwo is only five hundred miles from Tokyo. A few days before we reached the place, a party of Japanese had attacked the airport personnel who were living in tents beside the field and killed about thirty people with knives and swords.

When I got there, the army was making every effort to get the Japanese out of the caves at the north end of the island. A young Japanese lieutenant was used as interpreter. He would harangue the Japanese from the mouths of the caves, telling them they would not be hurt if they surrendered. One of his countrymen finally shot him through the shoulder and he lost his enthusiasm for the job.

The Japs, however, surrendered in fair numbers. The prisoners were living in a barbed-wire compound in the middle of the island. I saw a few being brought in and later walked around the compound with a sergeant of the military police.

The Japs, dressed in American khaki, were a strange-looking group, for all the uniforms were too big. They seemed happy with their lot and spent much of their time making rice balls which they cooked for themselves.

The attack on the airfield made all the sentries on the island trigger-happy, and I pulled a major bull by walking around after dark without having ascertained the pass word. Fortunately, I ran into a lieutenant named Jack Keating, former managing editor of *Cue*, who supplied me with the necessary protection.

The fighter attack on Tokyo took off early in the morning, and I spent most of the day riding a duck with a Negro private from an engineering company. A duck is an army truck which is also a boat. We went out to a ship and came back with loads of cargo in a net. At the supply dump the derrick unloaded net, cargo, and all.

To get up the steep black sand beach the driver had to deflate his tires. This he did with a neat little attachment on the wheels. He blew them up the same way and I'm still trying to figure out how the thing works.

The flyers came back from Tokyo that evening and reported good results and few losses. A string of ships had been spread over the route to pick up those who ran out of gas.

Security was rather feeble in the Pacific, and when Task Force 58.1 came into the fleet base at Ulithi, I heard about it and at once applied for assignment to one of its carriers. The transportation officer was shocked that I knew about ship movements but gave me authority to join the carrier *Hornet*, and I did so the next day.

We flew from Guam to Ulithi in a B-46 and the ensign in charge of the takeoff wasted an hour making sure of precedence—who should get on the plane first. This is the only time I ran into such nonsense. When we finally got aboard we discovered the plane was chock-a-block with big cases of whole blood. The pilot reassured us by saying, "If anything happens to this plane, it will be the bloodiest accident in the history of aviation."

We were palpably overloaded but we got off the ground somewhere near the end of the runway. For three hours we ducked and bobbed going through two weather fronts. As we came in for a landing I was looking down at the sea from my place in the rear. I was still looking at the sea when the front wheels hit the ground. The pilot told me afterward that the runway was a little too short for such a load.

I was welcomed aboard the *Hornet* by Captain Austin K. (Artie) Doyle, who had formerly played first base for Annapolis and was by any definition the best naval officer I ever encountered.

He got me aside. "I come from New York, Stanley," he said, "and I've been reading you for years. Now, I know you're aboard here for business and I authorize you to go anywhere in the ship: the radar room, the engine-room, or the bridge . . . I would just like to ask you for one favor: don't put my name in the paper. Publicity is the kiss of death for a professional naval officer."

The *Hornet* carried the flag of Admiral Jocko Clark, a bluff, burly man who was inordinately proud of having Indian blood. While we were at sea he sat for his portrait on the wing of the admiral's bridge. The artist was a young j.g. who had considerable talent. He also had talents of flattery, for he was making the picture redder than any admiral has a right to be. Jocko thought it was wonderful.

When I boarded the *Hornet*, Clark's code name was Bull Durham, which he liked. After a week or so it was changed to Romeo, which he hated. People with enough stripes would call him on the radio and say, "Oh, Romeo, Romeo. Wherefore art thou, Romeo?"

He would snort and shout, "Go to hell."

As soon as we got aboard the *Hornet*, Admiral Clark insisted we see the moving picture *Fighting Lady*, made aboard the *Yorktown* which he had commanded. It was an impressive picture and I thanked the admiral effusively for showing it. The CPO who had run the picture machine stopped the effusion with a stiff jab in the ribs. When the admiral went out of the room he explained, "If you praise the picture too much the old bastard will make me run it again . . . He loves it . . . Me . . . I've seen it nine thousand times and I'm sick of it."

We stayed in Ulithi two days and sailed the third. The

night before I had gone to bed in my quarters down below decks when a marine came to the door and asked for me. "Captain Doyle's compliments, sir. He requests that you come to his quarters."

I got dressed and went with the marine, wondering what Captain Doyle wanted of me. I soon found out. A Staten Islander, he wanted to talk about New York City with someone who had been there recently. He had been sailing the seas for many months.

The next day we sailed and as we proceeded north toward Japan the air freshened and the dismal heat of the Marianas was dispelled. The boys played ball on the flight deck. Sooner or later they would lose the ball over the side, then they'd all come over to the island and look up at the bridge. Captain Doyle would go in his quarters where he had a supply of baseballs and throw one out to them after an exaggerated wind-up.

"You just watch," he said to me. "We're heading north and in a couple of days it will be much cooler. You'll find them out there playing football," and so it turned out.

But there was no baseball or football when we got near the enemy islands. We attacked Honshu, Kyushu, and Okinawa. We would be at the front for a time, then we'd withdraw a couple of hundred miles to meet the oil tankers. On one occasion, a great clumsy tanker came alongside and grappled us. Her name was *Tallulah Bankhead*. It occurred to me that Talu would prefer to have something more delicate and shapely named after her.

When the fleet was out of trouble in the refueling area, times were comparatively gay. The carriers which had freezing plants would furnish ice cream to the destroyers, and the carrier's band would play what was then called gut bucket for the destroyer crew when the cans came up to the quarter to top off, i.e., take oil from the carrier as the carrier took it in larger quantities from the oil tanker.

Captain Doyle used to tell the destroyer men about his system of reward to crews of destroyers which picked up flyers from the *Hornet*. He explained it to me.

"We give twenty gallons of ice cream for every flyer they pick up," he said, "but only ten if he's a marine."

At this time the landing at Okinawa had been made and a screen of destroyers was acting as radar pickets at the northern end of the island. The Japanese kamikazes were knocking the destroyers to pieces; forty or fifty of them were hit before the screen was withdrawn.

Our first assignment was to hit certain airfields in Kyushu, from which the suicide planes were supposed to be coming. We got close to our objective before we got into trouble. But once it started, it was almost continuous with torpedo attacks at night and kamikazes in the daytime. Our force steamed steadily on for a time; the attacks were avoided.

I was in the pilothouse with Captain Doyle one morning when the executive officer who was scanning the radar said, "Here it is. There are fourteen attacks coming at once."

That day I saw my first kamikaze. It came astern of the *Bennington* which was on our port beam and aimed directly for us. I was standing on the wing of the bridge, gawking at him, when the five-inch gun in the turret just forward started to fire and knocked me flat on my face with its muzzle blast. I crawled into the pilothouse. By this time all the five-inch guns were going and the forty-quads had started.

It didn't seem possible for one Japanese boy to fly

through so much fire, but the kamikaze came on right for us. Then all of a sudden he burst into flames and plunged down into the sea. Captain Doyle spoke to his lookouts: "All right, he's gone. Now look around and find the others. Keep alert for the safety of the ship."

Kamikazes came at us for three days and the torpedo attacks, all preceded by brilliant flares over the fleet, occurred every night. I don't remember going to sleep for seventy-two hours. It was too exciting. There were occasional single Japanese night flyers over the fleet and I watched one episode on the radar screen.

A Jap was flying around the edges and a member of our CAP (Combat Air Patrol) was trying to run him down by following vectors (intercepting courses) furnished him by the radar officer. The two talked together.

"You should be able to see him now," said the radar officer.

"Don't see him yet," said the pilot . . . "hold on, there he is—tally-ho."

There was a pause of a minute, then the pilot yelled, 'I flamed him."

One night there was a bogey (Japanese plane) over the fleet and the CAP couldn't find it.

Admiral Clark spoke over the ship's loudspeaker. "I'm going to call off the CAP and open fire on this one," he said.

A j.g. standing next to me on the bridge muttered, "The old fool will outline the whole fleet."

But Romeo was right. A minute after the barrage opened the bogey came down in flames.

The *Enterprise* was in a different section of the task force and was the flag ship of Admiral Mark Mitscher, who commanded the whole task force. The next morning we could see her on the horizon approximately seven miles away. Her big square island marked her. The first kami-kaze wave hit the section in which the *Enterprise* was steaming. I was standing on the bridge with an Australian correspondent when the guns started shooting.

"You've got a grandstand seat, Woodward. For God's sake, make notes."

I got out my paper and pencil and looked at my watch. It was 7:05. I put down things as they happened with the time of their occurrence; made note of the time each kamikaze went into the water. I was looking right at the *Enterprise* when she got it.

There was a flash on her forward deck and something blew into the air. The old ship steamed on as if nothing had happened, but a moment later her captain talked to the fleet over the radio.

"I have suffered a hit abaft the forward elevator. I am inoperative. Losses are light."

After we pulled back from the front and were relatively out of trouble, I got myself moved to the *Enterprise* by way of two breeches buoys and a destroyer. I was two hours in the tin can, during which time I learned that the destroyer navy is the most uncomfortable that can be imagined.

At noon chow the skipper said to me, "You sit at the head of the table, Mr. Woodward, and be the father." All unknowing I took the designated seat. A minute later the destroyer made a forty-degree roll to port and I got all the plates plus the ketchup and mustard in my lap.

The *Enterprise* was a sad old ship when I got aboard over the stern. A kamikaze, whose name was Tomi Kai, was not one of the "fat, dumb and happy" flyers who generally manned a suicide plane. He was a good flyer who had hidden in a cloud cover over the ship awaiting his chance. When he saw he was going to miss the *Enterprise* with his dive he turned on his back, thus righting his error.

He struck her just astern of the no. 1 elevator, went through the flight deck and exploded in the elevator well, blowing the thirty-ton elevator several hundred feet in the air. All the men in the pump room below deck were killed; also some who took cover on the hangar deck.

Bud Wilkinson, now Oklahoma football coach and athletic director, lay down on the starboard sponson and dogged the steel door leading to the hangar deck. The explosion blew the door open, and it took off half the head of a sailor lying next to Bud.

When I got aboard the *Enterprise* I found my room so hot I couldn't stay in it. So I lived with the sailors who bunked in the corner of the hangar deck. One of my mates complained that there was something wrong with his back. I urged him to go to sick bay. The doctor took about one half a pound of steel out of his rump.

The toll of dead was fourteen; thirty were wounded. The kamikaze was blown into small pieces. A few remnants were found, his wristwatch, his shoulder patch with the cherry blossom emblem, his wallet, and a chunk of his shinbone. The *Enterprise* had a ripple in her foredeck which made launching planes impossible, and she was ordered to the shipyard at Bremerton, Washington, for repairs.

It was the end of her naval career. She had participated in every battle of the Pacific war except the Coral Sea and had more Japanese planes and ships to her credit than any craft in the navy. There were those of us who thought the Japanese surrender should have occurred on her flight deck rather than on the *Missouri,* a newcomer in the navy.

On her way home, the *Enterprise* went back to Ulithi, to unload ammunition. It took nearly a week, during which we melted in the equatorial heat. The carefree sailors who unloaded the bombs frequently dropped them on the deck with thunderous crashes, but the ship's company said it was all right, the bombs were not armed.

Ultimately we set out for home by way of Pearl Harbor at twenty knots. Twice we were called to general quarters because of a theoretical Japanese attack. But each time it turned out to be a lone B-29 whose pilot had neglected to turn on his IFS (identifying signal).

Approaching Pearl Harbor the *Enterprise* flew a homeward-bound pennant one hundred feet long. She was greeted by flights of planes as she approached Oahu, and when she finally came alongside at Ford Island, a company of Waves was drawn up on the pier to serenade her. The girls sang the "Song of the Islands" and other anthems very prettily, but they would have made the same impression if they had howled like Banshees. The guys on the *Enterprise* hadn't seen a woman for eighteen months.

The boys at the rails threw messages to the girls. One enthusiastic suitor was seized by the Jimmylegs for wrapping his note around a pair of pliers. A marine saw Commander Tom Hamilton on the dock and threw him a cigar, shouting, "Have a cigar on me, Commander Tom."

Hamilton caught the cigar neatly, held it over his head and yelled, "Thank you, mate."

It took us another week to get to Puget Sound. There the ship was anchored in the stream, and a ferry came to take the first leave party, half the crew, off the ship. The ferry docked in Seattle, and the party was marched to the railroad station, where each man was required to buy a round-trip ticket home before he was let out of the ranks.

I was the only civilian aboard and the executive officer had made a point of telling Customs that I would require inspection. My seabag was full of navy-issued cigarettes. I had heard about the shortage at home and didn't want to see the Customs man. So I put my seabag on my shoulder and marched off with the sailors, dropping out as we passed the first barroom.

My fiftieth birthday had occurred at sea between Pearl and Seattle. I had made great preparations for this anniversary, starting a few months before when I gave the chief steward in the Officers' Mess at Pearl Harbor a large tip to save my liquor allowance when I pushed off for Guam and the front. Consequently, I was able to acquire a seabag full of booze when I returned to Pearl. With this on my shoulder, I walked up the gangway to the *Enterprise*'s quarterdeck, saluted the colors and the officer of the deck.

"Just a minute, Mr. Woodward," said the OD. "What have you in the bag?"

"Oh, just a few trinkets for the children, sir," I said.

If I'd just paid attention to my own business and avoided compassion for the wretches who didn't get shore leave, I would have been all right. But after stowing the spoils in my locker I got out one bottle of whiskey and whispered to one of my bunkmates on the hangar deck that it would be on my desk.

That was the end of the booze. The next time I looked in my locker every drop was gone. I didn't get a chance to open one bottle. However, Jerry Flynn and some other young officers were able to round up some substitute material, so that my fiftieth birthday did not go wholly un-celebrated.

Flynn was the toastmaster at all *Enterprise* smokers. He had an arrangement with the captain that he could be as fresh as he wanted while acting as emcee. Jerry's position at general quarters was in the top, i.e., up the mast.

One day an unidentified plane flew over the big *E*. It was Japanese, but Flynn, who was in the best position to spot it, missed identification. It dropped a bomb on the flight deck of the *Enterprise*, which, fortunately, struck flat and did not explode; however, the admiral did. He called Flynn and blistered him for twenty minutes. In conclusion, he said, "Flynn, the *Enterprise* is a big ship. But, big as she is, she is not big enough for both you and me."

A few months later the admiral was transferred to a new command and the *Enterprise* gave him a send-off with a muster of all hands on the hangar deck. Flynn, as usual, was in charge of festivities. After various speakers had lauded the admiral, Flynn took the floor. "Admiral," he said, "a few months ago you said to me, 'Flynn, as big as she is, *Enterprise* is not big enough for both you and me.' Well, Admiral, we're all sorry to see you go."

I had been home about two weeks when I got an air-mail letter from Flynn. He said the *Saturday Evening Post* had a man on the *Enterprise* and apparently was planning to run a feature about the ship's career. He warned me that this was apparently the reason that the censors had refused to pass anything written about the hit on the old ship.

I had written the story three times—once for submission to the censors at Guam, sending it by air in care of Admiral Nimitz; once at Pearl Harbor; and once after I got back to New York. I told Joe Barnes, our foreign editor, that we were getting double-crossed and he took it up with the Censorship Bureau in Washington without success.

I was an eyewitness to the kamikaze hit on the ship. I had full notes on the attack. I wrote it immediately. That was May 14, 1945. On August 27, after the war was over, the *Saturday Evening Post* finally went through all the ponderous processes which placed it on the newsstand. That was the day the navy chose to release the story.

I also accuse the navy censors of throwing away at least a dozen stories I wrote about the army while I was a navy correspondent in the Pacific. But when you go ten thousand miles to get a good story and then find yourself in a dead heat with a magazine writer from Philadelphia you should get a full pardon for blowing your stack.

17

MRS. HELEN ROGERS REID BLEW HOT and cold on me at various times during my prewar and wartime career with the New York *Herald Tribune*. When I came back from the Pacific I felt I was in high favor. Not only had I written reams of copy about the nether side of the war but I worked largely by mail and so had not run up the hideous radio and cable bills the lady was used to receiving for war correspondence.

Mrs. Reid was extremely active in running the paper. She was the actual head of the Advertising Department but in the late stages of Ogden's life she played a role of increasing importance in the Editorial Department. He started to fail in 1945, and his death occurred on January 3, 1947.

My first day in the office after getting back from the Pacific theater, Mrs. Reid invited me to her office and asked me what I would like to do for the paper. I believe I could have had any job I named at that time. But I asked merely to be returned to the Sports Department which needed reorganization. I asked to go back as sports editor on the theory, held by myself at any rate, that I would be moved out of Sports after the department had been put on its feet.

The first move I made was to install Arthur Glass as head of the copy desk. Our selection of news had been poor during the war and our choice of pictures was abysmal. Glass improved the paper the first day he worked in the slot, which was September 4, 1945.

At this time Al Laney was the columnist and didn't like the job. He much preferred to handle assignments or to get up a feature series as he had in the case of "The Forgotten Men" before the war.

The first move I made was to attempt to get John Lardner to write our column. The first time we discussed it we renewed the old crap game argument and got nowhere. The second time I took along our publisher, Bill Robinson, and the talk was more businesslike. We met Lardner several other times but couldn't come to terms with him. The fact was he didn't want to write a newspaper column and kept making difficulties. So we dropped him, reluctantly.

Even before we talked to Lardner I had been scouting a little guy on the Philadelphia *Record* whose name was Walter Wellesley Smith. This character was a complete newspaper man. He had been through the mill and had come out with a high polish. In Philadelphia he was being hideously overworked. Not only did he write the column for the *Record* but he covered the ball games and took most other important assignments.

We scouted him in our usual way. For a month Verna Reamer, Sports Department secretary, bought the *Record* at the out-of-town newsstand in Times Square. She clipped all of Smith's writings and pasted them in a blank book. At the end of the month she left the book on my desk and I read a month's work by Smith at one sitting. I found I could get a better impression of a man's general ability and style by reading a large amount of his stuff at one time.

There was no doubt in my mind that Smith was a man we must have. After I'd read half his stuff I decided he had more class than any writer in the newspaper business.

At first I didn't think of him as a substitute for Lardner. Rather I wanted to get them both. When dealings with Lardner came to a stop I was afraid I would have to go back to writing a daily column myself, which I dreaded. I thought of myself at this time as an organizer rather than a writer, but Laney was anxious to have a leave of absence to finish the book he was writing (*Paris Herald*).

I telephoned Smith and asked him if he could come to New York and talk with me. We set a date and he arrived one morning with his wife Kay. She and Ricie paired off for much of the day while Smith and I discussed business.

It must be said that I was making this move without full approval of the management. George Cornish, our managing editor, knew I was looking for a man but was hard to convince when higher salaries were involved.

It is very strange to me that there was no competition in New York for Smith's services. He was making ninety dollars a week in Philadelphia with a small extra fee for use of his material in the Camden paper, also operated by J. David Stern. Nobody in New York had approached Smith in several years. In fact, he never had had a decent offer from any New York paper. I opened the conversation with Smith as follows—

"You are the best newspaper writer in the country and I can't understand why you are stuck in Philadelphia. I can't pay you what you're worth, but I'm very anxious to have you come here with us. I think that you will ultimately be our sports columnist but all I can offer you at the start is a job on the staff. Are you interested?"

"I sure am if the money is right," said Red.

We adjourned for lunch and I told him about the paper and what I hoped to make of the Sports Department. I told him that I had lost all interest in sports during the war but now I was determined to make our department the best in the country.

"I can't do this without you, Red," I told him.

I left Smith parked in Bleeck's and went upstairs to talk to George Cornish. With him it was a question of money and he blanched when I told him how much I wanted to pay Smith. I got a halfhearted go-ahead from George, but still I didn't dare make the offer to Smith.

He owned a house in the Philadelphia suburbs and would be under great expense until he could sell it and move his family to New York. I suggested that we would perhaps be able to pay him an "equalization fee" until he moved his wife and children into *Herald Tribune* territory.

I went back to see Cornish and broached this subject. No one can say George wasn't careful with the company's money. He argued for a while but finally agreed that if we were to bring Smith to New York, it would be fair to save him from penury during his first weeks with us.

I was able to go back to Bleeck's and make a pretty good offer to Red. I explained to him that his salary would be cut back after his family moved.

"But don't worry," I added. "You'll be making five times that in three years."

Of course, it turned out that way. As our columnist, Red was immediately syndicated. His salary was boosted within a couple of months and his income from outside papers equaled his new salary. Before anyone knew it he was making telephone numbers—and he deserved it.

I am unable to account for the fact that none of the evening papers of New York grabbed him. He could have been had, in all probability, for five dollars more a week than we gave him.

With him in hand I was able to let Laney take a few

months off to finish his book while I slaved at the column, in addition to other duties. I didn't want to put Red in too quickly. I wanted him to get the feel of the town first, and also I needed some of his writing in the paper to convince the bigwigs that he was as good as I claimed.

After Smith had been with us a month or so, I talked to Bill Robinson about making him our columnist. I wanted Bill to talk to Mrs. Reid about Smith so that Red would get away from the gate in good order. Bill had been reading him and was enthusiastic about his work. So not long after Smith had shifted his family to Malverne, Long Island, having sold his house, I told him that he was the columnist until further notice.

"I think that means forever, Red. And I'll go right upstairs and see if I can get you more money."

As a columnist Smith made an immediate hit and it wasn't long before the Hearst people were showing interest in him. I told Bill Robinson it was silly not to have a contract with Smith. He agreed and it was drawn up at once. It gave him a large increase in salary and half the returns from his syndicate, which was growing fast. It now includes about one hundred papers.

I'd like to go back to the question of why Smith wasn't hired by somebody else. My conclusion is that most writing sports editors don't want a man around who is obviously better than they. I took the opposite view on this question. I wanted no writer on the staff who couldn't beat me or at least compete with me. This was a question of policy.

I was trying to make a strong Sports Department and it was impossible to do this with the dreadful mediocrity I saw around me on the other New York papers.

The week the Smiths moved from the Main Line to

Malverne was memorable. The kids, Kitty and Terry, were dropped off at our farm for a few days so that the parental Smiths could move in peace. I think the kids had a good time playing with our little girls.

Terry, who is now a bright young reporter and a graduate of Notre Dame and the army, was satisfied to sit on the tractor for hours at a time. To be safe I blocked the wheels with logs of wood and took off the distributor cap. The tractor had a self-starter.

With the Smiths established in Malverne, the next move was to get a racing writer. I wrote about twenty-five letters to people in racing—horse owners, promoters, trainers, jockeys, concessionaires, and gamblers. I asked each one whom he considered to be the best racing writer available to the New York *Herald Tribune*. The response was nearly 100 percent and unanimous: "Joe Palmer."

I asked Smith if he knew Joe Palmer. He said, "Yes, and he's a hell of a writer."

I found that Joe had a regular job on the *Blood Horse* of Lexington, Kentucky, that he was also secretary of the Trainers' Association and was currently in New York tending to the trainers' business.

I got hold of Bob Kelley, my old Poughkeepsie associate, and asked him if he would make an appointment for Palmer to meet for lunch in Bleeck's restaurant at his convenience. Kelley had left the *Times* and had become public relations counsel for the New York race track. He got hold of Palmer and conveyed my message. Palmer answered as follows, "Tell that son of a bitch I won't have lunch with him, and if I see him on the street I'll kick him in the shins."

I told Kelley that his answer was highly unsatisfactory and sent him back to talk further with Palmer. This time

Joe came into Bleeck's with his guard up. What he didn't like about me was that I made a specialty of panning horse-racing. But once we got together we were friends in no time.

Joe liked the idea of working for the *Herald Tribune*. We came to terms quickly. It was agreed that he should go to work for us on the opening day at Hialeah, some months away. He needed the intervening time to finish his annual edition of *American Race Horses*.

I didn't know at this time what a remarkable performer I had hired. Palmer turned out to be a writer of the Smith stripe, and his Monday morning column, frequently devoted to subjects other than racing, became one of the *Herald Tribune*'s most valuable features.

I was misguided in the way I handled Palmer. I should never have tied him down with daily racing coverage. He would have been more valuable to us if I had turned him loose to write a daily column of features and notes as Tom O'Reilly did for us much later. But Joe was effective whatever he wrote. He even did a good job on a fight in Florida one winter, though he hated boxing.

He and Smith were at Saratoga during one August meeting, and Smith persuaded him to go to some amateur bouts, conducted for stable boys and grooms. On their way home Palmer panned the show.

"I'd rather see a chicken fight," he said.

"Why?" said Smith, outraged. "Chicken fighting is inhuman."

"Well," said Joe, "what we just saw was unchicken."

Palmer was a big man physically and as thoroughly educated as John Kieran. Joe had earned his master's degree in English in Kentucky and had taught there and at the University of Michigan where he studied for his Ph.D.

He could speak Anglo-Saxon. His knowledge of music was stupendous and he would have made a good drama critic for any newspaper.

He had started his thesis at Michigan when he discontinued his education and went to work for the *Blood Horse*.

He first attracted my attention with a St. Patrick's Day story in which he revealed that the patron saint's greatest gift to the Irish was the invention of the wheelbarrow, which taught them to walk on their hind legs.

Joe, himself, was of Irish descent and was brought up a Catholic. When he moved into a house in Malverne near the Smiths, he didn't like the public education and sent his children to the parochial school. He decided on this course after a long talk with the mother superior. She asked him if he wanted his children instructed in religion and he said he did.

One day Steve and young Joe were learning the catechism. One of the questions was, "How Many Gods Are There?"

"That's an important question and I want you to be sure to give the sister the right answer," said Joe. "Now say this after me: 'There is but one God and Mohammed is his prophet.'"

The story ends there. Nobody ever found out whether the boys told the sister what Joe told them. It's a safe bet, though, that their mother, Mary Cole Palmer, touted them off Mohammed.

A few days before Palmer came to work for us, we carried a special story by him explaining his credo of racing and a four-column race-track drawing by the distinguished artist, Lee Townsend. The main point of Joe's story was, "Horse-racing is an athletic contest between horses."

He was not interested in betting or the coarser skull-
duggery that goes on around a race track. For a long time
he wouldn't put the payoff in his racing story.

"Why should I do that?" he asked Smith.

"Because if you don't, the desk will write it in and
probably get it in the wrong place."

A few days before Joe went to work for us, Tom
O'Reilly, another great horse writer, heard about it. He
said, or so it was reported to me, "Holy smokes! Those
guys will be hiring Thomas A. Edison to turn off the
lights."

The advent of new writing material in the *Herald Tribune*'s Sports Department spurred the regulars to new
efforts and the paper got better and better. Arthur Glass
proved a fine head of the desk and everything would
have been great for me except that there was still a slight
tinge of alcohol around the place. Glass was no ab-
stainer and occasionally went on toots.

One day he called up my house and I was out. Ricie
said, "Can I take a message, Arthur?"

Glass would have told me that he was slightly over-
board and couldn't work, but he didn't think that was the
right thing to tell Ricie so he said he was sick. Ricie thereupon sent ten dollars' worth of flowers to him at the Albert Hotel where he lived before he married and re-
formed. Glass was so ashamed of himself that he never
gave me any more trouble.

He and I worked together a long time and I have never
known anyone with a better mind. He read Latin and
Greek for fun and once, somewhat later when he was as-
sisting me in editing the earlier *Sports Illustrated*, he
translated a five-thousand-word article from French after

telling me he didn't know anything about the language.

What he meant was that he had to look up about three or four modern idioms to make a perfect translation.

We lived on the farm until 1946, when we were almost forced to sell it by circumstances. Herb and Pete Hurley inherited a little money and decided they would leave me and turn to other work. Herb became a working co-owner in an apple farm and Pete undertook a job in a garage. They stayed with me until I could reduce the stock to a point where I could take care of things myself.

We sold the herd at auction in Trenton for a disappointing price. I had hopes for a young bull because I knew that Elizabeth Arden was interested in him. Her herdsman came to the sale with a great sound of trumpets and everybody else backed out of the bidding. As a result the bull went to Mrs. Mudpack for four hundred dollars. I thought I'd get at least twenty-five.

I didn't want to stay on the farm if I wasn't going to farm. Ricie favored keeping the house, a few acres, and selling the rest of the land. We hadn't really decided what we were going to do when a delegation from Princeton drove into the barnyard with a man who wanted to buy it.

It was raining and for some reason there was a taste of gasoline in our deep well water when it rained. I asked the gentleman if they would have a drink and they said, yes, with plain water. I had to sneak out through the trees to the brook to get a pitcher of decent-tasting water.

The prospective purchaser was the editor of two McGraw-Hill magazines on mechanics. He was accompanied by Hack McGraw and two other Princeton residents—Mr. Jeffers, who was my adviser when I bought the farm, and John Poe, president of one of the Princeton banks. They apparently had been discussing the farm while I was out for the water. When I came back Mr. Jeffers said, "Albert Hauptli here is interested in buying your farm. Do you want to sell it?"

"Well, Mr. Jeffers, it's a much better farm than it was when I bought it. The buildings are adequate and in good repair. So are the fences. The *ph* and the fertility has been brought up. I have a good deal of money invested in it, as John Poe will tell you. I will sell it for an inflationary price."

After a few more conversations with Mr. Hauptli he offered me an inflationary price and I sold him the farm, with great regret.

If the Hurley boys hadn't left me I wouldn't have sold in a hundred years. I couldn't get anyone to replace them.

The people who applied for the job, after Herb and Pete had given notice, were drifters whom I couldn't count on. Leroy Burgess and Isaac White were not available. Leroy had undertaken a career in the merchant marine and Ike had a Civil Service job in the post office.

Ricie sold our herd of pigs in Trenton to a man who had known her father in New Haven. She got a good price. Moreover, she drove our two six-hundred-pound sows to the purchaser in our little truck. Every time they shifted, she thought she was going to capsize. I was very fond of the sows and considered them beautiful. Therefore, I had named them Sonja Henie and Clare Booth Luce. This was considered uproarious in the stockyard.

In the spring we had not concluded the sale of the farm and I had a twenty-acre field prepared for corn, so I planted it in my spare time. I plowed it and harrowed it with and across the furrows and both ways obliquely. I had sold my own corn planter, so I borrowed one from Percy Van Zant.

In New Jersey rural area boys are allowed a number of days out of school for farm work, so I engaged a young fellow who lived near us to help me with the actual planting.

When my fertilizer was delivered I discovered it had been put in 150-pound bags instead of the customary 100. I nearly killed myself hoisting it onto my wagon. The boy was only twelve and too little to help.

In the field he drove the tractor and I ran the corn planter. After a few tours of the field one of the wheels came off. We tied it on with baling wire ten or twelve times and finally called Van Zant to send a man over. He fixed it by putting a dent in the axle which kept the end of the bolt from slipping on the shaft.

We planted corn faster after that and ten days later it came up in virtually unbroken rows, the finest field of young corn I had ever seen.

It was knee-high when I sold the farm to Mr. Hauptli and he told me that his decision to give me the price I asked was influenced by the prospective corn crop. He had farmed in Illinois before moving to McGraw-Hill's New York office. I felt compensated for lifting thirty 150-pound bags when he commented on the corn.

The Sunday *Herald Tribune* hit its all-time peak in October, 1946, when it sold 748,576 copies. Bill Robinson had scored a coup when he bought an extra supply of newsprint in advance of need. The *Times* was hard up for paper and the *Tribune* had an advantage. Our paper was stronger in all ways than it was at any other time in my experience. The morale was high despite low salaries.

The paper had done a wonderful job covering the war.

Homer Bigart, known to his associates as "Cannon's Mouth Bigart," was perhaps the outstanding war correspondent in the world and there were other good ones.

The *Herald Tribune* had a toe-hold on suburban circulation in those days, beating the *Times* in New Jersey, Long Island, and Westchester. Notwithstanding its daily circulation, it never got above 385,000; it passed that figure after the Reids sold it to John Hay Whitney. But in 1946 nobody wanted any more daily circulation; the excess paper was being used in the Sunday edition.

Late that year I noticed a change in the newspaper's atmosphere. Mr. Reid was sicker and seldom came in the office. One day an advertising man came into my office and gave me detailed instructions on how to run the Sports Department. I listened to him and started to think about what was happening. Apparently an unfortunate metamorphosis was beginning. The Editorial Department was no longer verboten to the commercial minions of Mrs. Reid. Mr. Reid lived until January 3, 1947, but before his death most of the things he stood for had been forgotten.

He was fearless. He was honest. And, like Nick Skerrett, devoted to the thesis that the American newspaper is the greatest institution in the world. Moreover he was loyal to his employees and when a complaint was lodged against one of them by a reader or advertiser, he took it directly to the man involved and got his view of the matter.

Once Larry McPhail of the Yankees wrote to Mr. Reid complaining about something I had written, suggesting that I be fired. Mr. Reid gave it to Wilbur Forrest to answer, and the latter did a nice job as follows—

"Dear Mr. McPhail: Mr. Reid is out of town and I am answering your letter of November 6 for him. Before leaving he suggested that I tell you that he will call on you in case he decides he needs aid in running his business."

This action by Mr. Reid was what we could expect during his regime—complete backing in anything we did as agents of the paper. Following his death I was given quick evidence that the policy had been discontinued. His elder son Whitelaw had succeeded him as editor.

I had written a column in which I panned Mike Jacobs for deliberately scheduling a heavyweight fight a few days before our Fresh Air Fund football game. I saw young Whitelaw in Bleeck's bar a few days later, and he stopped at my table and said, "I had to apologize to Mr. Jacobs for your column. I wrote him a letter today. I considered the column undignified."

This flattened me. It was the first time in eighteen years on the *Tribune* that anyone in authority had gone behind my back in a matter of office business. It was hard to believe.

I said, "Whitey, your father wouldn't have done that. . . . Incidentally, if you want a dignified sports editor you'd better get somebody else."

I received enough prior symptoms of the course the paper was steering to decide to get out. I could not resign without sacrificing about twelve thousand dollars in severance pay. I couldn't commit an overt act without the same result. I decided I would run the Sports Department as I always had and would refuse to follow orders which I thought were not for the good of the newspaper.

I saw Mike Jacobs at the Garden a week or so later and he pulled out Whitey's letter and said, "Who is this guy named Reid? Here's a letter he wrote me about you. He must be nuts."

It became obvious early that Whitelaw's performance as editor was going to leave much to be desired. It also

became evident that most of the principal decisions issued
in the name of Whitelaw or George Cornish actually came
from Mrs. Reid.

I soon found I was on the proscription list, though I
was not numbered among the victims of the first two
purges. One day, however, George Cornish called me in
and said, "Stanley, Mrs. Reid thinks we ought to cover
the women's golf in Westchester more fully. She wants
you to put an eight-column head on it in tomorrow's
paper."

I said, "George, it isn't worth it. You want me to use
my judgment on what we should play, don't you?"

"Oh, yes," said George. "But there is an advertising
angle here and Mrs. Reid is very keen on the subject. In
the future she wants you to send a good man to cover the
women's golf."

I went back to my office and wrote George a memo in
which I set forth: that the women's golf events in question
were of practically no news value; that I would not send
a good man to cover them because I felt that giving out
an assignment of this kind to an experienced reporter was
degrading and demoralizing; that I would like to borrow
a copy boy or copy girl to call up the club each week and
get the scores.

I assured George that a short lead with the scores would
comprise adequate coverage. At the end I asked him to
send me the name of the copy boy or girl who was going
to do the assignment.

This is what got me fired. No Reid dignified the Woodward departure by being present at the obsequies. George
called me in his office and executed the duty to which he
was committed. He said he didn't think I was interested in
my job as sports editor any more and that it would be just

as well if I withdrew.

I wanted to be sure of my ground, so I said, "Do I understand that you are going to pay me off?"

"Yes," said George . . . "When do you want to leave?"

That morning I had heard that Bobby Cooke had been appointed sports editor the previous day, meaning twenty-four hours before I was canned. I confronted George with this.

"You've already named a sports editor, George," I said. "All my business here is completed. I will leave now if it suits you." So I went in the Sports Department, poked my head in Smith's office to tell him the news, picked up my hat and coat and went down to Bleeck's.

The news spread around the shop and people started to drop into the saloon. I could see I was going to get into a mess if I stayed there so I went home. By this time we had moved out of the farm and had subleased an apartment at 77 Park Avenue. In half an hour the place was full of newspaper people. Some members of the staff announced they were going to quit, too. I dissuaded them from this, pointing out that I was going to get my severance pay and that anyone who quit would get nothing.

Joe Barnes, who had started the *Star* in the building formerly occupied by *P.M.*, offered me a job on the new paper. I was grateful to him, but I felt I didn't want to take up any new job immediately.

At this point Whitey Reid called me up and told me he regretted I had left so precipitously. I told him that I was an old and indoctrinated *Tribune* man and a loyal friend of his late father; that I didn't like the way the paper was going under his direction and that I was perfectly content to be out of it provided I got my severance pay.

I was right about the immediate future of the *Tribune*.

It started downhill with the Whitelaw Reid regime and continued when Whitelaw was benched and his younger brother Brownie was made editor. Under Brownie the downward rush attained terrifying speed. It is hard to pin a descent on any one cause, and it may be that factors other than management contributed to this one. However, it certainly would be hard to argue that management had nothing to do with it.

18

I VISITED THE STAR TO SEE IF I wanted to work there. I liked Joe Barnes, who had been foreign editor of the *Tribune* and therefore was my boss while I was a war correspondent. But I didn't like his paper and guessed after one look around the Editorial Department that it would have a short life.

I dropped in about four o'clock in the afternoon, when a morning paper should start to hum. I found small groups of intellectuals standing around discussing important questions and nobody doing any work. I was also afraid Barnes, a renowned liberal, would support Henry Wallace for the presidency and so die by hari-kari rather than by desiccation. So I thanked him for his very fine offer and told him I didn't want to work there.

Instead I went back to Circleville, New York, where we had rented a house for the summer and went to work in the vegetable garden. I got telephone calls now and then offering me bum jobs. But, for the most part, I hoed and dusted with rotenone. It was the best garden I ever had. My success with midget corn was spectacular.

The first financially satisfactory job that was offered me was at Dell Publishing Company, then located at Twenty-ninth Street and Fifth Avenue in the midst of a thoroughly sterile neighborhood. I called there and was received by Mrs. Helen Myer, a lady who reminded me painfully of Mrs. Reid.

She told me that Mr. Delacorte, proprietor of the business, was in Europe but she was empowered to talk to me about a rather secret proposition. It developed she wanted me to become editor of a new magazine to be known as *Sports Illustrated*. Its format was to be like that of *Life* and it was to specialize in pictures.

At almost the same time I got an offer to become sports editor of the Providence *Journal* and its evening counterpart. I liked the job in Providence better, but the financial cut I would have had to take was a deterrent, particularly since Dell had offered me somewhat more than I was getting at the *Tribune*. So I accepted Mrs. Myer's offer and turned to at the corner of Twenty-ninth and Fifth.

I found that conditions were rather disagreeable. Everybody in the place had to punch a time clock. I saw no sense in this or in the fact that the three newspaper people, who comprised the staff of the new *Sports Illustrated*, had to start work at nine o'clock in the morning. If you stayed more than ten minutes overtime, moreover, you found the stairs locked and had to wait for a single elevator to get out of the building.

I had taken Arthur Glass with me to *Sports Illustrated* and also Verna Reamer, who had been my secretary. Glass and I wrote some of the material in the book, but for the most part we bought it.

There was a long period before we published the magazine. We were supposed to get out what is known as a dummy which the advertising solicitors could take around to show prospective customers. We found that we could do things twice as fast as the magazine people were accustomed to doing them and, therefore, were out of work much of the time during the first six months.

The nine-o'clock starting time was anathema to all of us and we devised a system whereby only one of us came in at nine o'clock, punching the clock for all three. The others would get in about noon and I would make a show of consulting the Art Department or, if possible, Mrs. Myer. Then we settled down to working one of the double-crostics out of a book issued by the *Saturday Review*, which Verna brought in.

I got promises from some good people to write for the magazine and I engaged Bill O'Brian to do some drawings for us. He had worked for me at the *Herald Tribune* until Cornish made me drop him and was one of the most gifted performers I knew of. His characterizations of Branch Rickey and Leo Durocher were great.

Among others I engaged to work for *Sports Illustrated* were Red Smith, Joe Palmer, Al Laney, John Lardner, John McNulty, Dick Maney, Tallulah Bankhead (who wrote about the Giants), Jimmy Cannon, and Tom O'Reilly.

I turned down stories by Lucius Beebe and Bill Taylor after asking for them. They were slightly angry but when I turned down a story I had sought from Stanley Walker, he accepted my right to do this with good nature. I wrote an editorial and a story in each issue, also a good deal of anonymous material in the front and back.

I went into the foreign field with a boxing story by Frank Butler of the London *Express* and a story about Marcel Cerdan at home in Africa by one of the Paris sports editors whose name I can't remember. He accompanied the story with a fine selection of pictures, one of which we used on the cover of our second issue. The story about Cerdan in Africa was about five thousand words in French. That was the one Glass translated in a few hours one afternoon.

I got the contributions largely on the basis of friendship, because we did not pay much, but I devised a supporting system which I found valuable. I would say to a writer, "We don't pay much but we pay instantly."

So when I got the copy for a story I would read it,

take it to Mrs. Myer who had to initial the copy to authorize purchase, another indignity to which I was subjected, then I would gallop up to the cashier with a voucher also signed by Mrs. Myer, get the check, take it back to Mrs. Myer for authorized signature and put it in the mail before dark.

We got a good reputation through this system. A writer could mail his manuscript one day and get his check the next. The dilatory tactics of many magazines in payment furnished a contrast that made us look good.

After I had been working at Dell a couple of months, a slim, dark-looking man entered our office and said, "Mr. Woodward, I'm Delacorte." I rushed forward to greet the big boss. Unfortunately I had just thrown a match in the wastebasket and there was a towering burst of flame as I gripped the chieftain's hand. He backed off in alarm but I didn't even stop talking. I just took another wastebasket and fitted it into the first, thus smothering the flame. I don't think I made a very good first impression.

Later he would take me to the Harvard Club for lunch with some of his promotion and advertising men. They would think of all kinds of dodges to sell space in the magazine. I didn't say anything for three meetings and then finally blew up.

"Mr. Delacorte," I said, "I consider this a lot of nonsense. I believe the way to promote a magazine is to make it a good one. If you can appeal to enough readers, the advertising will come naturally."

Unfortunately, we didn't appeal to enough readers and such advertising as came to us was obtained unnaturally.

On several occasions I was forced to go with a solicitor and jolly up a reluctant huckster. I stopped just short of writing signed commercials for shirts.

Mr. Delacorte had started a small radio and television magazine a month or two before ours; at that time the Dell Company had a flock of rather lurid newsstand material. He closed down the television magazine in a day without advance notice to the editor. This caused me to worry about my own magazine.

So I went to Mr. Delacorte and asked him about our situation. He protested that our magazine was in a different category. It was, he said, a "coffee table magazine," by which he seemed to mean it was respectable. He said he would stick with it until it succeeded. He expressed confidence in its future and even praised me a little for the four issues we had already gotten out.

The fifth was then in the works, almost complete. I was working on football material for the fall because most of the college teams were having spring practice, and I could make the pictures I would need in the fall.

A man from the Pacific Coast told me that Eddie LeBaron of College of the Pacific was the best ball-handler in football.

"The way he hides the ball," said my informant, "it is absolutely impossible to see what he is doing. It looks as if he has it on a string and jerks it back after giving it to someone else."

I decided to make "guard's-eye" pictures of LeBaron in spring practice and made all the arrangements with the authorities at his college. The idea was to photograph a scrimmage with ten men on the defense and a camera in place of the left guard. It might have worked.

I had other ideas. I asked Colonel Earl H. Blaik at West Point if he would help me make some pictures of an offense I had devised with two quarterbacks under center. He agreed and suggested we build a platform on top of one of the practice goal posts for use by the photographer.

I was sitting in the office of Colonel Ockie Kruger, West Point graduate manager, before dinner one night when I got a call from Glass in New York.

"Man the lifeboats," he said. "We're done for."

"What do you mean, Arthur?"

"I mean old Delacorte just closed the magazine. You'd better come back to New York."

I did that immediately after telephoning Colonel Blaik to call off the double-quarterback pictures. I found conditions as Glass represented them. Our chieftain, after telling me of his utter devotion to our magazine two weeks before, had now given it the snicker-snee.

I set to work finding jobs for Glass and Verna; neither needed much help, because both were able operatives. Glass joined up with Joe Val at the *World-Telegram* and continued a good job he had always done for me. Verna went to the New York Racing Association and later quit to free-lance.

As for me, I had no written contract but I claimed a verbal contract with Mrs. Myer. It had three months more to go and it was agreed that I should spend this time at my regular salary getting out a one-shot called *Stanley Woodward's Football*. This was a forecast of the season that would begin in September. Its feature was a futuristic All-America team.

I continued to get this magazine out every spring for fourteen years, whatever my main job was. I finally quit in the spring of 1962 when the company told me that it was going to cut my pay in half. My garden didn't amount to much that year. I could only get to the country weekends and sometimes not then because I was working so hard for Dell Publishing Company.

In my last days there, in the spring of 1949, I was sitting in my office working on the football book when a rugged, youngish-looking man walked in and offered me a job.

This was Ted Thackrey, former husband of Dorothy Schiff and former editor of her newspaper, the *Post*. He told me that he was starting a new paper in the plant of *P.M.* and the *Star*, which had also folded, and wanted me to be the sports editor and columnist. I could go to work any time and the pay wasn't bad.

I asked for some particulars about the paper. It was to be called *The Compass*. Its policy would be radical but not Communist. It would be a tabloid paper issued six times a week. The sixth issue would be a so-called weekend paper. The backing was to be furnished by a sister of the Chicago *Tribune*'s Bertie McCormick. She (the sister) had definite leftist leanings.

I had written to the *Wall Street Journal* to see if they wanted me to start a sports column for them. Here was the exact opposite type of newspaper. But it didn't seem to me that a sports column would be any different whether it was written for one or the other.

I talked with Ricie about it and accepted the offer the next day. I found the paper was manned by a collection of good newspaper men. Thackrey had chosen his staff primarily on the basis of ability. The fact that many of the best men he had were barred by the other papers on account of leftist leanings was a help to him. We had some outright Communists, but the ones who couldn't do the work were quickly dropped.

The first couple of months I worked there I doubled in brass, coincidentally finishing the football book for Dell. I found that the Sports Department comprised three men —Bill Mahoney, Jack Orr, and me. Mahoney, an absolute whiz in the newspaper profession, did most of the copy-reading. Orr worked on the desk when Mahoney was off, and was our principal news writer.

Later we hired a bright young fellow named Stanley Isaacs, also Herb Goren, who had written "The Old Scout," the New York *Sun*'s baseball column. It was probably the most efficient Sports Department ever organized. It had some nonexistent members like Bruce Connor, whose writing had to be ghosted. We needed the names but not the help.

All I had to do was write six columns a week and supervise the department, which needed no supervising.

I had created "The Reliable Jersey House," a theoretical bookmaker while I was at the *Herald Tribune*. The *Compass* was full of horse bettors and offered a great chance to exploit the general subject, so I developed The House as a character and he appeared in my column two or three times a week.

This fellow was a tall, portly person who wore white piping inside his vest and carried black eyeglasses on the end of a black ribbon. In cold weather he wore a karakul-lined overcoat, a Homburg, and spats. He spoke in measured tones and boasted of his ancestry, which had been engaged in the "commission business" for several generations.

His paternal grandsire, it appeared, had taken the commitments of Albert the Prince Regent, while his maternal grandparent handled the bets of the Czarevich, Prince Ivan Petrovsky Pickoff. People around the *Compass* started calling the local bookmaker "House" and he was flattered by the name. He didn't deserve it because he wasn't as elegant as the true character.

I took some awful chances in my column by writing

about the police payoff system then in vogue (thirteen months—the regular ones and Christmas) and there was never a complaint from anyone.

I had a year's contract with the *Compass*. When it was up Thackrey said he regretted that he had to let me go. Bertie McCormick had had his radical relative declared *non compos mentis* and the financing was giving Ted trouble. The paper was finally operated on a short-term basis with different money behind it every six or seven days. You could tell the politics of the current angel by the editorial policy. Some weeks it was only light pink; others it was red as Marx.

I had bought a 125-acre farm near my former rental at Circleville, New York. And when I got canned I moved there and prepared to free-lance. I had bought this farm for a small price and now spent more than the purchase money putting it into shape to live in. It turned out to be a comfortable little house, after we had drilled a deep well and installed a bathroom, which it never had had. We built a fireplace in the kitchen and that's where we spent much of our time.

The kitchen was used for many things. Thelma cooked on one side of it; I occasionally ran the Gravely tractor in so it would be warm enough to start in the morning. One of the dachshunds had a litter of puppies on the davenport which was drawn up beside the fireplace.

I had good luck as a free-lance writer. With the able Max Wilkinson as my agent, I appeared in all the popular magazines and wrote four books for Dell, all in one year. I made more money than I ever had before and I should have kept it. What I actually did was to get bulldozers, power shovels, and trucks and build a new road and a lake in front of the house. It was a beautiful little body of water and soon as it was finished I started to stock it. There was a big pond below the house, mostly on another man's property. I got myself a three-foot round net which I baited with dog food and operated on the end of a pole. I would let it down for five minutes then hoist it up. There were usually three to ten blue gills in it. These and a number of full-size blue gills, which I caught with a fly rod, were dumped into the new pond. In the fall when the bass hit freely I put in fifty big ones. Other people gave me volunteer assistance. They would come up to the house with a bass and offer him to me for my pond. I became very choosy. I refused to take any more from the neighboring pond to avoid inbreeding. I made the fisherman go to more distant places.

The State of New York virtually gave away red pines in those days, but specified that they must be planted in rows as windbreaks or soil holders. I wanted scenic planting around the pond. I solved my problem legally by starting the rows of pines at the pond and taking them twenty trees deep in all directions. This made it possible to make an undulating border for the pond.

I also went into the chicken business, against my wife's advice, and blew more of my free-lancing pelf. The result of these operations was that I had to borrow money the next year to pay my income tax. I found, too, that the novelty of having my name in the magazines had worn off and that Max Wilkinson wasn't selling as much stuff as he did formerly.

However, Ted Thackrey, still getting out the *Compass*, offered me seventy-five dollars a week to write him two columns. These and the remnants of a newspaper's syndicate I had organized when I was at Dell provided enough revenue so that Ricie and I could push off for Florida. The girls by now were in boarding school. The educational advantages of Circleville were nil.

We had an old friend in Florida named Colonel Robles and he rented us a cottage on Siesta Key off Sarasota. I hadn't been there very long when the managing editor of the Miami *News* called me up and offered me the job of sports editor. A chance to get back in the newspaper business appealed to me strongly, though I knew the money would be poor.

Ricie and I drove to Miami and I had a talk with the managing editor. The result was that I agreed to go to work for the *News*. The fact that I stuck it out for two and a half years indicates that I was strong, well, and in the throes of idiocy. I discovered almost at once that I was expected to be at work at six thirty in the morning, that the Sports Department was insufficiently manned, and that the newspaper's standards were dreadful.

I was used to going to bed at two or three o'clock in the morning and I had trouble breaking myself of the habit. If I went to bed early I couldn't sleep. Because of the lack of man power, I had to do a great deal of the copyreading. We got out six evening papers a week as well as a Sunday edition. We had to work all week getting copy down for the Sunday, and we had to put in our first Sunday edition about two and a half hours after we had closed the Saturday paper.

God knows I tried to make a decent Sports Department. But my tenure started in the summer when there was practically nothing going on and the production of features, on which the improvement depended, was difficult. We had some good men. Joe Tannenbaum, the racing writer, was a good summer copyreader; Arthur Grace, a recent graduate of the University of Miami, surprised me by showing signs of education. He turned out to be a first-class writer. Carl Dillon was as good a copyreader as I have known and so was Abe Abikoff, who later worked for me in Newark and New York.

I found I had to sell the Circleville farm and it had to be at a loss because of all the money I had invested in it. I sold it by telephone, just before the first Sunday edition, to Joseph Kramm, author of *The Shrike*. The first thing he did after taking title was to open the drain in my pond and let all the bass and blue gills go down stream. Circleville correspondents said they had been biting savagely.

We had our children with us again in Miami. Ellen was in the university and Mary in Coral Gables High School. We lived first in a rented house, which was full of scorpions, in the pine boondocks of South Miami. Later with the customary show of business acumen, I bought a house in Coral Gables, across the Deep Water Canal from Cocoplum Plaza. It was a beautiful house. Ricie loved it, but each time she admitted it she added, "Too bad it's here."

The girls had a great time in Miami, but Thelma didn't, thanks to the nonsensical regulations curbing the actions of colored people. She wasn't even allowed to sit with the girls in our own car in a drive-in theater. No colored person could be in a white neighborhood after nine o'clock at night unless she had a note from an employer. We tried to give Thelma a life but there was practically nothing for her besides association with us, whom she regarded as her own family. Thelma made the break. It turned out that a gentleman named Samuel Sapp, a Jacksonville city employee, had wanted to wed her for ten years and at long last she accepted him and moved to Jacksonville. She had been with us almost twenty years. We still bring her North for family occasions.

Being an indoctrinated Yankee I never had much sympathy with Southern people, and I was positively warlike when I came up against any of the customs designed to hurt the Negro. I had no companions at the Miami *News* because every executive but me was from Georgia. When the Supreme Court made its antisegregation ruling, a bunch of them gathered around and one asked belligerently, "What do you think of this decision?"

"I don't like it," I said.

They were incredulous. "You don't like it? I thought it would be right down your alley, you being a goddamned Yankee."

"You call me a proud name and you may choose your adjectives. . . . The reason I don't like it is because it will force self-respecting colored children to go to school with you goddamned wool-hats."

They snickered without merriment and let it pass. We traveled back and forth to the North with Thelma several times and we were always having difficulties over accommodations for her. On one trip when Ricie and I were alone we had our dog Brownie with us. We carried a small saucepan so we could give Brownie a drink of water every few hours. I walked into a garage and was confronted by the customary white and colored drinking fountains. The proprietor, an ugly, gruff South Carolinian, was sitting in a chair tilted against the wall. I addressed him in my best Red Neck dialect.

"Suh, please tell me which fountain I should use to give mah dawg a drink. Yuh see, it's a brown dawg; but it belongs to a white mayun."

The garage proprietor made no answer. He just spit in the general direction of the gabboon. Receiving no answer, I decided for myself. I gave Brownie her water out of the white fountain and I drank out of the colored.

After I'd been at the Miami *News* a year and a half, the boss called me in and said that the *News* wished to run the Golden Gloves Boxing Tournament and wanted me to take charge of it. They had run it some years before on a lily-white basis.

I told the managing editor I would be glad to run the tournament but that I wouldn't have anything to do with it if it wasn't going to be open to all boxers, white, black, or green. The editors went into a huddle and finally decided we would run an integrated tournament.

It came off pretty well except for the fact that we had almost no Negro spectators. We had divided the house equally and fairly with seats in all classifications for both white and Negro. Under the law it was impossible to avoid separating the races. But the Negroes wouldn't buy in spite of the fact that half our boxing entries were colored. I didn't get the reason until Charley North, our only colored reporter, explained it to me. We were running the tournament in an arena in Coral Gables. Two weeks before, North told me, the Coral Gables police had shot and killed an unarmed colored drunk in the city police station. The colored people did not want to go into Coral Gables. We finally had to sell the best seats we had held for them to white people in order to "dress the house."

Billy Reagan, boxing coach at the University of Miami and the man who refereed the last Patterson-Johansson fight, was a great help to me in operating the show. Many of our entrees were from army, navy, marine, and air force bases, and couldn't get to Miami until the afternoon before the fights started. We could see that if we applied the weight restrictions closely we were going to lose half our entrees. We had an old A.A.U. man there who was making us plenty of trouble over technical details. So Billy and I jimmied the scale. We rigged it so it weighed 3¼ pounds light and we just made it with that allowance.

I've never seen better judging or refereeing in boxing. Billy Reagan gave the judges and referees an hour of instruction in which he said that this was the first time Negro and white boxers had come together in south Florida and that there must be perfect accuracy in deciding the bouts. Our officials responded well. I don't recall one bad decision. They didn't lean over backward in favor of the Negroes but they gave each man who fought a square shake. We came out of it with a fair financial success, but I was glad I never had to do it again.

To many people Miami is a beautiful land where it's warm and pleasant and free of northern winter bedevilments like snow. To me it was a pleasant place for a couple of months in the winter, then it lapsed into a hell hole. I spent part of three summers there and I don't want the experience again. Summer vacationers get by only because of air-conditioning. If you are contemplating a Miami vacation in the summer and wish to test the climate, I can recommend a method you can carry out in your own northern kitchen.

First you get five or six thousand mosquitoes and other assorted noxious bugs from an experimental laboratory and turn them loose in your kitchen. Then you heat the room up to approximately 96 degrees. Then, having obtained a pail of horse urine from a neighboring riding stable or race track, you put it on the stove to boil. You sit in the kitchen, and in about twenty minutes, you will know what it's like in Miami in the summer. Breathe deeply.

There are two Miami features which winter visitors

never experience because they happen only in the summer. One is the mango, a large and beautiful fruit which grows everywhere. It is delicious. The other is a royal poinciana, a tree which has magnificent scarlet blossoms in late June and July. South Miami Avenue is solid with poincianas all the way out to its intersection with Dixie Highway.

The summer swimming is like taking a hot bath, and you are in danger of running up against a Portuguese man-of-war, a blue jellyfish with trailing tentacles. Contact with them causes such severe pain that a doctor's first move in treating a case of man-of-war rash is to administer morphine.

Each summer I was required to substitute two weeks for Morris McLemore, our columnist. By rigging my own vacation to follow, I was able to spend a whole month in New York with my wife and children. It was a great relief, from the column-writing point of view, to have something to write about.

One day toward the end of my vacation in 1955, I received a letter from Mr. Welsh, my managing editor. He said that I was a wonderful operator but that my salary was too high for the *News* and therefore I was fired. I can't say I was terribly distressed, for I wanted to get North not only because I hated the South but also because I was afraid one of my girls might marry a Floridian. God knows enough of them were hanging around the house.

The next stop was Newark, that huge slum across the river from New York, where I found the people friendly and the standard of newspaper work high. Walt Kelley, who draws Pogo, got me my job on the *Star Ledger*, where I was sports editor and columnist for four years.

I didn't like the city of Newark particularly and we had no friends in any of the suburbs. So Ricie scouted around Princeton and found us a satisfactory apartment over a garage. Later we moved into university housing, which meant that we had a small, heated two-story house with acres of lawn in the rear and a parking space in front. It was ideal except for the daily hour's trip to Newark.

The make-up and head writing on the *Star Ledger* filled me with joy. It was not only pointed but it was frequently memorable. When a distinguished Briton who had doubted the age of the Piltdown man was laid to rest, the *Star Ledger*'s head was:

SKULL SKEPTIC
PASSES AT 83

Our own slot man, Les Malimut, had a great gift for his job and occasionally came up with an outstanding head. He got hold of a picture showing the horse Nashua in the winner's circle. A couple of track employees were trying to place a spray of flowers over his withers and he was raising hell. Malimut's picture caption was "Nashua says 'Neigh' to the Nosegays."

Phillip Hochstein, editor of the *Star Ledger* and all the other Newhouse papers, was one of the best newspapermen I have ever worked under. I've never been treated as well as I was on the *Star Ledger*. I was given two raises in four years and, although the paper did not have a retirement plan, I was handed a guarantee of two hundred dollars a month for life any time I wanted to quit active work. I was also made general sports editor of Sam Newhouse's seventeen papers. This didn't mean much but looked good in a biography.

I was so happy in Newark and Princeton that I was re-

luctant to move back to the *Herald Tribune* when my old
sparring partner, George Cornish, approached me about
returning as sports editor. All the Reids had been cleaned
out and it seemed likely that the paper would be a good
place to work now that it had passed into the hands of
Jock Whitney.

I met Cornish in Whyte's uptown restaurant. He saw
the need of secrecy in our dealings; that's why we went so
far away from the office. We sat down and the first man
who came over to speak to us was the circulation manager.
Nothing was done in our first meeting. Cornish said the
paper was interested in seeing me return and wanted to
know if I were interested.

I answered that of course I was interested, but that the
degree of my interest would be governed by the amount
of money the *Herald Tribune* wished to lay on the line.

George said that he could not make me a proposition at
that time but that he was going to talk to Mr. Whitney
soon and would have a definite proposition for me. Whitney was then ambassador to Britain. So we parted with
nothing done.

At this point, Mr. Hochstein made a move which com-
plicated my situation. He took a full-page ad in the *Editor
and Publisher* in which he announced that I had been made
sports editor of all the Newhouse papers and added a paean
of praise that was downright embarrassing. He also offered me more money to stay with the *Ledger*. The *Editor
and Publisher* scared George Cornish, who called me up
and wanted to know if that meant that I had decided not to
come back to the *Tribune*.

I told him that I had been sports editor of the Newhouse
papers for some time, but that Mr. Hochstein had just gotten around to announcing it. I said I was still waiting for

the proposition he was going to make me. He indicated that it would be ready in a week or so and I told him I would wait that long before making a decision.

It was a hard decision to make. I was sixty-four years old and comfortably set where I was. I did not feel my energy had been impaired but I could see a tough stretch ahead during which I would have to clean out some of the people with whom Bobby Cooke had garnished the *Trib* Sports Department.

In justice to Bobby, I would like to say that, though all his moves as sports editor of the *Trib* were not good, he had the good sense to engage Tommy Holmes and Sam Goldaper when the Brooklyn *Eagle* folded. He had also hired Hal Claassen for his copy desk. There were many good men on the *Tribune* including some who had been there eleven years before when I was given the boot. I talked a long time with my wife about making the move and we finally agreed that the thing that made it necessary for me to go to the *Tribune* was my own vindication. I had been thrown out and now I was being asked to return. The act of returning would be a severe punch in the eye for the surviving members of the Reid family.

Ricie loved our little house in Princeton and we had just been given permanent tenure, which meant we could stay till carried out. Up to that point we were on an indefinite basis because the University might need the house for a faculty member and theoretically might kick us out. It was a wonderful place to live because we were surrounded by interesting young people of many nations who had come to Princeton either to teach or study. Next door to us was a Chinese family in a house previously occupied by a Swedish physicist, his wife, and a little boy named Lars.

Every morning Lars would walk out back of our house

and look at our chimney. If there was smoke coming out of it, he would call to his mother, "Stanley cold."

The rent was low, the commutation wasn't too tough, even though the Pennsylvania had taken off some of the best trains and raised the fares. I had a good many friends in the town. And so did Ricie. Broadway tryouts frequently were held in the McCarter Theatre. There were concert series and other events which interested Ricie, if not me. She tried to get me to go to a concert by massed Italian violinists. But I rebelled and christened it "The Thousand Guineas."

The moment of decision came in George Cornish's office in the corner of the *Trib*'s city room.

"Will you take ——" —mentioning a telephone number—"to come back as sports editor of the *Tribune?*" he asked.

"God, George, I don't need all that money. However, I'll say I've decided to come back and, if you will alter your terms, I will do it. What I want is three quarters of that amount and I want the paper to put away one quarter in a pension plan for my retirement. . . . I hope you realize that I am sixty-four years old and can't go on working in this business many more years. I expect to last about five."

As a matter of fact, I only lasted three.

19 WHEN I ENTERED THE TRIBUNE ON February 16, 1959, it was in frightful shape. The old-timers on the staff didn't know what to expect and there was a new group of junior birdmen who had been taught the newspaper business wholly under the aegis of Whitey and Brownie Reid. Needless to say, they were confused. A look around the Sports Department almost caused me to return to Newark. There were some old associates on whom I could count, including Irving T. Marsh, my former assistant, who apparently had held the Sports Department together during the White-Brown regime. I could see that I would have to do some firing to bring the department up to its old standard. And I recognized that this was going to be difficult in view of the fact that every man who had been with the paper more than four months had earned the tenure guaranteed under the contract with the Newspaper Guild.

Getting rid of certain people, however, was essential. And I set out to do it. I returned one man to the desk from the outside staff, and when he balked, I asked for his resignation. I was surprised when I received it. He was a good man, incidentally, but his talents obviously were for copyreading rather than news writing. The staff included a lady named Denise McCluggage who had a good writing style and other assets but did not fit in my plans.

When I arrived in the shop she charged at me and told me she would like to do some "fun" assignments. I didn't want any "fun" assignments nor was I particularly interested at that time in her favorite sport, which was automobile-racing. She also had done skiing and other fringe sports. I had a plan to combine a man on several sports, including skiing, so that left her out.

I asked Eugenia Sheppard, the fashion editor, if she would like to have Denise in her department and she said she would. I got Denise into Cornish's office and told her that I had arranged to transfer her to fashions.

"To hell with that," she said. "Do I get severance pay if I resign?"

I said yes before George had a chance to interfere. So he had to back me up.

There were other tougher cases which I won't identify by the use of names. Two men refused to resign; one of them sat around the office three weeks glowering at me. I glowered at him and we had a mutually unpleasant time. He finally saw that I would not back off, gave me his resignation, and took his severance pay. Another man I threatened to take before the Guild and prove a case of incompetence. He battled gamely but ultimately turned in his papers. He was ready to see reason three weeks before he actually quit; but a pal of his, who was a *Times* sports writer, kept telling him that he had remarkable ability and that I was an old son of a bitch.

The last move I made was to elevate Harold Claassen from the rim to the position of head of the copy desk. This proved to be a strike—in the bowling rather than the industrial sense—for he improved the paper at once and succeeded me as sports editor when I finally left it. Boosting him into the slot involved the transfer of another veteran to the night desk. As soon as Claassen got into his new job, he and I made a survey of the composing room to discover what type was lying around downstairs. I wanted to change the appearance of the paper, for the better if possible, to show the readers that something new had happened. Just before I came in the page lines had been lowered from 42-point type to 36. I made them 48 points. We then started trying different type faces: Metro medium, Franklin Gothic, Caslon bold, Century bold, Memphis bold, and Poster Bodoni. My superiors screamed piteously over this departure from usage. But I pointed out that all this type was lying around downstairs, and we might as well see if any of it was usable.

I didn't know so many people knew so much about type until this interlude occurred. The screams were particularly piercing when sans serif faces appeared in the paper. Even readers wrote in about this. I finally agreed with Mr. Cornish that we would discard everything except Poster Bodoni, which was a blocky black type and a member of our main family. I found it useful for feature stories and for short, one-word heads to break up a long piece.

I found that the *Herald Tribune* had fallen into a rut in playing the news. If there was a basketball game or a hockey game in the Garden, that was automatically the lead. As a result, we had some sick-looking papers. When Claassen succeeded the old operative it was easy to change to something more vital. Not that we didn't occasionally lead with basketball or hockey, but we might come up with anything. In fact, we frequently, on days of scant news, spread an eight-column feature across the top of our page 1. At that time we were on the front of the second section every day. Later, after our sports pages had been shifted inside the second section, we carried out the same idea of make-up. In other words, we used our first sports page as the lead page, playing our best stories on it and sometimes jumping them to a subsequent page. This plan had its weaknesses but it worked out well when we had a right-hand opener. I did my best to persuade the men who assembled the paper to give us a right-hand break as often as possible. We tried all kinds of forms of assembly in the leading feature story. If Smith had a hot column we often would put an eight-column head on it and square it off in two-column indented type at the top, instead of using his regular column head.

At other times we would set a story with a one-nut indent for use in the same way. Another trick we developed was to set a column, full measure, and place it in seven of the page's eight columns, using the eighth *column* as white space between the others. In other words, we used our regular body type as indented type. This was a good dodge when you had a good late story coming and needed something to plug the first edition, which went in at eight thirty on week days and five thirty on Sunday, i.e., Saturday night. It could be an indented story in the first edition and a full-width story later on. This is a dodge I learned from Malimut on the Newark *Star Ledger* and it is not in general use in our business.

A couple of years ago, I made a speech in Toronto to a meeting of the Ontario sports writers and nobody in the place had ever heard about this system. They have been using it in Toronto, Hamilton, and other cities ever since.

Of course, you couldn't cut off all the men we lost and not replace them. And I strengthened the *Herald Tribune*'s Sports Department by bringing in three men from the Newark *Star Ledger*. Abe Abikoff had worked for me in Miami and I had brought him from there to Newark. I remember giving him detailed instructions for driving from Miami to my apartment in Princeton. The instructions were perfect as far as the last traffic light. He came in the winter and I even remembered to tell him to put antifreeze in his radiator. But I told him to turn right instead of left at the last traffic light and he went wandering off toward New Brunswick.

Jerry Izenberg was a man I had hired for the Newark *Star Ledger* from Paterson. He came to the *Herald Tribune* as a copyreader and was later shifted to the outside staff, where he did outstanding work. He is now back in the job I used to have on the *Star Ledger*, sports columnist. Lud Duroska, another desk man from the *Star Ledger*, also joined us on the *Herald Tribune*, subsequently moved to the *Times*, which offered him more money. I tried several times to persuade Malimut to cross the river but was unsuccessful. Another man I brought up from the South was Don Rubin, a young fellow who worked for the Miami *News* as university correspondent, then blossomed into a full-time reporter while attending the university. I got him a job on a Princeton weekly, pending an opening in Newark, and finally brought him to the *Star Ledger*. He stayed there a while after I left, then jumped to McGraw-Hill, where he is doing an excellent job, on one of their trade magazines.

Management was familiar when I returned to the *Tribune*. Cornish was the editorial head and Everett Walker, a gifted operator in any newspaper shop, was his assistant. Cornish resigned after a short time and was succeeded by Fendall Yerxa, former city editor of the *Tribune*, who had become editorial boss of a paper in Wilmington, Delaware.

At this point Mr. Whitney started hiring outside editors. His first choice was Bob White, a wonderful guy from Mexico, Missouri, where he and his father were owners of a daily paper. I never could figure out why Bob came to New York, because he had everything going for him back in Missouri. He was exuberant, almost bubbly, and quickly made everyone on the paper like him. He went to all the football games and sat in the press box with me sometimes. He knew a great deal about the game, having played at

West Point and at Washington and Lee University. But he didn't catch on to New York journalism and didn't seem to have many ideas for putting the *Herald Tribune* on its feet after the long years of Reidism. He was given to writing handwritten notes to reporters whose work he liked. He wrote a letter to me once about a column I had written; but he praised it for the wrong reason. He wrote a note to a photographer praising him for taking one of the worst pictures I had ever seen. The photographer showed it to me and I quickly furnished rebuttal, then wrote a note to Bob requesting that he stop commenting on things that appeared in the sports section until after I had passed on them.

In the end, he and Mr. Whitney agreed to separate and he went back to Mexico, Missouri. If he had had time to get his balance in New York, he might have made a great editor. Certainly he had human characteristics which few of them can offer.

With White gone, Yerxa became head of the paper and things went along satisfactorily for some time. Then, a typhoon hit the *Tribune* in the person of John Denson. He had been editor of *Newsweek* and assistant editor of *Collier's* magazine and no one can say that he didn't have ideas. The fact is the front-page make-up of the *Tribune* was largely patterned on his plan, which he put into full execution before he came a cropper for failure to get the paper to press on time. After putting up with multiple changes and delays for several months, the circulation manager finally went to Mr. Whitney and said, "I'm sorry to say, sir, that we are not going to be able to deliver your paper tomorrow morning."

This led to a notable ruckus. Denson quit and Jim Bellows, whom he had brought from the Miami *News* as managing editor, succeeded him. He is the fifth man who has been in charge of the paper in the four years Whitney has owned it, which seems to indicate that Jock, though he may be a stumble-bum in the matter of editorial judgment, is hell-bent to put the *Tribune* on the black side for keeps.

I didn't know Mr. Whitney until after I came back to work on the *Tribune*. The first time I talked to him was in the Embassy in London in the summer of 1959 during his tenure as ambassador. The *Herald Tribune* London Bureau made a date for me to have lunch with him but he had got stuck in the country where he had gone to see his English racing stables—he has two, one on either side of the ocean—and couldn't keep the date. Consequently I was constrained to a short interview in the afternoon. A dozen people were waiting in the outer office of the Embassy and I didn't think I should stop the nation's business, so I made a few cracks and got out. That's what he seemed to want me to do, anyway. During the time I was in his office, I promised him that I would try to improve the coverage of racing, which I had already decided was one of our weak points.

Improvement in this field ultimately involved the engagement of Tom O'Reilly as racing columnist and feature writer. He was an operator comparable to Joe H. Palmer, who already had made a mark for himself when he died after a year. The fact is that I might have hired Tom instead of Joe during my first tour with the *Herald Tribune*, except that one could handle his booze and the other couldn't. Tom, who wrote for the *World-Telegram, P.M.*, and the *Daily Telegraph*, was supremely gifted and very funny. But for many years he tried without success to outbox John Barleycorn. In spite of this fact, he wrote great columns and I was one of those who refused to miss his daily output. I saw him only occasionally.

Once when I was working on a temporary job as press agent for a Columbia picture called *Saturday's Hero* he dropped in at a preview. Halfway through the picture, which was a fairly routine job about a college football player who sold himself down the river to an intercollegiate fumble foundry, he started to cry bitterly. I went over to talk to him and said, "What's the matter, Tommy, old boy?"

"This is so sad it overpowers me," he said. "I've got to have a drink."

I had anticipated that some of the brothers that attended the preview would be in a similar mood after the showing. So I got out one of the bottles I had cached and gave him half a tumbler.

"Ah," he said, gasping. "I think I can stand the picture now. Lead me to my seat."

I talked to Tom during the early days of my *Tribune* return, but I wasn't ready to hire him. I told him what I had in mind, however, and he seemed to like the idea. But many wheels had to grind slowly before I could clear it. At that time Yerxa was the top editor and he was most careful with money. O'Reilly got good pay, and though I could probably have talked him into accepting less, I refused to do it. At this time he had been off liquor completely for four years. As a matter of fact, he never had another drink. We hired him in 1961. He started to score at once with feature stories and columns of notes which he wrote in the Pepys style.

Tom had a bad medical history. He had had a cancer removed from one lung five or six years before and I was frightened when he went back in the hospital for a series of examinations. I was afraid of a recurrence but the doctor found no evidence of bad trouble. Tom was back at work in a couple of weeks. He continued writing for us virtually until he died the next spring. His trouble ultimately turned out to be cancer of the larynx. He spent the last weeks of his life in St. Vincent's Hospital and showed the greatest gameness I have ever seen. On his back in bed, and dying of cancer, he kept up his column for the *Herald Tribune*, and he made it good, too.

Before Tom came with us I decided to apply the acid test to Mr. Whitney. He was a great enthusiast over Saratoga. He had a house there and loved to be on hand during August when the horses were running. It meant a great deal to him, I am sure. I said to myself, "I'll put Saratoga on the pan and I'll find out about my boss. If he shuts me off, I'll know I have no freedom. If he doesn't, I will be his devotee."

To me Saratoga was a nasty old hole where you were overcharged for everything and where the betting customers turned out in insufficient numbers to produce proper share of tax revenue for the state. At the same time, New Jersey's Monmouth Park, which operated for a few days at the start of each Saratoga meeting, always produced a tremendous pot for the state and beat Saratoga in attendance and handle by a considerable margin. I decided I would divide the coverage equally between Saratoga and Monmouth, running two one-column charts instead of the usual two-column chart on New York racing. I also engaged a man to rate the New Jersey horses just as Eye-Q did in New York. In addition, I printed a box in the paper showing the comparative attendance and handle at Monmouth and Saratoga. It was invidious from the viewpoint of a Saratoga-lover.

Mr. Whitney took this without a whimper or a comment and I concluded that, even though he didn't have the newspaper sense to make Rufus Stanley Woodward his top editor, he was a good guy and should receive my full support. However, he did shut me off once or twice in exuberant attacks on this and that. He once wrote me a note saying that I was unfair to Robert Moses after that noted whistle-blower had written him a letter blackguarding me. Previously, Mr. Moses had written a similar letter which I had printed in my column without comment. Later on I took a side blast at him and the letter I got from Whitney was the result.

The Moses-Woodward brawl started over the construction of the stadium in Flushing Meadow Park. I said that the stadium, as planned, was undersized and overpriced. I called it a little stinker and pointed out that it wasn't going to be big enough to house any show that would do New York any good. I thought New York should have a one-hundred-thousand-seat stadium rather than a fifty-thousand-seater.

And I still think the little round building which Moses and the city put up will be proved inadequate and unsuitable for most sports events. It's just another baseball field.

After spending approximately 23 million dollars on the new stadium, New York still is unequipped to handle such sports extravaganzas as the Olympic games, the Army-Navy football game, or shows of similar proportions. The existence of thirty- or forty-hundred-thousand-seaters over the country assures that New York will never get anything that is really big. Army and Navy don't relish playing annually in Philadelphia, but the capacity of the moldy old stadium at the end of Broad Street makes it the logical place. If New York had a decent site, the game would be back here in no time.

When I came back to the *Tribune*, I figured I would be active for five years and would stay around part of the next year to help the man who succeeded me. However, in March, 1961, there occurred an event which made it necessary for me to change my plans. As the *Tribune*'s fourth editor-in-chief, Mr. Whitney had chosen Denson, who, as I've said, was a dynamic character and had many ideas for change, some of them good. Virtually his first act was to get into a fight with Yerxa, who was designated as managing editor, and goad the latter into resigning. I regret to say I was indirectly involved in this.

One of the people I got rid of in the Sports Department purge was Ed Gilligan, rod and gun writer. Ed was capable in his field, also a skilled and meticulous writer. He had produced numerous books including some novels which were among the best-sellers. Despite all these qualifications, I felt he was not the man for us. He lived in Bearsville, New York, and came to town only occasionally. Too many of his columns were "think" pieces devoted to his dog, Mr. Toddy, and himself. I felt he was too involved in other writing to give us the best of his product. So I asked for his resignation and got it after promising Mr. Yerxa, then in full charge, that I wouldn't engage another regular man for the rod and gun beat until Mr. Gilligan's full severance pay had been met. This meant that we would have to go without a rod and gun man for approximately six months.

When Denson came in he asked me numerous questions about the Sports Department and I answered him honestly on all points, telling him that we were without a rod and gun man and that under agreement with the managing editor I wasn't going to engage one until the latter part of the summer. I had a man in mind; in fact, I had approached him. He was Art Smith, Red Smith's brother, who was a thoroughgoing newspaper man as well as an enthusiastic hunter and fisher. It turned out that Art and Denson were close friends. I don't know how much that had to do with what developed.

I had planned to cover such important events as occurred in the field, such things as the opening of the trout season, by putting in one of the regular staff members. Denson didn't like the idea of leaving the field uncovered and took the matter up with Yerxa. The latter was adamant about paying off Gilligan on a weekly basis before engaging anyone new in the same job. He and Denson got into a hassle and the result was that Yerxa submitted his resignation.

I doubt that Fendall would have stayed anyway. If he and Denson hadn't argued about a rod and gun writer, something else inevitably would have come up. Apparently, Yerxa, having been the head man on a paper in Wilmington, did not like the idea of being superseded on the *Herald Tribune*. Personally, I felt that I was going to come to grips with Denson in the end. At times he was very considerate of my authority in the Sports Department. At other times he walked over me. I had enjoyed complete freedom in my column. Now I found that I was operating under censorship. I wrote in my column one day that New York *Times* readers bought their Sunday paper by the pound and added that this great organ offered a wonderful buy for merchants who needed cheap wrapping for fish. As a matter of fact, you could get more wrapping paper out of a single Sunday *Times* than you could get for the price anywhere else. This column Denson squashed in its entirety, even though the fish-wrapping was an insignificant part of it.

The next thing I knew, a couple more of my columns came back marked "kill." I argued with Denson about one I had written about the Kennedy family in which I blasted Bobby for jumping on a passel of western bookmakers. In the same column I praised Caroline and the old man, also Jack. After some forensic he reinstated part of the column, but it was ruined. I had said in it that I used as an antidote for my Democratic leanings the *Herald Tribune* motto, "A Good Newspaper Doesn't Have to Be Dull." Denson said this was facetious and insulting to Mr. Whitney. I said I had no wish to insult Mr. Whitney and that I had found him openminded and fair in all ways. I said I was not trying to please Mr. Whitney; I was trying to amuse and entertain the readers of the New York *Herald Tribune*. I also said that I was a long-standing member of the *Herald Tribune* staff, even though I had broken time in my record, and that I claimed the same right enjoyed by Walter Lippmann to write what was in my mind, short of libel.

It was obvious, however, that I wasn't going to get along with Mr. Denson. He irritated me further by skipping me and going directly to my assistant when he had anything to say to the Sports Department. He made us give him a copy of every column on any subject that we intended to print. This was not only insulting, but also a damned nuisance. It sometimes involved copying a thousand words at a time.

I was now over sixty-five and eligible for Social Security. I also had a pension arrangement with the *Tribune*. I could get by on what I would have left if I quit the paper. So I decided to resign. It took me about a month to arrange a meeting with Denson to discuss the subject.

Finally, we met for Sunday breakfast and I told him, without revealing any annoyance, that I thought it was time for me to get out and make room for a younger man. I explained that what I would like to do was to give a year's notice. This would enable me to complete the reorganization of the department and to prepare my successor to take over the job.

"If you're going to quit, you might as well do it right now," he said. I sensed that he would be glad to get rid of me.

"All right," I said. "I'll leave at your convenience."

The matter lay dead for a long time. When I saw Denson in the city room he nodded to me and walked past. When I went to his office to advance the retirement plan, he was busy or out. I finally had to get Red Smith to get hold of him for me and tell him that I would like to make my arrangements to retire. He finally set a date for a meeting and made me a very generous proposition which I accepted with reservations. I wanted to conduct my last dealings with Mr. Whitney himself on the theory that he might overrule Denson and let me stay long enough to complete my job.

There was another long pause. My anniversary of reemployment by the paper came and went. I had to nudge him a couple of times more and finally he set up a meeting with Mr. Whitney and Walter Thayer, president of the company, in Mr. Whitney's office. Both sides accepted the conditions of my retirement almost exactly as Denson had outlined them. I felt that I was being treated royally. But even though Denson had set the conditions in an early meeting between us, I was grateful not to him, but to Mr. Whitney and Mr. Thayer.

Denson, himself, was gone from the paper in less than a

year. If I had known the imminence of his departure, I might still be working there. My sudden retirement was due to annoying dislike and the knowledge that Denson, though a parvenu on the *Herald Tribune*, had all the fire-power. I don't think anyone fully understood the situation.

So, I worked for the New York *Herald Tribune* for two stretches and left the paper in disappointment and rage both times. Denson once said to me, "Everybody on this damn sheet thinks he has a proprietary interest in it." His attitude was that people employed by the *Herald Tribune* should work there for the money he paid them, do what they were told, and shut up. But the proprietary interest which had weathered the late Reid regime, and Denson's own abortive tenure, was the true strength of the paper. Under Whitey and Brownie Reid it wavered, but held on. Under Denson, it flagged considerably. Not only was he transforming the appearance of the old sheet, which might have been a good thing, but he was uprooting the long-standing morale of the *Tribune*, which he described as the "employees' proprietary interest."

The old spirit of the *Tribune* still lives, however, and though the boys may never attain the freewheeling *joie de vivre* of the glorious days of Ogden I, Mr. Whitney's system of trial and error may ultimately return the paper to its old place as the number-one liberal Republican daily of the nation.

20

THE REST OF THIS BOOK IS CHEER-
ful. The paper kept me on for a
while as occasional columnist. Ricie
and I built a little house in the
woods at Brookfield Center, Con-
necticut, where we can live a peaceful life in the company
of foxes, raccoons, possums, squirrels, nuthatches, inch-
worms, and Republicans.

I have found that the theory that a man must work to
be happy is fallacious. The most pleasant occupation I
have found is sitting in a chair looking at the trees. I do
some work but it isn't compulsive work and I don't have
to worry about it through the night. I regret to say we
still keep newspaper hours. For a while neighbors came to
the door asking if we had been sick the night before. They
had noticed all our lights were on at two A.M. We were
just getting ready to go to bed as in the days of active
newspaper work.

After my retirement on April 1, 1962, the boys at the
Tribune threw a brawl for me in Toots Shor's and a lot of
old friends came. A couple of photographers from the
Tribune made pictures, and after a while Mr. Whitney
sent me an album with copies of all of them. In so doing,
he may have saved my life. For after scanning the cadaver,
which was supposed to be me, I concluded that I had some
frightful disease and went to the doctor for an examination. In the doctor's office I weighed 189 pounds, whereas
my regular weight was 220, with periodical excursions
up as high as 257. The doctor gave me some pills and I
am now back to 215 and have considerably more drive
than I had when I first came to the country.

Our house was designed by me with essential modifica-
tions by the builder, a local character named Clarence

Bristol, who was beaten narrowly for the State Legislature in Kennedy's year. He ran as a Democrat in a solid Republican district. One night at a party in my sister's house—she also lives in Brookfield—I laid my plan before Clarence. It was based on the hen house we had at Princeton; this was 20 × 20. By combining two hen houses I figured we'd have a house of approximately the right size; half would be a living room (20 × 20); the other half would be a bedroom, kitchen, and bath. In the end it evolved into a little more of a house than I had drawn due partly to the terrain on which we built it and partly on Clarence's ingenuity and long knowledge of the building business. Now we have a house whose upstairs is almost like the one I planned, with a good fireplace and a small entry. We looked for the land for quite a while and finally found a few acres on the edge of the woods. It was necessary to build a road into the place, which added somewhat to the expense but also to the attractiveness, for the house sits back nearly three hundred feet from the highway.

The building site on which we decided turned out to be a ledge which sloped to the south. This made it advisable to build two more rooms on the lower level; one is a garage and the other an office for me. There's no room for guests except on unfolding sofas in the living room and office. When our children and grandchildren come to see us, we haul out all the hideaways and everybody has a bed. If the guests are fastidious, we give them our room and sleep on a converted sofa.

Ricie and I worked long and arduously to get the place planted. I didn't want to run a lawnmower, so we substituted myrtle for grass. We dug through the ledge with pick axes and planted yew, lilac, forsythia, laurel, and syringa. We transplanted ferns and violets from the woods.

Ricie put in a couple of hundred bulbs last fall.

The front of our place alongside the road looked scrubby. So we ran a bulldozer over it and sowed rye. The next year I made a vegetable garden there, but my furry friends made a shambles of it.

The raccoons seem to know the exact day when the corn is going to be ripe. They eat it all the night before. After they have been in the corn patch it looks as if a battle had been fought over it. I was so angry with them that I almost decided to ambush and shoot them. But never having shot at anything unhuman, except rats, I withheld my fire. I was glad of it last winter, when the raccoons became friends. They would come up on the front steps to be fed. And when spring approached one of them made a habit of sleeping in the crotch of a slim maple on the edge of our myrtle. Lately a possum has discovered there are handouts at Woodwards' and shows no more fear than the raccoon. A gray fox occasionally sniffs around the house, but he is still suspicious of people. So are the squirrels, who run up a tree if you open the front door.

Everywhere we've been, except in Florida, we have fed the birds during the winter and this year we got rid of a couple of hundred pounds of sunflower seeds, suet, and chick feed. The Brookfield birds get fat in the winter because everybody feeds them, and some species which are not accustomed to staying north in the winter make the town their permanent home. A lady near me had blue-birds. Everybody had evening grosbeaks but me last winter. I got partly even by having a red-breasted nuthatch; the white-breasted ones are common, so are gold finches and purple finches. The ordinary varieties, chickadees, juncos, tree sparrows, white-throated sparrows, mourning doves, cardinals, hairy and downy woodpeckers, and other common winter varieties were present in bunches. I had a female snow bunting, fairly rare in Connecticut.

After half the winter was over, I found I was spending so much time watching the birds and beasts that I wasn't getting any writing done. So I moved to New York for the duration. I am going home tonight.

As I write, the disastrous newspaper strike seems to be almost at an end and all the boys and girls will start repaying the money they borrowed from the Friendly Home Loan Association. It's going to be rough for a year or more.

I am worried about the voracity of the newspaper unions, fearing that they will ultimately bring the business down with a crash unless they discover there is something to unionism beside rapacity. I hope to live to see the day when contract negotiations are realistic and are carried out for the good of the business.

It may be that I am talking out of jealousy, for it took me twenty years to climb to the salary a green reporter now receives. At the same time I note that Mr. Samuel Newhouse, for whom I worked in Newark, does not consider New York City Proper a good area in which to operate and has added no New York paper to his extensive holdings. He has had chances to buy, or so they tell me.

There was a time, which extended down to my early days on the *Tribune*, when newspaper owners paid employees as little as possible and every five-dollar raise was attended by a battle between the employee and the managing editor. The collapse of the News Writers' Branch of the Typographical Union, which occurred during my Boston days, was proof to me that editorial people can't do anything for themselves collectively.

The Newspaper Guild, of which I was a charter member, operated on a new principle. It included not only editorial people but also those of all other departments who were not associated with a craft union. This gave the movement strength, and the reporters rode along happily in the conditions it obtained for them. Still they contributed almost nothing to the strength of the Guild. If they had stood alone they would have thrown away their organization long ago.

For a long time, the Guild exerted a beneficent influence on the newspaper business. It got the salaries of useful people up to the point where they should have been many years before. I hesitate to say that the Guild has become a menace, but I believe it will cooperate with the craft unions to wreck the newspaper business in New York.

It has not as yet attained the viciousness of the Typographical Union, which seems hell-bent to block progress by resisting automation and by insisting on the old bogus clause in its contract. This is a provision which makes it necessary that matter set outside the plant be reset and thrown away. The continuance of bogus reveals the Typographical Union as an organization which is neither respectable nor aware of modern trends.

It may be that residence in a Republican community has made me a reactionary, but I don't like to see the pendulum swing too far. There was a time when anybody who could put up with the newspaper employer's philosophy was a scoundrel; but it has passed. It would be nice to see a session of negotiations between management and employees where all the cards were on the table face up. The unions would recognize the right of the employers to get a decent return from their capital and the employers would recognize the union's right to decent wages and conditions. If this doesn't happen, there will be more newspaper combinations and thousands more people will be thrown out of work. Ours is a shrinking business. In most American cities it has shrunk down to a monopoly.

It doesn't make any difference to me what happens to the newspaper business; that is, it doesn't make any difference to me economically. But I can't bear the thought of a general newspaper collapse. For I still believe what Nick Skerrett told me when I was a cub reporter—

"The American newspaper is the greatest institution in the world."

INDEX